# ENVIRONMENT
## IN PERIL

Edited by Anthony B. Wolbarst

Smithsonian Institution Press
Washington
and
London

Copyright © 1991 by the Smithsonian Institution.
All rights are reserved.
Chapter 11, copyright 1990 by Carl Sagan.
Library of Congress Cataloging-in-Publication Data
Environment in Peril / edited by Anthony B. Wolbarst.
    p.   cm.
    ISBN 1-56098-092-3
    1. Man—Influence on nature.   2. Environmental protection.
    3. Environmental policy.   4. Population.   5. Pollution.
    6. Conservation of natural resources.   I. Wolbarst, Anthony B.
    GF75.E56   1991
    383.7—dc20                                                    91-17500
                                                                      CIP

British Library Cataloguing-in-Publication Data is available.

∞The paper used in this publication meets the minimum requirements of the American
National Standard for Permanence of Paper for Printed Library Materials Z39.48–1984.

Printed in the United States of America
10   9   8   7   6   5   4   3   2
200   99   98   97   96   95   94   93   92

# Contents

# Foreword

It is hardly news that the environment is in peril, but what *is* constantly new is what people are doing about it. The Smithsonian in association with the Environmental Protection Agency takes pride in publishing presentations by some of the most eloquent American voices in the field of environment, with all the spontaneity that EPA's seminar series was intended to foster.

The contributors to this volume represent no Greek chorus, but rather a medley of creative individual offerings. Those who have worked as long and hard as these authors might well have become hardened and cynical, ultimately naught but voices of the Apocalypse. Rather, these are profound optimists, perennially engaging and engaged in what Ralph Nader terms the "battle for people's minds."

The book reflects the relative homogeneity of the profession of environmental protection although that is changing. Most of us, myself included, are male and privileged by education. I do not raise this to detract in any sense from these individuals, but rather to emphasize that we need all the help we can get. Environment will never rise to its truly proper place on the national agenda until it is a high priority for us all.

The press of human numbers and the accelerating toll we are taking on the environment constitute a challenge of overpowering magnitude. Time is short indeed, and society is seriously entrenched in its ways. How possibly can a bureaucracy such as EPA maintain the flexibility and openness necessary to cope? One way is to continually refresh by listening to unfettered viewpoints from outside. That is what this volume is all about. We would all do well to emulate.

THOMAS E. LOVEJOY
Assistant Secretary
Smithsonian Institution

# Preface

The physical, economic, and social problems that lead to deterioration of the environment are as complex and difficult to resolve as they are significant. Their solution requires not only hard work and the commitment of valuable resources, but also the exercise of intelligence, imagination, and good judgment.

In the United States, environmental protection is largely the responsibility of the U.S. Environmental Protection Agency (EPA). Soon after his arrival, Administrator William Reilly spoke of the importance of infusing the agency's work with wisdom: "The very health and well-being of millions of people depend on the decisions we make and the effectiveness with which we pursue our mission." It is therefore essential that those who carry out this mission be exposed to a broad spectrum of responsible opinion on environmental issues.

To that end, EPA's Office of Radiation Programs is sponsoring an ongoing series of seminars, in which distinguished men and women are invited to speak about critical environmental issues. The objective is to provide a stimulating, thought-provoking, and balanced forum, representing a variety of viewpoints relevant to environmental protection policy-making. Participants are asked to discuss what they consider to be the most serious of environmental problems, and to think of the seminar as an opportunity to convey to the management and staff of EPA the most important messages that need to be heard. The addresses they have delivered, in response, have demanded most careful consideration.

The seminars are open to all EPA employees. It has become clear that they would be of interest to others as well, so the videotapes of the seminars have been transcribed, edited lightly, and brought together to form this book.

These are the transcriptions of seminars delivered before large EPA audiences. Some of the talks were nothing short of electric. In an effort to capture the excitement of the moment, the transition from the spoken word to the written has been made with as little change of substance or style as possible. The speakers have had the opportunity to review the transcripts, and to make the final editorial decisions. But the book is a compilation of essentially oral, often spontaneous presentations, rather than of pieces polished for publication.

The operation of this seminar series and the preparation of the book have involved the ideas and energy of many individuals. We would like to thank Miles Allen, Brenda Bell, Dan Bell, Rem Brown, Don Clay, Dave Cohen, Tom Darner, Margaret Donogan, Bill Gunter, Michael Kane, Sheldon Meyers, Don Nantkes, Gene Paget, Barry Parks, Skip Price, Chris Rice, Allan Richardson, Michael Scott, and the others at EPA and in the offices of the speakers who helped to make it all work.

We are very pleased that the Smithsonian Press, which is known for the high quality of its publications and for the effectiveness of its distribution system, will be publishing *Environment in Peril.* Our thanks to Peter Cannell, Ruth Spiegel, and our other friends at the Press who have worked so hard and effectively to bring this project to fruition.

We at EPA wish to express our deepest appreciation to our speakers. Receiving no honoraria or even travel support, they have taken precious time out of their busy schedules to prepare outstanding talks. Their reward, perhaps, is the knowledge that *Environment in Peril* may help spur on people everywhere in their efforts to create and maintain a world that is environmentally safe, habitable, and pleasing for us all.

Anthony B. Wolbarst
Seminar Coordinator
Office of Radiation Programs


Richard J. Guimond
Deputy Assistant Administrator
Office of Solid Waste and Emergency Response, formerly Director,
   Office of Radiation Programs
U.S. Environmental Protection Agency


The views expressed in this book are those of the seminar speakers, and do not necessarily reflect those of the U.S. Environmental Protection Agency.

# ENVIRONMENT IN PERIL

# The Management
# of Environmental
# Violence

## Regulation or Reluctance?

I would like to convey a few observations on the state of environmental regulation. I want to illustrate how some of the hopes we had, when we worked so hard on this legislation in the 1970s, have not been fulfilled; why they haven't been fulfilled; and what we can do about it.

Any regulatory regime has to have a basic philosophy behind it. And what EPA is all about, as I see it, is the management of violence: preventing it, reducing it, anticipating it, counteracting it in ways that liberate more humane technologies, and informing people about the risks, so that they can join in the effort. Unfortunately, that is not EPA's image.

EPA functions very much in the tradition of the Public Health Service. It operates in a pattern similar to that used so effectively in the eradication of malaria and other public health diseases. We looked for the source of the mosquito, where it breeds, and found the pools. We went after the breeding environment, and reduced the agent that conveyed the malaria.

Here, we're looking for the sources of the pollution, for ways to prevent it in the first place. And if we cannot prevent the pollution, we need to find "mosquito nets" and ways to alert people to avoid the "pollution mosquito" as it is about to enter the immediate human environment.

But the image of the agency is one of being either regulatory or deregulatory, depending on your philosophy. When the Reagan admin-

RALPH NADER is an attorney, author, consumer advocate, social critic, and founder of and inspiration for a number of public interest groups.

istration came into office in the 1980s, the president's intention was very clear. Basically, it was to switch the agency into a mode of greater deregulatory activity. Not by abandoning programs outright, but *de facto:* by lessening the velocity of enforcement actions and the stringency of standards and, most unfortunately, by reducing the collection and publication of data at the sites where it is most needed. This, you all know, ended up with the brouhaha involving top officials of EPA prior to the second advent of William Ruckelshaus.

But the impact is still there, because it is fostered by the presence of OMB [Office of Management and Budget]. (If anybody wants to analyze raw government these days, they ought to look at OMB, and not just the NSC [National Security Council].) The people at OMB subscribe to the cost-benefit theory. That means they analyze cost as defined by industry and ignore benefits as achieved by people.

Take automobile safety as an example. The intellectual corruption of the cost-benefit yardstick as used by OMB was revealed by OMB's failure to approve a single safety standard, with the exception of the rear-light standard. No approval of any other standard has come forward, not even the so-called air bag standard that Nordhaus at Yale said had a cost-benefit ratio of about 10 to 1. The air bag standard was revoked in the first year of the Reagan administration, only to be reinstated a few years later, following a unanimous 9 to 0 Supreme Court decision that the revocation was arbitrary, capricious, and illegal.

This kind of extra-agency rule via OMB has resulted in a mercantile dominance over what should be a recognition of humane values in the context of practical technological alternatives. The approach carried the day because it was bolstered not only by the political support of the White House, but also by the political impact of business and industry devolving to local Chambers of Commerce and local manufacturers' associations. It is further bolstered by the so-called "think tanks"—if we want to grace them with that word—like the Heritage Foundation.

What this illustrates is that humane movements go in cycles, and nothing should be taken for granted. Today, polls around the country are showing much greater public support for environmental pollution controls, even when the controls result in higher costs. There is growing evidence that concerns about environmental violence are no longer in the professional grasp of a few full-time environmental groups, but are becoming more and more decentralized, down to neighborhoods and rural areas. Middle-class America is now really leading the way in terms of grassroots support, particularly in the area of toxics.

So on the one hand, the public is calling for stronger enforcement measures, and millions more people understand what pollution really is in terms of emphysema rates, property damage, and cancer rates. On the other hand, the so-called representative government in Washington has been going essentially in a direction opposite from that of the environmental trajectory of the 1970s. You would have expected the government to be way ahead of the 1970s, because there's an incubation period for standards and for data collection. The 1970s were involved in standards and data collection, and should have presaged an even stronger, heightened degree of activity in the 1980s. But that's not how things worked out.

EPA's mission is the management and reduction of violence. Environmental violence, however, is a silent form of violence. It does not immediately provoke pain on the part of the people exposed to it, and it therefore tends to be less dramatic than, say, a fire or a tornado. This silent form of violence invites an intellectual response, because our sensory capacities of saying "ouch" and "stop it" are not up to the kind of particulate matter or gas or chemicals that are harmful over a longer period of time.

We are talking about a battle for people's minds. The issue should not be confused with competitiveness or productivity, as defined by the mercantilists. You can define productivity in the steel industry purely in terms of output, sales, and profits. But you can also define it in terms of the decrease in the levels of injury and disease afflicting workers and people in the community. That kind of intellectual embrace has not been forceful enough because it has not been coming forth from the government or from many of the well-heeled institutions that back up the Reagan administration. Yet anybody who looks at it will agree that the productivity should account for the associated mortality and morbidity rates.

I think we're going to see, in the next few years, a decreasing reliance on the courts to get environmental protection moving. This will come about because of the change in the judiciary, through the appointment powers of the president. By 1989 President Reagan will have appointed 50 percent of the federal judiciary. You can see the effects already in the D.C. Circuit Court, represented by decisions of Judge Robert Bork, who, to some, appears to be a reflector of judicial restraint. But in the cases we've analyzed, when business challenges government regulations, Bork is very hard on the government agency. And when citizens or community groups challenge government inaction, he is very protective of the government agency. Bork also does not like people to have much standing to sue. Not only does he disagree with environmentalists substantively on many occasions, he also doesn't want to let them through the door to argue their cases.

If that kind of judicial philosophy spreads, you're going to find less recourse to the courts. When there is less recourse to the courts, the pressure has to emerge somewhere else. One example of that is the new hard-line, earth-first type groups that are starting to grow in this country and abroad—direct-action groups such as Greenpeace. And also, you're going to see more political pressure at the community level, on city councils and state legislatures. Whenever the doors to the courtroom are blocked, the pressure will focus more on the legislature or on the direct-action arena.

The Clean Water Action Group, for example, is canvassing over 4 million homes a year. Those of us who wonder why Congress is so good on clean-water legislation may begin to realize it's because they're hearing more and more from their local constituents, and they're noticing all those trucks with bottled water clogging up traffic on their way to constituents' homes. I think there's now more bottled water than milk being delivered to American homes, by a considerable volume. Today, bottled water is a business of over $2 billion a year.

So I think we're going to see a more exciting period ahead—if you define excitement as uncontrolled and unstructured popular disappointment with government about what needs to be done.

Now, enthusiasm has a lot of consequences, and when you measure an agency's enthusiasm, you can draw some pretty interesting conclusions. You detect an agency's enthusiasm, for example, by asking people at colleges and graduate schools, "Where do you want to work in government?" When I was in law school, the students wanted to work at the Securities Exchange Commission, the Justice Department, and the National Labor Relations Board. Certainly in the 1970s when I talked to students around the country and asked where they wanted to work, EPA was always right at the top of the list. I don't know if that's true now. Why would they want to work in the EPA? Because they want to get something done. What else would be the reason for joining EPA?

In the past, these students would have been overcome by euphoria from the exciting speeches being made by environment officials around the country. They would have heard an EPA assistant administrator or an EPA administrator speak in almost Kennedy Peace-Corps terms about the great mission awaiting the current generation to toilet train big industry and clean up the air, water, and soil; about the chance to apply their knowledge of physics, engineering, biology, economics, public administration, and public health to these goals. We don't get that anymore, unfortunately. One of the punishments I have assigned myself is reading speeches by high administration officials. And we do not get that message.

Why? Because so much of what is done here is with an antenna sensitive to OMB and the White House, and the general political supervisory role exists. There's always a kind of apologetic approach to the work you do now. It's almost as if you have to apologize to the perpetrators of violence.

One reason is that a lot of your work deals with trying to curtail a problem just before it hits the environment, right out of the pipes, so to speak. We really have not developed, for government administrators, an adequate philosophy of preventing a particular chemical from being produced in the first place. This is especially true if the chemical doesn't have that much redeeming value, and if another substance that would perform the same economic mission more safely can be substituted.

A clear example is nuclear power. There's no form of energy more substitutable than nuclear power, nor with better reasons for seeking substitutes. Yet we spend a great deal of time asking where are we going to find the radioactive waste disposal sites with geologic stability for forty thousand years. And what are we going to do about transporting radioactive waste, about low-level emissions and low-level wastes? Those are enormously complicated problems, involving great political, economic, and technical struggles. Nuclear power, after some $250 billion investment, gives us less energy than wood, and we're not exactly a wood-burning society. It gives us about 15 percent of our electricity, yet we waste about half of our electricity. We have all kinds of other ways of using existing resources more efficiently, including small hydro plants. There are hundreds of other sources and efficiencies outlined by Amory Lovins and others who have worked in this area both in government and business. So why are we expending so many government resources and personnel on this program? Why don't we just phase it out? Why did we start it in the first place, before we at least tried to solve many of the technical problems that now plague this industry?

The same is true with the petrochemical industry. We really must ask ourselves how much of the petrochemical industry is socially redeemable. Suppose you saw 100,000 tons of plastic swizzle sticks for stirring drinks. And you realized that fuming petrochemical plants produced the substance that was extruded into swizzle sticks. Surely you would ask if it is really worth the worker exposure to that level of toxicity, or worth the toxic-waste problem, to produce plastic swizzle sticks. So also with arsine, a very risky gas. An accident with an arsine gas transport container could be one of our country's greatest catastrophes to date. To what extent is arsine gas substitutable? We don't even ask those questions.

It's almost equivalent to trying to deal with poverty by opening up more soup kitchens, rather than dealing with the causes of poverty to begin with. That's why I put an emphasis on speeches and writing as the educating function of a regulatory agency, whose mission should be much like that of a physician. Physicians are equipped to try to treat the disease, but their highest ethic is prevention.

Now, the Office of Technology Assessment, which once in a while comes out with a report on what agencies are doing, has questioned the end-of-the-line solutions to hazardous waste, and what is happening in the area of solid waste. There is a great push now for waste incinerators, and talk about regulating emissions as a solution to the air-pollution problem. Yet incinerators are breeding real community mobilization and conflicts all over the country. It's almost like a replay of the fights over nuclear power plants. Years ago, even environmentalists thought incinerators were the way to go. Frankfurt, Germany, supplied 15 percent of its electricity by burning its solid waste. Now we know a little more about these incinerators, and about the extent to which they convert our waste into certain harmful gases that then come back into our lungs.

What's the way to go? An incinerator is better than a landfill, isn't it? We're running out of landfills, and the waste is getting into the ground water. Let's get the incinerators going; we'll put the latest emission control technologies on them. But a lot of pollution still will get out, and we'll have to do something with the ash, which is full of heavy metals and quite toxic in its own right. We have a real struggle here.

The sensible approach, of course, is recycling. But recycling requires a different degree of social organization. Instead of dealing with x number of incinerators, you're dealing with millions of households, which need to separate their waste into paper, organic material, metal, and glass before the garbage trucks pick it up. Then the waste must be taken out and subjected to various recycling technologies so we can reduce the amount that goes into the incinerators, if we are going to have incinerators.

But that's not enough. We'll have to go back to the packaging industries, to the product designers, back to the disposable philosophy. We have disposable razors and disposable contact lenses: you put them in, you throw them out a week later. The auto companies have been giving us disposable cars for a long time. Who knows what's next.

But the merchandising strategy of industry has very little concern about what happens to the waste afterwards, with the possible exception of the aluminum industry. As a result, we're on a treadmill. The faster we go, the more we stay in the same place. That's why I think it is important to hold recycling referendums like those in Massachusetts, Connecticut, and elsewhere to get recycling bills through and to develop incentives for more biodegradable materials to go into packaging. More than just recycling the few bottles or cans out of the totality of solid waste, it is even more important to get people *thinking* in those terms.

I doubt that many people realize that American consumers pay as much again for food packaging as they pay the farmers. Guess which one is going to be ahead in another five years.

A plea, then, for a more preventive philosophy and a higher level of educational visibility for government agencies in this respect. Some of you may have read a recent article in the *New Yorker* [June 15, 1987 issue] by Barry Commoner, who expressed his view that the greatest improvement in the environment comes when a polluting substance or activity is banned outright, removing it from the environment, instead of just moving it around the environment from river to landfill, or to an incinerator, to the air, to human lungs, to the food. An analogy in the area of street crime would be EPA arresting the criminal after the crime had been committed (and not doing a very good job of finding and arresting the criminal) instead of preventing the crime and setting up programs to change the environment for the producers of the crime.

I think there have to be lines of activity other than regulatory ones. (I don't give these examples to say the regulatory system won't work. It can work; It has worked. We have a book out called *Freedom from Harm: The Civilizing Influence of Health, Safety, and Environmental Regulations*. It's the only book of its kind I've seen that brings together the benefits of regulation. We sent the first copy to OMB.) There is a lot we could do about the deficiencies in statutes that lead to problems in regulatory performance. For one thing, you must have deadlines, and you must enforce the filing of reports based on those deadlines. This government is full of reports that are overdue to Congress, regularly, chronically, sometimes a year or two years overdue. There's too little enforcement of deadlines.

Our environmental statutes should provide for systematic disclosure of *capability* data as well as harm data. Harm data deal with the effects of toxics, for example. Capability data deal with such things as recycling technology and the accompanying need for a vigorous public information program.

An environmental statute should provide for citizen suits, mandamuses, and injunction actions, settling the question of legal standing and providing for a kind of legal aid to groups—such as a poor rural group in North Carolina that a few years ago was opposing the dumping of PCB-contaminated waste. This would be a kind of legal aid for petitioners to regulatory agencies. During the Carter administration, this aid got under way at the Federal Trade Commission, National Transportation Safety Board, and the Civil Aeronautics Board. All aid was abolished when the Reagan administration took over.

Another provision in the ideal statute should be civil service accountability. Who ever thought civil servants, especially at a higher level, could be accountable only vertically, that is to their superiors, or to the cabinet secretary or to the White House? There also needs to be horizontal accountability to the citizenry, under prudent standards. You don't want to develop too insecure a posture for civil servants, or they'll be afraid to do anything. But you don't want a situation where civil servants and political appointees are not accountable.

The way to make a bureaucracy accountable, in my judgment, is to hold bureaucrats accountable personally. For example, there is a provision in the Freedom of Information Act to impose a thirty-day suspension sanction on a really officious government official who went out of his or her way to block the public's right to know. There needs to be more of that in environmental statutes.

Another provision in statutes that would make regulation work better, I think, is a more refined protection of internal dissent. There has been some advance in that area, but much of it is nominal. I am speaking about protection of whistle blowers. I thought when Ronald Reagan became president he was really going to stand up for those whistle blowers who are taking on the government and trying to get government off people's backs, but I haven't seen much protection of whistle blowers from the White House.

A final provision in the workable statute should be an affirmative-action duty by the agency to inform and facilitate the establishment of citizen groups interested in these areas. You can become too partisan in that respect, and I'm not talking about going to extremes. I'm talking about what was done in the early years of the air-pollution program, before EPA, when federal employees traveled around the country encouraging and helping establish citizen groups devoted to air-pollution control. They'd provide information to the groups, tell them what the standards could be and how bad air pollution was, and help the groups in other ways. I think there's a legitimate role for government in that respect.

Of course, the one provision we all would like, but never seem to get adequately funded, is the technical capability to encourage and test innovations in pollution controls. It's a way to appeal to the great inventiveness in our country, the "lone inventors," and give those inventors an evaluation capability, the way the Department of Energy was supposed to in the area of energy-conservation inventions. To have an R & D capability and an invention evaluation capability is a way to get around the constant industry complaint that companies don't have the technical know-how to achieve reductions in pollution, that they don't know how to achieve air standards.

Now I'd like to discuss a few specific environmental matters, the first of which is pesticides. As you know there is legislation pending in

Congress to strengthen the Federal Insecticide, Fungicide, and Rodenticide Act (FIFRA). EPA supports some of the provisions. The worst provision in existing FIFRA law is the provision saying that removing a pesticide from the market requires indemnification. Removing one particular pesticide from the market could cost EPA $160 million. The cost of removing other pesticides, as cited for the committee, are $80 million, $50 million, $30 million, and so on. It adds up to real money, as Dirksen used to say, especially when you look at the budget of the pesticide section here at EPA.

In 1986, EPA estimated that at least seventeen pesticides had been found in the drinking water wells of twenty-three states. We have been gathering all the data we can get a hold of concerning the kinds of chemicals being found in drinking water and drinking-water sources, such as surface water and ground water. The numbers are far greater than the official experts would indicate. (Why do we have to do this digging for information? It's EPA's job.) The slowness with which the 1974 Drinking Water Act has been implemented has been very, very discouraging, except for the 1986 Act, which maybe will give the process a higher level of metabolism.

The administrator ranked pesticides as one of the most urgent problems facing the agency. It has been staggering to total up how little has been achieved in all these years under FIFRA, compared to the number of pesticides that are being sold and misused. There are forty-seven carcinogenic pesticides registered for use on food, according to the agency. The General Accounting Office [GAO] has noted that EPA has generally taken two to six years to complete Special Reviews of chemicals that may pose significant health or environmental risks, even though these reviews are supposed to be conducted more rapidly.

Since the mid-1970s many congressional, GAO, and other reports have documented the failure of EPA and the Food and Drug Administration [FDA] to protect the environment from pesticides. For example, in 1972 Congress directed EPA to reevaluate the safety of about six hundred older chemicals licensed for use before current requirements for health-effects testing were enacted. By the spring of 1986, according to the GAO, EPA had not completed a single final safety reassessment of a chemical. The GAO also criticized EPA's failure to regulate inert ingredients in pesticides, some of which are toxic in their own right.

We are witnessing advertisements for termite control by pesticide applicators, and we know these companies are using chlordane. The struggle to remove chlordane from that use still goes on. One TV ad shows a couple listening to the termites consuming the beams on which their home rests. You get the impression the home is going to collapse unless the termiticide firm comes on the scene. And it does. Then everything is fine, and the termites are gone and the couple is seen, in the last seconds of the ad, smiling. They're not seen breathing chlordane.

EPA is in favor of repealing the indemnification provisions of FIFRA, particularly since it has only a $60 million budget for indemnification, and if EPA invoked an emergency suspension of chlordane alone, indemnification would cost $53 million.

I want to give an illustration of what I think is going to happen in confronting these regulatory delays. Take the pesticide Alar. The first studies casting suspicion on Alar came out in the late 1970s, and there may be five or six reliable studies. Alar, as you know, is a chemical applied by growers to apples to make them rosier and to make them mature about the same time. These are some of the greatest objectives of the Western world, I want to tell you.

Alar is a systemic chemical. You can't wash it off. It gets into applesauce and it gets into apple juice, which are heavily consumed by infants, who are particularly susceptible to toxic chemicals. EPA moved over a year and a half ago to ban the chemical. The science advisory committee to the EPA said that the data weren't strong enough. So EPA put it on a three-year review status. That's when some of us got fairly upset, and I decided to try something. So I called up the chairman of Safeway, the grocery chain. He was, at the time, almost totally preoccupied with the Haft takeover attempt, so I got him at just the right time, from my point of view. I said, "Why are you selling people apples and applesauce with Alar?" He said, "What's Alar?" I told him what Alar was, and suggested his people probably had information on the subject. "Why don't you just voluntarily state that you will not buy any Alar-treated apples or apple products?" I asked. He said he'd let me know.

Within a week he sent me a press release saying that Safeway had notified its growers and suppliers that it would not accept any Alar-treated products. We then went to A & P. It got easier after that with the other major supermarket chains. I've always sought some value to economic concentration in our society, and I finally found it. If you deal with a dozen supermarket chains, you cover a good deal of the retail supermarket food dollar. Anyhow, six or seven major chains made the same announcement.

Around the same time, the Apple Commission of Washington State and Michigan informed their growers that it would be advisable not to use Alar, even though the commission believed it was harmless. Then the National Academy of Sciences presented its study, in which Alar came out pretty high on the harm index. We're trying to get some of the supermarkets to test their products to make sure their wishes are being carried out. Even so, I think there's been a very significant reduction in the use of Alar.

This approach is going to be tried in other areas. Citizen groups, locally and nationally, need to try to get voluntary withdrawal of these chemicals by using big buyers against the suppliers or against the growers. Not all projects will work as easily as Alar, which is largely a cosmetic chemical. But on the other hand, the strategy could be a little bit more sophisticated as well.

Again, to illustrate the value of citizen suits, have you noticed the spread of these suits against the violation of water-pollution permits? The Natural Resources Defense Counsel [NRDC] and other groups now have hundreds of cases under way. Many of them are settled or won. As a matter of fact, one group in New Jersey has found that court suits have led to settlement nine times more often in favor of the environmental group than against. So we're going to see more action of that sort. NRDC apparently has its specialty in this now; it's handling these like workman's compensation cases. They've made it a very routine pattern of litigation.

Let's look into the subject of hazardous waste and Superfund. This one is really challenging environmentalists. They don't know quite what to do, other than to try to get Congress to appropriate more money, increase the penalties, and provide for citizen suits. Indeed, it is one of the most difficult and intractable areas to deal with, if the approach is to deal with hazardous waste in palliative or clean-up ways, instead of a preventive way.

An intriguing hypothesis is that if, in effect, you pay people to comply rather than penalize them, you might get further. That would turn our jurisprudence upside down. But we do know what happened a few years back when a hazardous-waste deadline was coming up and many companies hired midnight truckers to dump the stuff in ravines and streams. So we do need some new thinking here. We may have to bite our lip and develop an incentive rather then a penalty system. This is particularly true since the violation pattern can be so surreptitious and so successful and so deadly to so many unsuspecting persons, as well as encouraging a violation pattern of organized crime activity to relieve respectable business polluters of their droppings.

In January 1987, the GAO released a report that contained the following details: A decade after Congress directed EPA to regulate the handling of hazardous waste, the agency had imposed federal controls on less than 10 percent of the five thousand types of waste regarded as potentially hazardous. The EPA expanded regulatory loopholes, and when Congress directed the agency in 1984 to reconsider 150 exemptions that EPA had granted, the EPA upheld only 32.

For fiscal year 1986, EPA's enforcement activity was significantly lower under the Resource Conservation and Recovery Act [RCRA] [the federal law dealing with disposal of waste] and Superfund than in other programs. In 1986 EPA referred 44 cases in these areas, an increase of only 4 from 1985. Under Superfund, the number of administration orders [corrective measures] declined from 160 in 1985 to 139 in 1986. Under RCRA, administrative orders declined from 327 to 235 in these two years.

So we're seeing greatly reduced enforcement levels. This is a theme, I might add, that has persisted in the last six years through many other regulatory agencies.

A few comments on the drinking-water issue. Last year we met with then-Administrator Lee Thomas and his assistants for drinking-water matters. One of the things that came out of the meeting was a proposal to put out a clearly written pamphlet about an individual's rights under the drinking-water law, and what a person should watch out for. Very quickly, it was drafted and the agency was kind enough to circulate it for comment, and we did comment. That was early in 1988. I haven't seen anything since, and it hasn't come out. In the meantime, we've come out with our own pamphlet. Copies are available today. In just eight pages it gives comprehensive, readable information about drinking-water safety and laws. It answers questions about home-water treatment systems, bottled water, investigating your water quality, lead in drinking water, and what your rights are as a citizen regarding your local water supply.

Even though EPA has the authority to do that job, you're surrounded by all these corporate law firms and trade associations and political action committees working on Congress, and you're sat on by the White House philosophy of minimal regulation—or what I call minimal law and order applied to corporate violence. I think that's closer to the mark than the word "deregulation."

So where are you going to look for help? We are talking about a political process, not just a technical, administrative, legal process. You've got to receive help from an *organized* citizenry. No law whose beneficiaries are unorganized is ever going to work very well when up against organized opponents. The citizenry must become organized, which is what the Clean Water Action group has been doing in many areas around the country. Somehow, within your particular minimal flexibility under the present administration, you've got to find a way of alarming people properly about what is going on in terms of lead, or benzene, or any number of contaminants in their environment.

If anyone wants to write a classic analysis of the failure of important laws to be implemented, the two leading candidates are the pesticide law, FIFRA, and the Safe Drinking Water Act. Both were enacted with a lot of fanfare and hope, and both failed because of something they have in common: There are very few groups around the country, apart from some here in Washington, monitoring and suing EPA. There are very few groups around the country—there is one in Texas—organized to deal with pesticide contamination or with drinking-water safety.

People who are concerned about unsafe drinking water buy bottled water, assuming that if it comes in a bottle it's okay. That takes away the people who are most likely to agitate and organize. Wherever you have an easy exit system from a perceived abuse pattern, you're going to have increased difficulty in organizing people. That doesn't mean it's insurmountable; there are millions of people in this country who aren't able to afford bottled water. But it does mean that the economic system is ingenious at providing exits for disgruntled people. If there's air pollution, give them air conditioning. As long as it's cool, they'll take the gas. There are all kinds of sensory exits operating here. But that doesn't do any good for a person's lungs or eyes or body. Those parts of the person are still very sensitive to pollutants. They don't exit. But the psychology of dissent and demand for change does exit.

Enforcement of drinking-water standards is poor. Thirty-five percent of the systems in this country are in violation of one or more of the standards, yet the federal government and state governments do not take action. We still don't have a single major city in this country with a granular activated carbon water treatment process, yet they're all over Europe.

If, in addition, you don't have adequate detection systems to build data in the drinking-water contamination area, you have less ability to trace the pollution back to the water source, and back to the particular polluter who is responsible. The lack of data-gathering for drinking-water sources has been very troublesome to people who want the safe-drinking-water law to work.

Acid rain. That one will go down as the Reagan-Mulroney duet. Canada is pushing us to do something about acid rain. It started out with David Stockman [then head of OMB] asking why we should spend billions of dollars to save a few fish in the Adirondack lakes. Stockman never let knowledge interfere with his judgments. The general attitude was that this is nothing serious—we had acid rain twenty thousand years ago, and it's not important enough to warrant this kind of expenditure.

Then the first advisory panel to Mr. Reagan came in, saying that we don't know everything we need to know about acid rain, but we know enough to start acting. That was ignored. So now we're in a research mode which, it happens, will be completed just after the end of the second term of the Reagan administration. There may be some information yet to be discovered that will mitigate what some people think are the serious impacts of acid rain. But I don't see this quest for more knowledge as being particularly innocent. I see it as being a way of avoiding the problem. You can have a quest for knowledge here and a quest for knowledge there, but you have to look at the motivation if we're going to see whether the quest is really sincere and having a beneficial effect, or whether it's just a technique for delay.

In December 1986, EPA's Office of Solid Waste suffered a wave of staff trauma and low morale. Staff turnover was at an all-time high, according to the office's employees. Turnover was at 25 to 33 percent over the period from July to December, and the agency's annual average is said to be 12 percent. (In some EPA offices there isn't any staff trauma or morale problem—in the indoor air-pollution section, for instance, because there's very little activity.) But bad morale is a function of leadership that is not stimulating or supportive. It's also a function of the press paying very little attention to people in these offices who are trying to do a good thing under great pressure. These people ought to be highlighted. They're not likely to get the civil service awards, but they should get citizen awards for this type of activity. The problem is, if you finger them, then they're really in trouble. One of the best ways to lose your job in government is to do it properly. But rest assured that those of you who qualify for that designation are very much appreciated—as are your brown envelopes and other communications that fulfill the public's right to know about nonsecurity matters.

We have come a long way in public information. I remember in the early 1960s, the navy resisted a demand by the Department of Interior's water-pollution section to disclose how much sewage from naval bases was being dumped into bays. The explanation by the navy was that if it announced the amount of sewage dumped, some agent from communist China with an abacus would be able to figure out how many sailors there were at the bases. The disclosure of pollutants and sewage from naval bases was deemed classified data. Imagine the navy saying that now.

So things have improved. Around 1964, *Life* magazine was sitting on two stories about water and air pollution. *Life* didn't want to do a big story on air pollution until there was an inversion disaster. *Look* magazine didn't want to do a story on air pollution because they couldn't find a way to do it without mentioning the auto companies, which had great full-page ads in the magazine before it folded. So things are getting a lot better in that respect.

On the other hand, we have an increased awareness of the difference between what we deserve, in terms of a safe environment, and what we're actually getting. The gap has never been greater. We are concerned that we're not getting out many reports like "Toxic Chemicals and Public Protection" [a report to the president by the Toxic Substance Strategy Committee issued May 1980], since Mr. Reagan took office.

Whether from the environmental council at the White House or from EPA, we're not getting enough public reports that scientists, citizen groups, community organizations, and the press can use. I hope we don't look back on these eight years as a kind of Dark Ages in terms of the gathering and dissemination of environmental information, but we may well have to.

## Questions from the Audience

Q   Do you see a shift toward more environmental action by state and local governments instead of the federal government? Are citizen groups becoming more active?

A   Environmental action by states is uncertain. It depends on the governor. The governor in one state may be very active. Then you find another governor, as in California or Arizona, and down it goes again. So there is no uniform expectation of increased activity by states.

I think you're going to see more detecting and measuring instruments in the hands of citizens or groups who will make their own pollution measurements and take action. Already companies are pushing that: Test your indoor pollution, test your home for radon, etc. That alone, because of the commercial thrust behind it, is going to get more and more people buying these instruments, testing, and then saying, "What's wrong? There's lead in the drinking water." More and more people now are taking samples from their faucets and sending them to labs for analysis.

Then they feed information to the press. They ask the mayor, "What are you going to do about lead in the drinking water?" It happened here in Washington, for example, in a certain part of the city. Sometimes a mayor will respond; sometimes a governor will respond. I believe you'll see an overall increase in this activity.

At the same time, this is one country, and EPA is the cement that binds it together environmentally. EPA is viewed as having greater technical capability than the states do.

Q  Even though citizen groups are pushing to get funding from EPA, you should be aware that a lot of EPA resources are not being devoted to the Agency's professional staff, but to private contractors seeking to turn a profit. We at EPA take an oath to serve the public interest when we come to work for the federal government, whereas the contractors, who do work similar to that of the professional staff here, are profit-motivated. We hope your people are carrying the message out to the public that the professional staff at EPA is subject to a lot of political pressure and budget limitations. We need help from the outside to keep the high standard of professionalism and public service alive. It's very important for you on the outside to help us.

A  That's a very good point. You'll notice I mentioned the importance of in-house R & D capacity and analytic capacity. You should have your own laboratories.

Three things happen when you contract out: First, you let someone else, a private firm, help shape policy. Let me assure you it does shape policy.

Second, the firm often has a conflict of allegiance. It's working for various kinds of interests and companies, and that creates problems.

Third, the more contracts these firms get, the more offers they make to people like you to leave EPA and join them. They're draining you. People are leaving EPA to earn more money doing similar work without any harassment from Congress. This kind of delegation is insupportable. It has built up a kind of government outside the government that isn't accountable. Trying to deal with these consulting firms is one of the toughest problems in the republic. It's like trying to get waste out of the defense budget. Basically, we are seeing a privatization of environmental protection. We'd like to help you in any way we can on that. Maybe we can get the Senate moving again on this problem.

You know what happened to the Agency for International Development [AID]. They built a whole series of consulting firms to do development studies and other agency work. Then they started losing their best people to these firms, and pretty soon you had two AIDs, one more accountable than the other.

*Q* EPA management is talking about the possibility of taking scientific work out of EPA and transfering it to some other federal agency. For example, some of our analysis of hazardous chemicals has been shipped off to Atlanta to the Centers for Disease Control. Would you comment on this?

*A* Obviously federal agencies can't have heavily overlapping labs and work, but I know both EPA and FDA labs are very shorthanded. Most people think the FDA does its own drug testing. Look what happened when EPA hired that outfit in Chicago to test pesticides: the company is now bankrupt, and data for pesticide registration applications were falsified.

I think it's a good use of taxpayers' money to have in-house capability. It's also a good way to attract young people who just want to do "research that's good," not research that leads to lethal weapons. You build up a scientific corps that way, from which comes scientific management within the agency.

*Q* Would you comment on the relative difficulty of motivating effective government responses to global environmental problems, as opposed to those that have a local character?

*A* In the 1950s you heard a lot about world federalism; then you didn't hear much about it. But I believe we will see international agencies with enforcement teeth, possibly ad hoc agencies, to deal with problems such as ozone depletion, the greenhouse effect, the Mediterranean, the Amazon area.

We have international cartels in commodities such as coffee and cocoa and diamonds. They're all pretty well networked. You have the "law of the merchant," which for hundreds of years has been a kind of common law that international traders abided by quite efficiently. There is great immediate need, and we're just dickering around with a treaty about ozone depletion. We really have to push for that. We got rid of our aerosol fluorocarbons in 1978. To my knowledge, no other country has banned fluorocarbons in aerosols. And that's just the beginning step.

The point is that if the Soviet Union and China ever developed a GNP per capita similar to ours, would this world be in the sink! Can you imagine a General Motors-type gas-guzzling car in every Russian and Chinese garage? The only thing that's saving us now is the fact that huge areas of the world are low per-capita consumers of polluting materials. That provides a little space and a little time. But if our economy is replicated across the globe, we'd be in very serious trouble. We've got to give more thought to supranational authorities in these areas. There are some models, binational and bilateral—Interpol, for example. But we've got to go much further.

Q  You expect the use of judicial remedies by environmental groups will decline. We've had a lot of legislative activity in the last decade. Do you expect this will increase during the next presidential term? And what kinds of legislation would you envision?

A  Instead of broad new grants of authority, I believe we should concentrate on improving existing legislation in light of experience. For example, we should get rid of the indemnification provision of FIFRA, improve the flexibility of sanctions, provide more opportunities for citizen suits, and develop better data-collection or in-house research ability. That's the kind of thing that needs to be done.

There will still be suits filed, but environmental and citizen groups are going to win fewer of them. A majority of the judges in the D.C. Circuit are Reagan appointees. They're not very responsive to these things—I doubt whether some of the great environmental lawsuits of the 1970s would prevail under this D.C. court—and after a while environmental groups will get the word. It's the reverse of what happened in the civil rights arena back in the days when Earl Warren headed the Supreme Court. Civil rights groups got nowhere with legislatures, so they went to the courts. If it hadn't been for the Warren Court, there might have been an insurrection in our country. But the groups kept going to the court, and they kept winning desegregation and civil rights suits.

That's the way it goes, back and forth. But we hope we'll go more forth than back with an informed constituency. You ask yourself what it will take to get a strong implementation of the drinking-water-safety law. How many citizens organized in how many congressional districts doing $x$ hours of citizen work will it take? Nobody has analyzed that, you know. Just how many does it take, a hundred thousand? Give me twenty thousand people ready to make safe drinking water their specific hobby and willing to devote three hundred hours a year to the activity—that's what the average confirmed bird watcher devotes to his hobby, I'd imagine—and you'd see a remarkable difference.

It comes back to the need for access to our mass media, the air-waves. We just can't allow the public airwaves to be licensed, twenty-four hours a day, to television and radio stations without payment or public control. It's the stations who now decide who says what and who doesn't say what. We have a proposal for an "audience network." This would involve an hour of prime time reverting back to a network made up of viewers and listeners. The network would be congressionally char-tered, nonprofit, financed by a small fee contributed by members of the network—people who, through a staff of producers and reporters, would put together their own, professional-quality programs.

The public has never had an electronic voice. It's always been that if you don't like a TV program, you switch it off. Not, "Hey, we want some of our time back so we can talk about these important health matters." Do you know how fast things would move if we had a few documen-taries on national TV about drinking-water safety, complete with ad-dresses people could write to for more information? The show format should be controversial, something like *60 Minutes*. You'd have a lot of people writing in, a lot of people getting involved.

The biggest single obstacle to people becoming involved in environ-mental health matters is ordinary apathy. People don't know what to do, or feel it wouldn't make any difference if they did know. But if people are given the information and tools and shown what they can do, then they can start achieving progress—progress that builds on itself. Otherwise people are apathetic and despairing. Apathy is the other side of powerlessness. When you're powerless you're much more likely to be apathetic. The people who are most energetic are the ones who have won a few victories. They see that action works.

When the administration tried to weaken the Voting Rights Act, there were groups around the country who had won a few victories, civil rights groups, and remember how fast the members of Congress back-tracked on that. And remember that in 1981 they eliminated social security payments to 3 million Americans, $120 a month, so that they could fund the latest missiles. The Senate approved the cut by about 94 to 4. But then the elderly groups found out about it, and within less than a year the Senate reversed itself by about the same vote. That's what we have to look for.

Q   How can EPA, and other agencies for that matter, really get their message across to the public?

A   Well, the *New York Times* and other papers should start doing front-page features on the constriction and contraction of information dissemination. Business complains that sufficient data are not being collected by the Census Bureau. Scientists complain. It's also a complaint of environmental, consumer, and labor groups that data are not being collected. What is collected is not being put in a form available to the citizen without paying for it twice. We pay for collecting the information through taxes. We shouldn't have to pay for it again in order to read what was collected.

The price of publications from the Government Printing Office [GPO] has skyrocketed: the *Congressional Record* is now over $225 a year; the *Federal Register* and the technical documents are also way up. If you want to get on the mailing list for Federal Communications Commission [FCC] or Interstate Commerce Commission [ICC] documents, you are referred to five or six private groups who have been authorized to sell you the ICC and FCC public statements, notices, and press releases. Some of it may be $200 or $300 a year.

We're trying to get the media interested in this; that's the first step. But I think they are much more likely to listen to calls from you on this issue than from us. Meanwhile, our calls will continue, and we are about to prepare a report on this as well.

When I was growing up in Connecticut, I got the *Congressional Record* from my senator, Senator Prescott Bush, father of George Bush. I got records of hearings; I got reports. Later I met Senator Bush after he retired. He said, "Oh, I know you. Your letters came in every other day asking for information." So here I was just a schoolboy in Connecticut, getting this information and devouring it. But now you can't do that. It's a tremendous expense, and the hearings usually are quickly out of print.

You know what the average print run of a congressional hearing is now? Unless there's a special directive to increase it: 300 copies, for the congressional committee. GPO is selling things like a seven-page pamphlet on hyperactive children for a $1.75 or $2. Hearings are now going for $20 or $30. That's why private publishing companies are putting out government materials. They can undercut GPO prices and still make a big profit.

GPO is shredding materials: 1,500 copies of the Watergate prosecutor's report were shredded by GPO. They say they're prohibited from giving away left-over reports that aren't selling. In Congress, there's a joint committee on printing that you should call. Some of the staff are very interested in getting something going. They would like to hear from people in federal agencies about this situation. They speak very authoritatively on this issue.

The feeling of the Reagan administration on the subject may have been epitomized by Ed Meese when he was a presidential aide. You remember a big press conference was held in the White House at which administration representatives showed all the reports they had Xed-out and would no longer publish. They ridiculed the publications. It was a very anti-intellectual session that went beyond saying that this report for veterans is outdated, or that pamphlet is no longer appropriate. It was more like, "Come on! Let's get rid of this stuff! Who needs it!"

We shouldn't underestimate. You may send out 1,000 reports, and 990 may be casually read or not read, but you're going to score here and there, and that's going to have a big multiplier effect. A schoolboy here or a homemaker there gets alerted to a problem and does something about it. These things happen. There was a homemaker, originally from a town on Lake Superior, who returned there with her kids and looked at the lake where they used to play. She couldn't see the bottom because of pollution coming out of Silver Bay [a facility for processing iron ore]. She kept pressing and pressing, "What's in this, what's in this?" Eventually a lab analyzed the waste water and found a form of asbestos in it, and there was a big cleanup. So a lot of scientific inquiries are prodded by very nonscientifically trained people who have a gut feeling that something is wrong.

You have to believe that information is the currency of democracy, that it's essential. You can't have an enlightened citizenry if you're going to cut a few million dollars from the information budget at the same time you're projecting hundreds of billions of dollars in weapons systems. I mean, where are we going to go with that kind of attitude?

So I really urge you to call the press or try to get people inquiring into this matter, because it's very serious: The noncollection of scientific data, the nondistribution of what is collected, or the overpricing of what is collected and distributed.

The environment is a cause that affects not only the intellectual sensitivity of people who care, but also their aesthetic sensitivity. That's one of the reasons environmental subjects rank higher in the public's interest than consumer-protection subjects. Environmental issues involve the wilderness, beauty, birds, cleanliness. These elements possess a real aesthetic dimension that fortifies the hard-core realization that you're dealing with a major public-health challenge as well.

Civilized societies, under the rule of law, are in accord about the need for management reduction of violence, are they not? We're going to see a lot more effort here. There will be a better day, and it's up to you to hang on and stimulate the next generation.

[JULY 16, 1987]

Ralph Nader first made headlines in 1965 when his book *Unsafe At Any Speed* exposed safety defects in U.S. automobiles, which led to auto recalls credited with saving many thousands of lives. His subsequent efforts in the areas of tax reform, energy, and health have inspired eight major federal consumer-protection laws.

In 1969, Mr. Nader founded the Washington-based Center for the Study of Responsive Law. In 1971, he established the consumer lobbying group, Public Citizen. He has set up a number of national networks of citizens' groups, including the Aviation Consumer Action Project, the Center for Auto Safety, the Clean Water Action Project, and the Disability Rights Center, and he is chairman of the National Citizens' Committee for Broadcasting, a media watchdog group. Mr. Nader also helped found Public Interest Research Groups, student-funded and student-controlled organizations on college campuses.

# The Economic
# Case for the
# Environment

I was first made actively aware of environmental problems, as I suppose
many of us were, by Rachel Carson; she and I even shared the same
publisher. I then served for a number of years on the Environmental
Task Force of the Governor of Vermont, a state which, along with
Hawaii, has perhaps been as successful as any in carrying out its environmental responsibilities.

I also became interested in the environment when I was working on
*The Affluent Society.* I wrote much of it in Switzerland, and one morning I finished the draft of a passage which I regarded as being just a little
too vivid, a little too far out and gothic. So I left it on my desk for a day
or two to see whether or not I could use it. It went as follows:

> The family which takes its mauve and cerise, air-conditioned, power-
> steered and power-braked automobile out for a tour passes through
> cities that are badly paved, made hideous by litter, blighted buildings,
> billboards, and posts for wires that should long since have been put
> underground. They pass on into a countryside that has been rendered
> largely invisible by commercial art. (The goods which the latter adver-
> tise have an absolute priority in our value system. Such aesthetic
> considerations as a view of the countryside, accordingly, come second.
> On such matters, we are consistent.) They picnic on exquisitely pack-
> aged food from a portable icebox by a polluted stream, and go on to
> spend the night at a park that is a menace to public health and morals.
> Just before dozing off on an air mattress, beneath a nylon tent, amid

JOHN KENNETH
GALBRAITH, author of
*The Affluent Society,* is
Professor Emeritus of
Economics at Harvard
University.

the stench of decaying refuse, they may reflect vaguely on the curious
unevenness of their blessings. Is this, indeed, the American genius?

At the time, I regarded this paragraph as going a bit over the edge,
but in the end bad judgment prevailed, and I included it in the book. I
think I can honestly say it has been quoted at least ten times more
frequently than anything else I have ever written.

Today, however, I would like to examine some of the larger environmental and associated public concerns, looking first at the protection of
the countryside and then at the underlying influences in the evolution
of the modern city as these stir environmental and other worries.

I want to emphasize that the benefits of a well-protected environment are worthy in themselves, something worth having quite apart
from any functional justification. They have their own enjoyments,
including that of good health. But I'm also going to argue that there are
concerns having to do with countryside and urban life that are also
increasingly functional. We inevitably find ourselves defending environmental concerns more and more for their positive, affirmative support
to economic life in the later stages of economic development.

Let me say a word first about what I mean by economic development. This is of the utmost importance. We must always think of economic life as a process—a continuing, ongoing process of change. There
has always been, and is now, a view of economics that seeks to find its

ultimate, enduring, stable, unchanging truths. This search for enduring principles is an empty, invalid effort, one to which I take stringent exception.

There is no great mystery to the central feature of economic development. It is a process that moves economic life from producing things that are concrete to producing the less tangible objects of public consumption. In the elementary society (such as that in the United States until relatively recent times), the economic requirements of the standard of living were hard artifacts of one sort or another. These artifacts, these objects, were food, clothing, shelter, furniture, accoutrements, the components of the household establishment, and the means for travel and transportation.

Overwhelmingly, these constituted what we call the standard of living. And, indeed, they are central to the standard of living in poorer countries to this day. But with economic change, with the movement that is intrinsic in economic life, the importance of artifacts—the hard objects of production—gives way increasingly to the importance of less tangible things. In the simplest terms, we move to intangible enjoyments—from food, clothing, shelter, and travel equipment to education, television programs, the arts, music, libraries, and other public services. We also move to the enjoyments associated with the surroundings in which we live.

This is the process, and I emphasize it because it runs counter to the very deep commitment we all have to hard consumer goods. It perhaps seems unnatural that we move to the less tangible forms of production and away from what have been regarded since ancient times as the very substance of economic life.

But this change is related to another one—one that is extraordinarily important today. That is the differential capacity in the provision of these two broad categories of economic products between the older countries and the newer. With economic development there is a tendency for the production of hard goods to move to the newer countries—not everything, but a great range of things such as textiles, clothing, chemicals, steel, machinery, and the like. Production of all these moves away from the advanced, developed countries to countries newer on the economic scene.

This comes about partly because of lower wage costs—wage costs that cover a lower standard of living—but also partly because of the particular qualities possessed by people who are new to industrial life, new to a life away from the more egregious toil on the farm. They are, on the whole, more effective producers. Industrial life, we must always remind ourselves, is a wonderful thing for people who are just escaping the self-exploitation of peasant agriculture.

And there is another change of which we should be aware, a tendency in the older industries to become sclerotic. There is a certain hardening of the arteries among them that further accentuates the movement of the production of the goods they produce to their newer competitors.

The movement of the modern economy to the less tangible production that now characterizes the older countries strongly invites, in turn, a general invasion of the countryside because the latter offers particular advantages to the next stage of development. There is need for recreation—for skiing, hunting, biking, hiking—all activities for which the countryside is important and necessary. In this stage of development, there is also the obvious rise of travel, of the tourist industry— people who simply go to enjoy rural surroundings, to see the mountains, to rejoice in scenery that is not available in Manhattan.

And in this stage of development we also see the rise of an industry devoted to the needs of living, what we may perhaps call the "living" industry. It is one that is very important for all modern environmental concerns. Given this stage of development and the associated changes in consumption, a very large part of the population can now live away from a fixed place of work: people who live on social security or other pension entitlements, people who have accumulated savings or enough wealth to exempt them from a daily job. And there are also an incredibly large number of modern occupations, especially in the arts, where one can live and work with no fixed identification with a workplace. The living industry is now particularly important in some parts of the United States: in New England, New York, and on the Eastern Shore of Maryland. It is not uniformly distributed over the country, but it has become significant in large parts of it.

This living industry is associated also with other things, such as a second residence and the desire of people at a certain level of affluence to have a seasonal escape from neighbors or the tedium of local obligations, from all the things that encourage one to say, "Well, I'm off to Maine for the weekend."

However, this new industry also creates problems that we must address in the days to come; that we must, indeed, begin addressing now. These are the problems that come from tourism and recreation, from part-time residence, from the activities that are not a fixed part of work.

What encourages and supports the industries arising from the intangibles of life? What makes the living industries—the recreation industry, the tourist industry, and the like—important? And what do these portend for the countryside? What do they involve for its environmental protection?

There are many things that are important for the living industries. One is good government services. Many of the amenities of life in the countryside are associated with the services of government; accordingly, the latter must be easily and amply available.

It is important also that full attention be paid to the range of cultural amenities that support and give depth to the interest of life. I have in mind schools, colleges, libraries, museums, and other sources of educational and cultural activities.

A year or so ago, my wife and I were in the Clinch River Valley of Virginia. I imagine that very few at the EPA—even though you are required to venture into the least salubrious parts of the republic—have ever been to the Clinch River Valley. It is deep in the heart of Appalachia, a coal-mining area, a countryside of great physical beauty. A singular feature of this part of the Commonwealth of Virginia is that nobody wants to live there, and that is because government services and the amenities of life generally are not available, as all who live in that unfortunate valley will be quick to tell you.

The next thing that is important in this stage of development, and to which I come at last, is the assurance of environmental protection or, more precisely, of environmental wisdom.

We are dealing here with industries and with a style of life that have, among other things, a self-destructive capacity. One obvious example of this is tourism. The tourist industry, as it reaches out for customers, as it advertises, as it litters the roadsides, has an extraordinary capacity for destroying the very attractions that created the industry in the first place. What is advantageous for the individual enterprise in seeking a share of the business culminates in disaster for all enterprises.

It is encouraging that Vermont and a few other states now recognize this self-destructive tendency and are taking steps to correct it. In Vermont, where I go in the summer, we have been exceptionally cautious about billboards and have given a lot of thought over the years to the protection of the roadsides. This is something about which we are going to have to be even more conscious in the future. It is a deeply functional matter, for it will keep the tourist industry from destroying itself.

Here and in the companion problem area of designing and controlling the real estate development that serves the living industry, there is an extraordinary tension. The unspoiled landscape, the unspoiled environment, initially sustains and encourages the development. But that development, particularly if it is unwise, then repels the people who were initially attracted.

One of our greatest problems lies in this field of economic design. We want the living industry, and we want it to satisfy and serve us. But we need to realize that this industry, by its very development, must be designed and controlled to avoid its own self-destructive character.

In consequence, we must accept that there will be tension, and that the tension will be between what is good and appealing in the present and what is functionally necessary in the future. We must not have opposing groups, one side against the other. We must be wise enough to see that there is a common, long-run advantage in good developmental design: in zoning, building restrictions, architectural control, and other key matters.

At the same time, if I may digress a moment, the subject can also be a source of mild amusement. Along with other full-time and part-time residents of Vermont, I have been observing, not without interest, an episode that by now must have come to an end. One of the great conflicts we have had in Vermont is over the so-called Killington Development.

Killington is a lovely mountain in the central part of the state, excellent for skiing. A large complex of condominiums, by no means of bad design, sprang up on the side of the mountain, but the project ran into serious difficulties over a proposal to purify the sewage from the development and have it sprayed as artificial snow on the slope. That produced a somewhat unfortunate bumper sticker widely seen in the state: "Killington, where the affluent meet the effluent."

But that wasn't all. A workman appeared at the building site with the sticker on his car and was promptly sacked. He then instituted a well-publicized lawsuit for improper discharge. The local newspaper added still further to the wonderful controversy with a cartoon that showed a skier going hell-for-leather down the slopes of Killington carrying two toilet plungers as ski poles. So much for the living industry and its conflict with environmental needs.

Let me now go on to the second part of my comments and look at urban development and economic development in the modern city as we see them in their connection to the environment.

We customarily measure economic development by the level of economic product or income, also called the gross national product or national income. We could just as well measure it by the extent of the urbanization of the society. In the advanced industrial society, nearly everyone lives either in or near a city. In the industrially undeveloped lands, the overwhelming number are still in the countryside, still in agriculture.

At the beginning of the present century, the as yet industrially undeveloped American republic had nearly 40 percent of its workers employed in agriculture. It now has 2.9 percent, whereas in India some 65 to 70 percent are still so employed. In other countries of the Third World—many of the African countries, for example—the percentage is even larger.

The test of the quality of life in an advanced economic society, in consequence, is now largely in the quality of urban life. Romance may still belong to the countryside—the future may still belong to the countryside—but the present reality of life abides within the city.

The "city," however, is not a single entity. Historically, there have been three quite distinct types, and it is important to recognize the differences among them.

To begin, there has been, over time, the political or ecclesiastical city—the capital. Second, there has been the city founded on mercantile trade—the merchant city. The first two cities have been very successful and serve to show what the city *can* be. The third, the industrial city, has not been successful.

The capital city was and remains a place with a reputation not only for success but for grandeur. In past times, it was the extension of the personality of a ruler or a ruling family, or it reflected a priestly tradition. In modern times, the capital city is or can be the expression of the democratic ideal and recruits attention for that reason.

In architecture and urban planning, the capital city was and is a place of style, even magnificence, as well as a community where, quite evidently, even the humble want to live. The older of these capitals—Rome, London, Paris, Vienna, Peking, Delhi, Agra—still draw tourists from around the world. The younger political households—Washington, Leningrad, Islamabad—are places of distinction.

Also successful has been the second of the great city types, the merchant city. While the political and ecclesiastical centers have the grandeur of controlled design and creation, the merchant cities exhibit the controlling influence of a shared purpose. To be a merchant was, presumably, to have some perception of style. Accordingly and in keeping with that, the merchant city was also a place of distinction and pride. Thus the cities of the Venetians and the Florentines, of the Belgians at Bruges, of the Dutch at Amsterdam, and the towns of the Hanseatic League.

To the merchant centers—as to the capital cities—tourists went in dense numbers. And the modern merchant city, as also the capital city, still generally attracts interest, approval, and people. The shopping areas of New York, London, and Tokyo are regarded with pride.

I now come to the industrial city. Its reputation is much less. The industrial city suggests a world of mean streets, mean houses, poor services, and poor air. In the last century, it was the city of the dark, satanic mills. The industrial city is seen as a world of social tension, anger and occasional outright conflict, and of an affluent minority who are wisely absent in the suburbs or behind guarded doors.

That is the reputation and in no slight measure it is still the present reality of the industrial city. To the industrial city, the tourists do not come—only the sociologists. Unlike the capital and merchant cities, the industrial city does not have a reputation for social, cultural, or political success. The question is: What can be done to redeem its reputation and its reality?

In fact, the industrial city is now changing everywhere in the world, especially in the older industrial countries. It is changing its productive enterprises; it is changing its products and its economic and social structure; and all of these changes are for the better.

The patterns at hand for further improvement of the industrial city are not abstract and theoretical. On the contrary, they derive in part from the solid experience and reputation of the successful cities and also in part from recognizable changes that are already happening in the components of modern industrial life.

Even in industries that produce hard industrial products, industrial life increasingly involves automation, robotization, and other technical processes. In general, such changes have the effect of blurring the old class structures of the industrial cities. Is the man or woman who serves by watching a computer screen a member of the working masses or a member of management? The answer is not clear, and the society becomes less contentious because of the muting of class conflict.

Changes are also under way in cleaning up industrial processes, reducing industrial pollution, and brightening the external aspect of the industrial city. Working to achieve these changes, against more than occasional resistance, is a greatly improved public conscience in these matters. Thirty years ago, when I argued the importance of urban environmental protection in *The Affluent Society*, the subject was perceived by most people in terms of a rather distant vision. The public perception has changed considerably since then.

Clearly, to overcome its past and present reputation, the industrial city must continue its escape from the environmental disorders that are so much a part of its history. It must do so not for compassionate reasons but because clean air, clean water, clean streets, and a healthy workplace are economic imperatives. Simply stated, economic development occurs where people—including executives, engineers, scientists, and the sponsors of new business enterprises in the arts—want to live. And they do not want to live amidst industrial debris and gloom.

However, this is not all. The industrial city must also escape from the social and cultural environment of its past. In the past, its social environment reflected the broad industrial commitment to laissez faire. Apart from some exceptional cases, no one took responsibility for the city's overall design and development—for anything beyond its mere habitability. Its growth was autonomous, an act of nature or accident. In contrast, the higher reputation of the capital city or the merchant center depended on the overall authority that, explicitly, assumed responsibility for its design and ongoing development.

The industrial city, to repeat, has lacked the kind of foresight and planning that went into the foundation of the capital and merchant cities. It must, as a very practical matter, have these things in the future. Let there be no doubt; there is no really good and perhaps no really habitable city where growth, development, and redevelopment are not subject to a competently administered design.

The industrial city must escape tradition in still another respect. Historically, the city was meant to house people cheaply for employment in the factories and mills. Public services—schools, libraries, hospitals, parks, public sanitation, even the services of the police and the courts—were deemed good insofar as they were cheap. To support such services, levies had to be borne either directly by the industries or indirectly by the wage earners of the city. Such services were seen as costs that affected the competitive position of the industrial firms, something to be kept at a minimum.

In other words, the public standard of living was seen as a threat to, or a deduction from, the private living standard. Some of these attitudes persist. We still seek to maximize the private standard of living; we still seek to minimize the public standard of living. A TV set is a valued amenity; public schools are a social cost. Privately purchased books are part of our living standard; public libraries are a burden on the public budget. Clean houses are essential for our quality of life; clean streets are not. The affluent accept the private cost of security guards but resist the public cost of the police. These attitudes, we must now recognize, are among the obsolete legacies of our industrial past, and they must be changed to accord with the present reality.

In the postindustrial city, the public living standard must be seen as no less important than the private. Public services must in their quality be wholly on a par with private consumption. It follows that the great modern city, the postindustrial city, will be expensive to develop and maintain. As a society, accordingly, we must face facts concerning the expenditures that will be required to sustain it. The costs of public services do not simply rise proportionately as urban populations increase; sometimes they rise exponentially. Nevertheless, these expenditures will be economically functional; they are necessary if we are to ensure the further development of the industrial city.

The quality of life in all our cities will be decisive to our economic future, and the quality of urban life depends heavily on the quality of its public services. We must outgrow fears concerning the adverse effect of the burden of taxes on industrial growth. Instead, from a wholly pragmatic political standpoint, it is time to focus all our attention on the quality of life, the nature of the demands of modern industry, and the quality of our educational and other public service systems.

A central responsibility for urban design and development, environmental protection, a high standard of public services, including education: all of these, to repeat, are vital steps toward redeeming the future of our industrial cities. In addition, we need also to have positive economic support for some of the central contributors to advanced economic development. In particular, there is the importance we should now attribute to the arts.

There is a long-standing belief that out on the cutting edge of economic development are the engineers and the scientists. I don't want to diminish their role, but beyond the engineers and the scientists, there are the artists. After things work well, people want them to look well. After good function comes the rather more difficult problem of good design, and beyond well-designed products there are entertainment and the enjoyment of life.

Artistic enterprises, like environmental controls, are central to our future, part of our means of escape from the failings of the urban industrial past. Clean air, clean and safe streets, good public services, serious attention to artistic endeavor: all of these are imperatives if we are to succeed in bringing our industrial cities up to the standard that has been achieved in our merchant cities around the world and even more particularly in our capital cities.

*Professor Galbraith's prepared talk ended here. Unfortunately, the sound recording was terminated after only one question.*

## Question from the Audience

Q You have stressed aesthetic values, intangible values. One of the things that we at EPA must do is deal with very tangible things, like health. And one of the binds we get into has to do with something that economists give us, the quantitative analysis of socioeconomic aspects of health policy. Would you comment on the validity of trying to balance costs against benefits, of valuing life, and of even going so far as to discount (in the financial sense of the word) future life?

A I learned something a couple of years ago as a fellow of the University of Chicago (an honor which they bestow upon you from time to time, and which mostly requires you to give a lecture and to spend a few days "on the midway"). One day I dropped in on a lecture by an old friend of mine on cost-benefit analysis. It was a superb lecture, and I sat there looking at the Chicago chapel, which many of you know is one of the purest examples of good gothic architecture anywhere on this continent, and my mind was diverted between the excellence of the cost-benefit discussion and the fact that the chapel would never have survived a cost-benefit analysis.

I hate to retreat into subjectivity, but I'm firmly of the view that these are matters where we must not trust to arithmetic calculations and algebraic equations—that we must trust our consciences as public citizens. We shouldn't hesitate to do so.

But when somebody is making a cost-benefit analysis, don't stop him from doing it. He or she probably needs the job.

[NOVEMBER 12, 1987]

John Kenneth Galbraith is the author of *The Affluent Society, The Anatomy of Power, A Life in Our Times, The New Industrial State,* and *The Age of Uncertainty.* Apart from intervals of government service, he has spent most of his life teaching at Harvard University, where he is Paul M. Warburg Professor Emeritus of Economics.

During World War II, as deputy administrator of the Office of Price Administration, Professor Galbraith was the principal organizer of the wartime system of price control. In 1945 he served as director of the U.S. Strategic Bombing Survey. For his wartime work, he was awarded the Medal of Freedom.

Professor Galbraith served on the campaign staff of Adlai Stevenson in 1952 and 1956. From 1956 to 1960 he was chairman of the Economic Advisory Committee of the Democratic Advisory Council. An early supporter of John F. Kennedy, he was the Kennedy administration's U.S. ambassador to India from 1961 to 1963.

Professor Galbraith is a past president of the American Economic Association, a member of the American Academy of Arts and Sciences, and a member and past president of the American Academy and Institute of Arts and Letters. He is currently vice-chairman of the American Committee on United States-Soviet Relations, an honorary Fellow of Trinity College, Cambridge, and a commander in the French Legion of Honor.

# The Failure of the
Environmental
Effort

I feel, as perhaps a number of you do, that there is a crisis in the development of the country's environmental program.

In 1970, with enactment of the National Environmental Policy Act and the creation of EPA to administer it, the country marked a turning point in its environmental history.

Beginning in the 1950s, new forms of environmental pollution had appeared and rapidly intensified: photochemical smog, acid rain, excess nitrate and phosphate in water supplies, pesticides and toxic chemicals in the food chain and in our bodies, dangerous accumulations of radioactive waste.

Then, in 1970, pressed by a newly aroused public, Congress began a massive effort to undo the damage. Now, nearly twenty years later, the time has come to ask an important and perhaps embarrassing question: How far have we progressed toward the goal of restoring the quality of the environment?

The answer is indeed embarrassing. Apart from a few notable exceptions, environmental quality has improved only slightly and, in some cases, has become worse. Overall improvement since 1975, when most of the consistent environmental measurements began, amounts to only about 15 percent.

Table 1 summarizes the story for air emissions (other than lead) since 1981—coincidentally, the advent of the Reagan administration. The annual rate of improvement has dropped from 1.52 percent per year

BARRY COMMONER is the founder and director of the Center for the Biology of Natural Systems at Queens College, City University of New York, and professor in the Department of Earth and Environmental Science.

to only 1.16 percent per year. At that rate, it will take nearly a hundred years to undo the environmental damage created over the past twenty years.

Next, look at water resources, as shown in table 2, based on a comprehensive assessment conducted by the U.S. Geological Survey. Here, it's a question of whether the trends are improving or deteriorating. For all the standard water-pollution items, measured at several hundred reporting stations across the country, improvement occurred at only 13 percent of the stations. In another 15 percent there is deterioration. At the bulk of the stations there is no change.

All the environmental news is not gloomy, however. You can find a handful of very significant improvements, as illustrated in table 3. Reduced lead emissions in the air, reduced DDT in body fat, PCBs in body fat, mercury in Great Lakes sediment, strontium-90 in milk, phosphate in isolated rivers such as the Detroit. For these pollutants, improvement has been in the range of 70 to 90 percent in the last decade or so.

There is a lesson here.

These are the only pollutants for which the control measures have been not high-tech devices but a very simple solution. In every case, the nation simply banned the production or use of the material.

Air emissions of lead have declined by 86 percent because much less lead is now added to gasoline, and therefore that much less is in the environment. The environmental levels of DDT and PCBs have dropped

TABLE I

### Changes in Emissions of Standard Air Pollutants
### United States, 1975–85

| Pollutant | Emissions (million metric tons/year) | | Percent Change |
| --- | --- | --- | --- |
| | 1975 | 1985 | |
| Particulates | 10.4 | 7.3 | −29.8 |
| Sulfur dioxide | 25.6 | 20.7 | −19.1 |
| Carbon monoxide | 81.2 | 67.5 | −19.1 |
| Nitrogen oxide | 19.2 | 20.0 | +4.2 |
| Volatile organic compounds | 22.8 | 21.3 | −6.6 |
| Average | | | −14.1 |
| Lead | 147.0 | 21.0 | −85.7 |

sharply because their production and use have been banned. Mercury is much less prevalent in the environment because it is no longer used in the production of chlorine. Strontium-90 has decayed to low levels because we and the Soviet Union have had the simple wisdom to stop the atmospheric testing of nuclear bombs that produce it.

The lesson of both the few successes and the far more numerous failures is the same: Environmental pollution is very nearly an incurable disease, but it can be prevented. What you do when you take lead

TABLE 2

### Water Quality Trends in U.S. Rivers 1974–83

| Pollutant | Trends in Concentration (Percent of Sites) | | |
| --- | --- | --- | --- |
| | Improving | Deteriorating | No Change |
| Fecal coliforms | 14.8 | 5.2 | 80.0 |
| Dissolved oxygen | 17.1 | 11.1 | 71.8 |
| Nitrate | 7.0 | 30.3 | 62.7 |
| Phosphorus | 13.1 | 11.3 | 75.6 |
| Suspended sediment | 14.1 | 14.7 | 71.2 |
| Average | 13.2 | 14.7 | 72.1 |

TABLE 3

## Significant Improvements in U.S. Pollution Levels

| Pollutant | Trends in Concentration (Percent of Sites) | | Control Measure |
| | Time Period | Percent Change | |
| --- | --- | --- | --- |
| Lead emissions[1] | 1975–85 | −86 | Removed from gasoline |
| DDT in body fat[2] | 1970–83 | −79 | Agricultural use banned |
| PCB in body fat[2] | 1970–80 | −75[3] | Production banned |
| Mercury in lake sediment[2] | 1970–79 | −80 | Replaced in chlorine production |
| Strontium 90 in milk[2] | 1964–84 | −92 | Cessation of atmospheric nuclear tests |
| Phosphate in Detroit River water[2] | 1971–81 | −70 | Replaced in detergent formulation |

Notes
[1] Measured as amount emitted per year.
[2] Measured as concentration.
[3] Change in percentage of people with PCB body fat levels greater than 3 ppm.

out of gasoline is to prevent its entry into the environment. Once you allow lead, nitrogen oxides, or other pollutants to be released into the air, you've got a lot of trouble getting rid of them.

As it turns out, environmental degradation is built into the technical design of modern instruments of production. A high-compression car engine is not only high-powered, it's a smog generator. A farm that uses chemical fertilizers and pesticides is not only productive, it's also an uncontrollable source of water pollution. We call it a "nonpoint source," and a nonpoint source is uncontrollable. A trash-burning incinerator not only produces energy, it produces dioxin as well, and so on.

The environmental hazard in these cases is just as much the outcome of the facility's technological design as is its productive benefit. For example, high compression is the cause of both the auto engine's power and the production of nitrogen oxides. Nitrogen oxides trigger smog. The extensive use of fertilizer and pesticide accounts for the productivity of the modern farm, and also for the pollution of rivers and ground water. The same combustion process that extracts energy from trash also releases the precursors that combine to produce dioxin.

Most of these technological changes that have brought us both high productivity and pollution are the results of sweeping change after World War II. That's when we got the new, large, high-powered, smog-generating cars. That's when there was a shift from fuel-efficient railroads to trucks and cars. That's when we began to substitute undegradable and hazardous petrochemical products for the biodegradable and less toxic natural products. That's when we substituted chemical fertilizers for manure. It's hard to believe, but before 1950 practically no inorganic nitrogen fertilizer was used in this country. It's all a postwar development.

By 1970, it was clear—some of us wrote about it—that these changes in the technology of production are the *root cause* of modern environmental pollution. This conclusion has been confirmed by the sharply divergent results of the effort to clean up the environment.

If I may allow myself a bit of retrospection here, in my book *The Closing Circle*, I analyzed the upsweep in pollution since 1950. I came to the conclusion then that the situation was due to the design of the technology of production. I'm not happy about the situation, but I feel personally pleased that theory has been confirmed by what has happened since 1970, as we tried to push pollution back.

Only in the few instances in which the technology of production has been changed—by eliminating lead from gasoline, mercury from chlorine production, and so on—has the environment been substantially improved. When the technology of production is unchanged, as when you take the same car engine and try to put a control device on it, you don't get very good results.

The point I want to make from the data is simply this: When a pollutant is attacked at the point of origin in the productive enterprise, it can be eliminated. Once it is produced, it is essentially too late.

Unfortunately, the legislative base of the whole environmental program was created, according to my reading, without reference to the origin of the crisis it was supposed to solve. You do not find in the laws any discussion of the origin of environmental pollutants—of *why* we have been afflicted with the pollutants that the laws were designed to control. This is true of every country, incidentally, and it goes back to the U.N. environmental conference in Stockholm in 1972. You were pretty much forbidden to talk about the origin. That was put off to the side in a separate forum, where some of us radicals were.

Back when our environmental laws were originally conceived, there was no shortage of theories being offered the legislators. Go back to the record, and you'll find Paul Ehrlich saying pollution is all a matter of population. And I put my side forward. Some theories, I have to tell you, were greeted with a great deal of skepticism.

For example, I well remember the incredulity in Senator Muskie's voice when he asked me whether I was really testifying that the same technologies that generated post–World War II economic progress were also the cause of pollution. I was. I don't believe I convinced him.

Because environmental legislation has ignored the origin of the problem, it has dealt only with its subsequent effects. And having to define the disease as a collection of symptoms, the legislation mandates only palliative measures. But preventing pollution, as the data show, is the only thing that really works. And prevention is an approach that appears only fitfully in the environmental laws, and has never been given any administrative force.

It is with some trepidation that I address people at EPA about the impact of this fundamental fault in our environmental laws on the operation of the agency that is chiefly responsible for administering and enforcing those laws. But that's really what I want to talk about.

To show exactly what I mean, look at the notorious record of environmental pollution racked up by the modern automobile. The failure to deal realistically with this enormous pollution source was commemorated on December 31, 1987, when dozens of urban areas were once again allowed to miss the deadline for meeting air-quality standards for carbon monoxide and ozone, pollutants for which the automobile is largely responsible.

Where has the effort to rid the environment of its automotive nemesis ended? What has been the result of the massive amounts of environmental analyses, emission standards, rulings, and litigation coming from EPA on the subject of automotive pollution?

For more than twenty years we have understood the origin of photochemical smog. The high-compression engines, introduced after World War II to power the suddenly enlarged American cars, will necessarily run hot. It's a law of physics that they do. At elevated temperatures, engines convert the oxygen and nitrogen in the cylinder air to nitrogen oxides. Once out the exhaust, nitrogen oxides are activated by sunlight, react with airborne fuel and other hydrocarbons (many of them otherwise relatively benign) and convert this mixture into ozone and all the other noxious components of photochemical smog. This is well known. It's been reported over and over again.

What has EPA done about it? EPA has tried to deal with the smog problem by aiming at everything except the crucial target, which is the engine's production of nitrogen oxides. That's what was new. We had hydrocarbons in the air before smog. What we didn't have was nitrogen oxide. But what EPA has done is propose regulations to reduce emissions of hydrocarbons from a bewildering array of sources, from gasoline pumps, the corner dry cleaner, house painters, body shops, and so on. The approach has clearly failed. I think there is no question about that.

Now let me suggest another approach—that you are better off attacking the problem at its origin. What could be done to deal with the production of automotive nitrogen oxides? You stop producing it.

It's worth noting that this approach accords well with a corresponding approach to health: prevention. Rather than trying to cure a disease, or tolerating it, you prevent it from happening. The preventive approach to disease, of course, is the source of some of the major advances in public health. The classic example is smallpox. Widespread use of a preventive measure, vaccination, has now completely eradicated the disease. There is a zero incidence worldwide. That's a real accomplishment.

Like smallpox, the great majority of the assaults on the environment are, in fact, also preventable. After all, nearly every environmental health hazard (the major exception being natural radiation) has been created since 1950 by introducing inherently polluting forms of production technology, including the modern chemical farm, the high-powered car, and so on. These health hazards are not the result of natural processes, but of human action. Human action can once again change the technologies and undo their harm.

Is this approach to the automotive smog problem really practical? Can smogless engines that do not produce nitrogen oxides be built? They can. Indeed, they have been. Every pre–World War II car was powered by such an engine; that's why the country was then free of smog.

But production of nitrogen oxides can be prevented without giving up the American car's precious over-powered engine (which is, nevertheless, a good idea in its own right). The so-called "stratified-charge" engine can do just that. According to a 1974 National Science Foundation [NSF] study, prototypes were then already operating in Detroit, and tests showed the engines would meet the 90 percent reduction in nitrogen oxide emissions required by the Clean Air Act amendments.

But the NSF report also said the engine would need to be considerably redesigned, requiring a new fuel injector, fuel pump, sparkplug system, cylinder head, piston, and intake and exhaust manifolds. Unlike adding a catalytic converter to the exhaust system of an existing engine, this would mean extensive retooling in the manufacturing plants. According to the report, had the auto industry decided in 1975 to take this course, the stratified charge engine could now be powering most U.S. cars. And automotive nitrogen-oxide emissions would have been sharply reduced instead of increasing.

In short, the goal established by the Clean Air Act could have been met instead of allowed to slide back, but only if EPA had confronted the auto industry with a demand for fundamental changes in engine design. EPA was unwilling, or unable, to take on this task. EPA's reluctance or inability to tell the auto industry what kind of engine it should build has helped undermine the goal of the Clean Air Act.

There are other examples of how pollution can be attacked at its source, and thereby prevented or considerably reduced.

Had American farmers been required to reduce the present, often unproductively high rate of nitrogen fertilization, nitrate water pollution would now be falling instead of increasing. If farms were required to shift from blindly repeated pesticide applications to integrated pest management, the rising level of pesticide pollution could be checked.

If the railroads and mass transit were expanded; if the electric power system were decentralized and increasingly based on cogenerators and solar systems; if the pitifully small percentage of American homes that have been weatherized increased, then fuel consumption and attendant air pollution could be sharply reduced.

If brewers were forbidden to put plastic nooses on six-packs of beer; if supermarkets were not allowed to wrap everything in sight with a film of polyvinylchloride, and then to stuff that into a plastic carrying bag; if McDonald's could rediscover the paper plate; if plastics were cut back to uses where they are really needed, such as in artificial hearts and video tape, then we could push back the petrochemical industry's toxic invasion of the biosphere.

Of course, all this is easier said than done. What I am proposing is no small thing easily accomplished by bureaucratic fiat. It means sweeping changes in the major systems of production—agriculture, industry, power production, and transportation. But the undertaking would have a social purpose: environmental improvement.

As I pointed out in some detail in a recent article in the *New Yorker* [June 15, 1987 issue], this represents social, as contrasted with private, governance of the means of production, an idea that broaches the infamous "s" word, socialism. It's an idea so foreign to what passes as our national ideology that even to mention it violates a deep taboo. I'm waiting for a thunderbolt because I used the "s" word right here in Washington, D.C.

But it's not my purpose here to argue the merits of undertaking such a sweeping change in the country's deeply felt concept of political economy. Rather, I am interested in discussing the consequences, especially for EPA, of our failing to address the issue of environmental quality in these fundamental, if highly disturbing terms.

But first I want to at least mention a major consequence of failing to take needed action in the fields just noted. The matter lies a bit outside the realm of the environment, but is closely allied with it. I am speaking of the efficiency of the national economy.

By now it is depressingly clear that the U.S. productive system, despite its past gains, is in a state of decline. Among the industrial nations of the world, the United States has one of the lowest rates of annual improvement in a fundamental economic parameter: productivity.

A good deal of this decline derives from the fact that new, highly polluting post–World War II production technologies were based on large-scale, centralized, capital-intensive, and energy-intensive facilities. The country's overall economic efficiency is now heavily encumbered by the low productivity of these facilities in terms of return on capital and low output per unit of energy used.

For example, compare the output per unit of capital invested in a nuclear power plant and in a cogenerator. Compare the productivity per unit of energy used between truck freight and railroad freight. Railroads are notably more energy efficient.

These and a number of other forms of post–World War II production technologies are very capital intensive and very energy intensive, and contribute greatly to the decline in productivity of our capital and energy. As a result, our economy has one of the poorest rates of development of any country in the world. So the change in the technology of production has had much more pervasive an effect than simply doing damage to the environment.

Now let us turn to the impact on EPA of the taboo against social intervention in the production system. A major consequence of this powerful taboo is the failure to reach the goals in environmental quality that motivated the environmental legislation of the 1970s.

The present, largely unsuccessful, regulatory effort is based on a now well-established process. First, EPA must estimate the degree of harm represented by different levels of the numerous environmental pollutants. Next, some "acceptable" level of harm is chosen. For example, a cancer risk of one in a million. Then you establish emission standards or ambient standards that presumably can achieve the risk level you've established.

So, you set up the ambient standards, and polluters are then expected to respond by introducing control measures such as automobile exhaust catalysts or power plant stack scrubbers that will bring emissions or concentrations to the required levels. If the regulation survives the inevitable challenges from industry (and in recent years from the administration itself), the polluters will invest in the appropriate control systems. Catalysts are appended to the cars, and scrubbers to the power plants and trash-burning incinerators. If all goes well, as it frequently does not, at least some areas of the country and some production facilities are then in compliance with the regulation.

The net result is that the "acceptable" pollution level is frozen in place. Industries, having heavily invested in equipment designed to just reach the required level, are unlikely to invest more in further improvements. The public, having been told the accompanying hazard to health is acceptable, is likely to be equally satisfied. Some optimistically inclined people will look upon exposure at the so-called acceptable level as a kind of guarantee of health. Others, perhaps aware of the linear relation between pollution level and the risk to health, will conclude we are doing as much as we can, and they will, in most cases, accept the remaining risk fatalistically.

Clearly this process is the inverse of the preventive public health approach. It strives not for the continuous improvement of environmental health, but for the social acceptance of some, hopefully low, risk to health.

In a way, this is a return to the medieval approach to disease, when illness, and death itself, were regarded as a debit on life that must be incurred in payment for original sin. Now we have recast this philosophy into a more modern form: Some level of pollution and some risk to health are the inevitable price that must be paid for the material benefits of modern technology.

The preventive approach aims at progressively reducing the risk to health; it does not mandate some socially convenient stopping point. The medical profession, after all, did not decide that the smallpox prevention program could quit when the risk reached one in a million. In contrast, the present regulatory approach, by setting a standard of "acceptable" exposure to a pollutant, erects an administrative barrier that blocks further improvement in environmental quality. This, I believe, is a major cost of our failure to confront the environmental crisis at its source.

But how do you decide when to stop, where to set the standard? The current fashion is called "risk/benefit." Since a pollutant's ultimate effect can often be assessed by the number of lives lost, let's say from cancer caused by an environmental carcinogen, the risk/benefit analysis requires that a value be placed on a human life. Some economists have proposed that the value should be based on a person's lifelong earning power. It then turns out that a woman's life is worth much less than a man's, and that a black's life is worth less than a white's. In effect, the environmental harm is regarded as smaller if the people killed are poor—a standard that could be used to justify situating heavily polluting operations in poor neighborhoods. And, in fact, this is an all too common practice. No one puts a toxic dump on Park Avenue.

Thus, thinly veiled by a seemingly straightforward numerical computation, there is a profound, unresolved moral question: Should poor people be subjected to a more severe environmental burden than richer people, simply because they lack the resources to evade it? Since in practice the risk/benefit equation masquerades as science, it deprives society of the duty to confront this moral question. It seems to me, therefore, that one result of failing to adopt the preventive approach to environmental quality is that the regulatory agencies have been driven into positions that seriously diminish the force of social morality. It may be a harsh thing to say, and it's not the fault of the people at EPA, but I think this is what's happening.

What is the result when, by whatever means, standards are set, but for the reasons described earlier, the required control measures fail to achieve the standards? Something has to give, as witness the scandalous situation in air pollution.

In 1970 the Clean Air Act Amendments called for a 90 percent reduction in levels of urban carbon monoxide, hydrocarbon, and ozone, setting a 1977 deadline for achieving this goal. The penalty for failure was very severe: loss of federal funding for development projects. In 1977, with compliance not even in sight, the deadline was moved to 1982. And when that also was missed, the deadline was once more delayed, to December 31, 1987. Now, with urban areas in which 100 million people breathe substandard air still in noncompliance, it is my understanding that some of these places will be given another twenty-five years to comply—to meet the standard, if they can. Step by embarrassing step, because we are unwilling to adopt the measures that can prevent air pollution, enforcement of the laboriously constructed standards evolves into a distant hope.

It hardly requires a sociological survey to determine the response to this retrogressive policy. The polluters can justify their inaction and the public its apathy. It erodes the integrity of regulation and diminishes public faith in the meaning of environmental legislation. This is part of the price we pay for failing to attack environmental pollution at its origin.

Confronted with such environmental failures, regulatory agencies have become remarkably creative about finding new ways to retreat. The latest is what I call the Humpty-Dumpty approach. You will recall that in *Through the Looking Glass*, Alice gets into an argument with Humpty-Dumpty, who claims that the word "glory" means "a nice, knock-down argument." When Alice objects to this arbitrary redefinition, Humpty-Dumpty says: "When I use a word, it means just what I choose it to mean." Alice replies: "The question is whether you can make words mean so many different things." Humpty-Dumpty's response is unanswerable: "The question is, which is to be the master."

I'm afraid Humpty's freewheeling linguistic philosophy has begun to take hold in regulatory circles. Not long ago, for example, when tests of fly ash from trash-burning incinerators showed that it was sufficiently contaminated with toxic metals to qualify as a hazardous substance, as defined by EPA, the New York State Department of Environmental Protection issued a remarkable pronouncement. Metal-contaminated fly ash is not a hazardous substance, it was declared, but a "special waste." This didn't change the lead or cadmium content of the fly ash, of course. What it did mean was that fly ash, unlike an ordinary hazardous substance, need not be consigned to an expensive Class I landfill—an additional cost that, according to a New York State official, might cripple the incinerator industry.

EPA and other regulatory agencies have put a great deal of effort into defining a hazardous substance. Clearly the public must rely on the integrity of this definition in dealing with Superfund sites and a whole range of contaminated materials. The linguistic detoxification of fly ash may be a handy expedient for New York State—which, from what I understand, may soon be emulated by EPA as well. With Humpty-Dumpty in charge, the public has good reason to doubt who really is the "master" that decides what environmental regulations mean. The loss of public confidence is a price we pay for the failure to regulate the *cause* of environmental pollution instead of its symptoms.

Another hazard is that conflicts between the stated goals of environmental regulation may be resolved at the expense of the facts.

A number of EPA divisions have done this country and the world a great service by devising and operating wonderfully effective fact-gathering systems—those dealing with air pollution, toxic substances, and radiation, for example. One of the most effective EPA programs, which uniquely meets EPA's mandate under the Toxic Substances Control Act "to assess chemical risks to the U.S. population," is the National Human Adipose Tissue Survey, carried out by the Office of Toxic Substances. The latest survey, for example, provided data on the distribution of dioxins and furans in the adipose tissue of the general population. Clearly, the adipose tissue data were an enormously valuable way of directly assessing toxic risks, and a valuable factual counterweight to the shaky assumptions so often involved in indirect risk assessments. These data enabled us at the Center for the Biology of Natural Systems to show that the cancer risk from this general dioxin exposure was even higher than the risks used by EPA to trigger regulation of airborne carcinogens under Section 112 of the Clean Air Act.

I was aware at the time that this posed a dilemma for EPA. To be consistent, EPA would need to regulate the sources of dioxin (largely, trash-burning incinerators), an action vigorously opposed by the incinerator industry.

Recently a way of seemingly resolving the dilemma has been discovered: Cancel the survey! This is perhaps the most pernicious consequence of the current misdirected regulatory approach—the attempt to shield ourselves from difficult facts by destroying the instrument that produces them. I hope this action by EPA will be reversed.

Finally, I wish to discuss the impact of the current approach on science. It is hardly news that scientific decisions about environmental hazards have consequences that extend far beyond the objective domain of the weekly department seminar. Although the scientific participants may be convinced that their decisions are even-handed and objective, the consequences are not.

Each such decision means that some people will save a good deal of money and others will spend more; that some people will be more concerned with their children's health and others less; for a few people, the decision creates a political problem, and for a few others, a welcome political opportunity. These are simply the facts of regulatory life.

In this situation, there is an understandable tendency to find purely scientific grounds, which appear to be free of economic or other judgments, for unequivocal standards of exposure—a firm line below which there is a simple message: healthy! The so-called NOEL, or no-effect level, is such a standard—a threshold level below which it can be said on presumably objective, scientific grounds that all is well.

On the other hand, if there is a linear relation between dosage and effect, with no such threshold, then determining the allowable standard moves from the seemingly solid realm of science to the more arguable domain of judgment, of policy. When a linear, no-threshold relation does exist, every level of exposure, no matter how small, will result in a corresponding degree of medical risk. In that case, an "acceptable" standard must somehow balance the expected harm against some other value—the supposed worth of a human life, or the cost of controlling or cleaning up the pollutant.

An instructive example is provided by one of the most difficult, and controversial, problems: the cancer risk from exposure to polychlorinated dibenzo-dioxins and -furans which, for the sake of simplicity, I shall lump together in the common term "dioxin." At present, the only EPA-promulgated standard on dioxin exposure is the criterion for cleanup of dioxin-contaminated soil: 1 part per billion (1 ppb). This action guide is derived from the detailed dioxin risk assessment produced by EPA in 1985. Based on a modeled linear relation between dioxin dosage and cancer incidence, this assessment determined that a dosage .006 picograms per kilogram per day would represent a lifetime cancer risk of one in a million to the exposed population.

This risk level—one in a million—has commonly been used as a measure of acceptability. It is, of course, a social judgment and not a scientifically derived value. However, if the risk assessment is changed (for example, by increasing the dosage that is expected to generate a one-in-a-million risk), the standard can be altered without changing the social judgment, thus avoiding this contentious area of discourse.

For Syntex (USA), Inc., the company liable for the dioxin cleanup costs in Missouri, this is a matter of money. That was made explicit in a 1986 paper by Paustenbach *et al.*, then of the Syntex staff. Their figure 1, reproduced here (figure 1), shows that if cleanup standards were relaxed from 1 ppb to 10 ppb, cleanup costs would fall by 65 percent—a con-

Figure 1

Estimated Cost of Soil Removal and Cleanup at Castlewood Site, Missouri

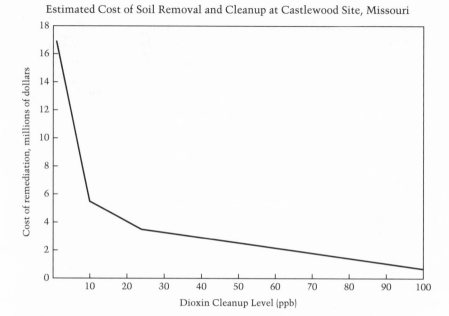

Note: Plot is based on EPA estimates of the number of yards of soil contaminated at various concentrations of dioxin and their estimated cost for incinerating soil.

Source: J. D. Paustenbach, H. P. Shu, and F. Murray, "A Critical Examination of Assumptions Used in Risk Assessments of Dioxin Contaminated Soil," Regulatory Toxicology and Pharmacology 6 (1986): 284–307.

siderable saving. The Syntex paper calls on regulatory agencies such as the CDC [Centers for Disease Control] and EPA to give careful consideration to the "methods and assumptions used in any risk assessment of dioxin-contaminated soil. The primary reason is the cost of remediation varies dramatically with the degree of cleanup."

In this and a subsequent paper, the Syntex scientists develop reasons why the 1985 dioxin risk assessment is wrong. They disagree with this assessment's assumption that dioxin is either a cancer "initiator" (also known as an "inducer") or a "complete carcinogen" and therefore governed by a linear dose/effect relationship. They claim, instead, that dioxin is a "promoter" and, therefore, a threshold exists below which dioxin will have no effect on cancer incidence. The Syntex scientists conclude that the EPA 1985 risk assessment should be sharply reduced.

Now, some of you may have heard about a recent draft report, prepared by an EPA task force, which develops a rationale for a new dioxin cancer risk assessment that is sixteen times lower than the risk assessment published by EPA in 1985, and which (unless changed) may become the scientific basis of any regulatory action on dioxin. As the Syntex people have made quite clear, such a reduction in the cancer risk would have powerful consequences. It would not only reduce the cost of cleanup in Missouri and at many of the Superfund sites, but also enhance the environmental acceptability of trash-burning incinerators, weaken the claims of Vietnam veterans who were exposed to Agent Orange, and affect the outcome of numerous court cases.

Moreover, the scientific issues go to the heart of the division between the preventive and the jiffy-bandage approaches to environmental regulation. As it happens, I have been asked to review the new report. And believing as I do that the public is entitled to be privy to scientific disagreements on such issues, I want to discuss it now.

The scientific disagreement relates to the role that dioxin plays in the biological process that leads from exposure to a chemical to the appearance of a tumor. According to a well-known theory (which, as the draft report quite properly points out, is yet to be established for any specific substance), this process is characterized by two main sequential steps. First, a substance (an "initiator") causes an irreversible genetic change in the exposed cell that creates the potential for the cell to proliferate into a tumor. Then, another substance (a "promoter") causes such previously induced cells actually to proliferate and produce a tumor.

It is generally agreed that the dose-response relationship exhibited by an inducer is linear down to very low doses. That is, every increment in dosage generates a corresponding increase in the carcinogenic effect. It is also generally agreed that, in contrast, promoters exhibit a threshold below which there is no effect.

Mathematical models have been developed to estimate, from the results of animal experiments, the risk of cancer in people exposed to given amounts of dioxin. Some models assume dioxin is an initiator (or a complete carcinogen, capable of both effects), and others assume it is a promoter. In general, the risks computed from initiator-based models are considerably greater than the risks computed from promoter-based models. The 1985 EPA risk assessment assumes that dioxin is not a promoter but a complete carcinogen.

Thus far, we have dealt only with assumptions and mathematical models based on them. Now, for a quick review of the experimental facts.

Dioxin, by itself, induces cancer in rats and mice, acting as though it were a complete carcinogen capable of both initiation and promotion. However, it clearly lacks the diagnostic property of an initiator: It is not genotoxic—and it does not cause mutations. This suggests to some specialists that dioxin must be a promoter, and indeed it does sharply increase the carcinogenic effect of a previously applied initiator. But dioxin also lacks the diagnostic property of a promoter: There is no clear evidence that it causes cell proliferation. According to the actual evidence, then, dioxin is neither an initiator (or complete carcinogen) nor a promoter. This means the initiator/promoter scheme is not a sensible way to try to account for the effect of dioxin on cancer incidence, and that risk assessment models based on either of these assumptions are not valid.

But there remains the unassailable experimental fact that rats and mice that are exposed only to dioxin exhibit a significant incidence of tumors, in proportion to the dose. According to the initiator/promoter theory, this is the behavior of a complete carcinogen. But since dioxin is not mutagenic, it is not an initiator and therefore (in terms of the theory) not a complete carcinogen. It acts like one, but does so in ways not encompassed by the theory.

Fortunately, there is an extensive body of data that does account for this apparent paradox about dioxin's very powerful effect on cancer incidence. This is the fact that dioxin greatly enhances the activity of an enzyme known as aryl hydrocarbon hydroxylase, or AHH, that is a necessary participant in the action of most environmental carcinogens, converting them chemically to the actual active agents.

Accordingly, exposure to dioxin will considerably increase the effective concentration of a complete carcinogen. This effect is so powerful that, apparently, dioxin can sufficiently increase the activity of the small amounts of carcinogens present in the laboratory food, water, and air as to generate the increased tumor incidence observed when dioxin alone is provided to the test animals.

Thus, the presence of dioxin translates into an increased concentration of the carcinogen—the effect of which is best estimated from a linear model, such as that used in the EPA 1985 risk assessment. In effect, dioxin influences tumor production by enhancing the activity of carcinogens. These relationships are delineated in table 4.

With this brief background in mind, let us examine how the EPA task force decided that the 1985 EPA risk assessment was sixteen times too high.

TABLE 4

Characteristics of Complete Carcinogens, Promoters, and Dioxins

| Property | Complete Carcinogen | Promoter | Dioxin (2,3,7,8-TCDD) | AHH Inducer |
|---|---|---|---|---|
| Mutagenesis (e.g., *in vitro*) | yes | no | no | no |
| Cell proliferation | yes | yes | no | yes |
| Reversibility | no | yes | yes | yes |
| Autonomous tumor production | yes | no | yes | |
| Enhancement of carcinogen-induced tumor production | no | yes | yes | yes |
| Multiple tumor types | no | no | yes | yes |
| Antitumor effect | no | no | yes | yes |

Their draft report notes that in addition to the complete carcinogen-based risk assessment, there are several others, developed by other agencies, that yield risk assessments nearly five orders of magnitude lower than the EPA 1985 value. These lower risk estimates are based on the assumption that dioxin is a promoter. There are five risk estimates considered by the task force. The estimates range in value (of the dioxin dose expected to generate a one-in-a-million risk) from 0.006 to 10 pg/kg/day. The lowest estimate, a reference dose of 0.006 pg/kg/day, is that of the EPA 1985 risk assessment. The task force decided the proper risk assessment is the midpoint of the range, which is 0.1 pg/kg/day—a value sixteen times higher than that derived from the EPA 1985 risk assessment (figure 2).

There are two very basic things wrong with this conclusion.

First, accepting that the procedure of averaging the different risk values is valid, the data base is grossly deficient. The draft report mentions two additional risk assessments that are also acknowledged to be equally consistent with the data and that yield, respectively, risks that are 10 and 100 times *greater* than the EPA 1985 risk. Inexplicably, the draft report does not include these values in the range used to compute the midpoint. If the values are included, the midpoint is more nearly 0.01 pg/kg/day, rather than the report's choice of 0.1—and thus a reasonable confirmation of the EPA 1985 risk of 0.06.

But I find *the method itself* a more grievous violation of scientific

Figure 2

Lifetime Daily Dose of Dioxin (2, 3, 7, 8 – TCDD) Estimated to Give a Plausible
Upper-Bound Cancer Potency of One in a Million

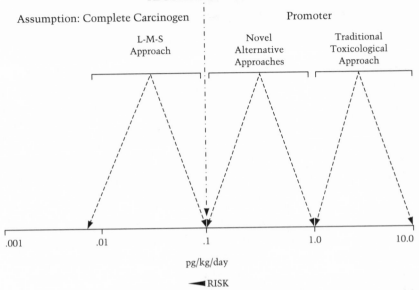

RECOMMENDATION

Assumption: Complete Carcinogen | Promoter

L-M-S
Approach

Novel
Alternative
Approaches

Traditional
Toxicological
Approach

.001          .01                    .1                    1.0                10.0

pg/kg/day

◄ RISK

procedure than even the strange shrinkage in the data base. Perhaps I
can best explain my concern with a parable.

Let us suppose there is an animal in a closed room, and from pre-
vious experience the animal is known to bite, but with an undeter-
mined severity.

A scientific task force is called in to evaluate the bite risk. Opinions
differ. One group says, "If we assume the animal is a lion, and apply an
appropriate mathematical model, we can compute that the risk from its
bite is 10 in a million." The other group prefers to assume the animal is
a dog, and its model yields a risk of 0.001 in a million.

The scientists engage in a bitter debate, and in an effort to resolve
it, they manage to provoke some sound from the unseen animal. It
neither barks like a dog nor growls like a lion. Finally, since a report is
due, they reach a consensus: The risk is midway, logarithmically, between 0.001 and 10, or 0.1 (figure 3).

Now, what's wrong with this picture? What about the method,
averaging the two types of risk estimate? Clearly, if the animal is a dog,

56

Figure 3

Delineation of Dog vs. Lion Parable

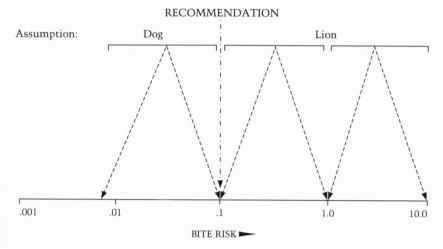

it is not a lion, and vice versa. Logically, this leads to the conclusion that at least one of the two classes of risk estimates is wrong, but we don't know which. At this point, the task force has two estimates, at least one of which is certainly wrong, and the other of which may be right or wrong. It hardly makes sense to average the two values. But in fact, since the animal neither barks nor roars, both sides are wrong. Which destroys the logical base of both risk models. This is a defect that surely cannot be cured by averaging the results.

The end of the story is this: Some particularly hardy soul decides to open the door and actually look at the animal. It turns out to be a monkey, which then playfully slides open a door at the back of the room, turning loose a loudly roaring lion.

In case my parable remains unclear, let me suggest that the monkey (which, unlike the two assumed animals, is *really* in the room) represents the actual observations about the enzyme-enhancing role of dioxin in carcinogenesis (as contrasted with the initiator/promoter assumptions). What dioxin—the monkey—does is release the serious effects of the complete carcinogen(s)—the lion.

I believe the new draft report on the dioxin health risk fails to meet certain rudimentary requirements of scientific discourse. However, it may be that that is not the proper standard for judging the report. It is not entirely clear that the draft report is to be regarded as a purely scientific document. The report itself yields a mixed reading on this issue, for it speaks of the conclusion as representing a rational *science policy* position for EPA.

I have emphasized this last phrase because in some sense there is an inherent contradiction between science and policy. In the present context, the relevant attributes of science are, first, its demand for rigorous, validated methods that are independent of the expected results, and second, its objectivity, or the independence of the data and analysis used to reach the results from the interests of those affected by them. By contrast, Webster defines policy as "prudence or wisdom in the management of affairs . . . , management or procedure based primarily on material interest."

If the new dioxin risk assessment is a purely scientific exercise, then, for the reasons discussed, the conclusion that the EPA 1985 assessment should be greatly reduced falls under the weight of its seriously inadequate methodology. If it is, instead, a policy document, or some undefined hybrid, then the document fails to meet a different obligation: It fails to specify what "material interest" was intended to govern the outcome of the exercise.

Was it the explicit interest of Syntex, Inc., in reducing its Missouri cleanup costs? Was it the often-expressed interest of the Office of Management and Budget in balancing health risks against the costs of achieving them? Or was it the interest of the American people in minimizing the risk to their health?

None of us are ready to prescribe what should be done to remedy the environmental failure. This will require the courage to challenge the taboo against even questioning the present dominance of private interests over the public interest. It will require good science and wise policies. But I suggest that we know how to begin—by an open public discussion of what has gone wrong and why. That is the necessary first step on the road toward realizing the nation's unswerving goal: restoring the quality of the environment.

## Questions from the Audience

Q Over the years, and again today, you have called for government control over the country's system of production. You say this will prevent or reduce pollution. But aren't the socialist countries, where production is strongly controlled by the state, in greater environmental trouble than we are?

A  For a radical like me, it's a tragedy that the Soviet Union and other socialist countries violate one of the basic precepts of Marxism: that various aspects of a culture—technology, art, etc.—should reflect, to some extent, the fundamental relationships of production. They violate this precept. I'll give you a somewhat humorous example.

I was invited to Poland for a meeting of their chemical industry. The Polish government had just bought—lock, stock, and barrel— DuPont's plant for making Corfam, a synthetic leather. Du Pont had sensibly closed the plant because you couldn't make good shoes from Corfam. They pinched and sweated and did other unwelcome things. But the Polish government bought the whole blooming plant.

I said to their officials: "You've got more horses than people in Poland. Horsehide makes excellent shoes. Why do you need a Corfam factory?"

They said: "It's modern technology."

Corfam is another product of the petrochemical industry. And the petrochemical industry is organized—through its physical structure, the kinds of reactions that are carried out, and the kinds of products it makes—to maximize profits. It is strange, but the Soviet Union and the socialist countries haven't quite picked up on this. Maybe that is what the socialist countries want to do: maximize profits. But every time you maximize profits, and think only of that, you get into trouble environmentally.

The reason we're in trouble with automobile pollution is big cars. As Henry Ford said, "Mini cars make mini profits." The reason Detroit went to big cars is not that people wanted them—until they were told. It was because big cars were more profitable.

Still, the issue always comes up: Isn't it up to us? Isn't it our fault that we buy the big cars, for instance? Well, no it isn't.

Let me give you my favorite example of why the consumer is not really to blame in most cases. I wear size 12 socks. That's an intimate fact I will share with you. Not long ago, I went into a well-known New York department store and asked for a pair of size 12. They said, "Oh, that's a special order. But over there you can get size 10-to-13."

Today it is very hard to get sized socks. Is this because of consumer demand? Do you know anyone who went into a store and said: "Listen, my feet change size every week. I need a variable-size sock?"

That is not why it was done. It was done to reduce inventories and maximize profits.

I'll give you a less facetious example. You go to the store to buy a refrigerator. You and the storekeeper have no idea how the thing was delivered from the factory. It could have come by railroad or truck. If it comes by truck, it causes four times as much pollution as if it came by railroad, because the fuel efficiency is four times lower. But what am I going to do, go into the store and say, "Listen, I'm an ecologist. I must have a refrigerator delivered by railroad"?

My response to that kind of situation, and I tend to be somewhat practical, is to get into politics. You have to rebuild the railroads, and you're not going to do that by saying: "Oh, well, we should not buy these silly refrigerators."

Certainly there are consumer efforts that are important. For example, I think the plastics industry is going to go into conniptions soon over growing consumer rejection of plastics, and I think that's fine. But let me tell you, you're not going to get the petrochemical industry, the Dows and Monsantos, to roll over the way McDonald's did, because Dow and Monsanto don't sell directly to the public. There are no fast-plastic-selling joints.

So there you are. I tend to see the issue as social, economic, and political. I simply refuse to blame us consumers. Mind you, I have a sort of religious preference for natural fibers over plastic ones, but that's about as far as I go.

Q   How many lives would be saved by eliminating pollution from automobiles?

A   I don't have those figures in my head. What I do know is that in the 1970s there were a number of public health surveys, and the figures were quite substantial. I think it would be in the tens of thousands of lives a year, easily.

What you are dealing with, in the case of carbon monoxide, for example, is a stress on the cardiopulmonary system, pure and simple. Clearly, people who are in distress because of heart problems or circulation problems are under very severe risk from carbon monoxide.

Or take sulphur dioxide. Sulphur dioxide inhibits the action of the cilia of the cells that line the lungs and clear the lungs of pollutants, and so on. That has a sort of negative catalytic effect on the intensity of what you experience from all air pollutants.

There have been figures, on mortality and morbidity, but I'd prefer not getting into that. Rather, we should adopt the position of the preventive physician. Pollutants pose a risk to health. Our job is to do everything we can to reduce the risk.

Q   You have called for sweeping changes in the means of production as a way to reduce pollution, among other things. But will these sweeping changes be possible without a preceding period of crisis, such as the Great Depression and World War II? Much more crisis than we have today?

A   I believe that our economic fortunes are going to indicate the need for rebuilding our productive system. At that point, if we're smart, we will step in and say, "Good! We've got some new production systems that are environment-friendly. Let's put them to work."

We are capital poor in this country. We have a much lower rate of reinvestment in our productive system than does Japan. That is why there aren't any American electronics on the market anymore. We don't reinvest. If you don't build up the system of producing goods, you're going to get in trouble with the growth of your economic system.

There will come a point, I believe, where the economic problems will grow so acute that people will be ready to listen, to break economic taboos, as they were in the Depression.

In the book by Berle and Means, *The Modern Corporation and Private Property*, written during the Depression, they raised the issue of social governance of corporations. People then were under such pressure that they were willing to think forbidden thoughts and break taboos. My guess is that it will be economic problems that bring people to the point of introducing environment-friendly production systems. We should be prepared for that eventuality. Meanwhile, don't hold back on the work you are doing.

Q   Isn't the basic cause of the global environmental problems simply that people and nations have rising economic expectations that are butting up against a finite biosphere with finite resources?

A   I absolutely disagree with the whole "limits to growth" approach.

Why do I say that? There's no doubt that the planet is a finite ecosphere. It does have a limited capacity to support activity. But it is also argued that this is a closed system. Spaceship Earth. That is a highly misleading concept.

No spaceship is self-sufficient. A spaceship has those big wings of photovoltaic cells, and that's the only thing that keeps the spaceship going. The only thing that keeps the globe operating is the sunlight falling on it from outside earth. So the real issue is, what is the limit on the accessibility of solar energy?

You understand that the material resources of earth are not a problem, not if you have enough energy, because matter cannot be destroyed. For example, we still have most of the gold ever mined because it is so precious that we use a lot of energy to regather it. We can do the same with copper and various other things. So the issue is the limit on the availability of energy to recycle material things.

How close to the limit are we? Roughly, we now use globally—speaking of human manipulated energy—about a thousandth of the solar flux falling on the land area of the world.

Let's say only 10 percent of solar flux is available, and we can't get to the rest. We are nowhere near the limit on the access to energy sufficient to generate more human activity. So I simply reject the notion that it is lack of availability of resources that's causing the problem.

Take the simple question of food. Britain doesn't produce enough food to support its population. But it has enough money to buy food.

Haiti doesn't produce enough food to support its population, but they are too poor to buy food. The issue is not the availability of resources, it is the maldistribution of resources. Do you know there is enough food produced on the globe today to provide every living human being with twice the physiologically required diet? Why are people hungry? Because they are poor.

If you detect a certain amount of passion in what I'm saying, it's because I think the issue has been misdirected. The issue is not these fancy things they talk about, like the Gaia hypothesis and so on. The issue is the poverty of the underdeveloped countries of the world. Their poverty was imposed on them by us in colonial times. I think that we owe them reparations which, incidentally, we ought to pay by cutting the military budget.

Q   For the past several years EPA has played a very subdued role, but are you also saying the agency is simply on the wrong track?

A   Don't get me wrong. I am not blaming you people at EPA. I think all of us were locked into a wrong course by the way in which the environmental laws were written, and EPA went along.

The benefit of the hard work that's been done by the agency over the last twenty years is that we now have good numbers—environmental facts and figures we can use productively. Now we need to say to the public and Congress: "Here are the numbers. They tell us something is wrong. Let's fix it."

We're getting into politics, but I've said this publicly and I'll say it right here: I think when the next president comes in, EPA is going to have to be rebuilt. Rebuild, that's my answer.

There has been a lot of damage done and it comes directly from the White House. I can say things like that because I'm a radical.

Q   How would you suggest getting the environment more on the political agenda? Most polls show the public supports environmental protection, but that is not being translated into political action.

A   The environment isn't a driving issue except on the local level. You have community groups everywhere now. I'm not talking about the Natural Resources Defense Council or the Environmental Defense Fund. I'm talking about Love Canal-types of citizens' groups.

Everywhere, people are concerned with the environment. What needs to be done is to open up the subject to the kind of discussion we're having here. Somebody must say: "The environmental effort has largely failed, and here is what we ought to do to rebuild it." I hope you'll hear that soon in politics.

[JANUARY 12, 1988]

---

BIOGRAPHY

Barry Commoner, described by *Time* magazine as a "professor with a classroom of millions," is the author of *The Closing Circle* and many other environmental policy and scientific works. His most recent book is *Making Peace with the Planet*. He reached perhaps his widest audience in 1980 as a candidate for president of the United States on the Citizens party ticket.

In 1965, Dr. Commoner organized the Center for the Biology of Natural Systems at Washington University in St. Louis. The center, a research group devoted to environmental and energy problems, is still under his direction, though its location has changed to Queens College, City University of New York.

Dr. Commoner has served as a member of the board of directors of the American Association for the Advancement of Science, and as an advisor to the scientific advisory boards of a number of agencies and commissions, both governmental and private. He is currently a scientific advisor to the New York Legislative Commission on Science and Technology, to the Scientific Advisory Board of the Vietnam Veterans of America Foundation Council on Dioxin, and to the Committee on Responsible Genetics.

---

# "Can the World
Be Saved?"

In an amusing scene in a recent popular movie, the intrepid Captain
Kirk awakes from the sleep of time travel and, gazing out, sees that his
starship is, as hoped, orbiting Earth. "Earth!" he says, "but when?" To
which the genetically unflappable Spock, checking his instrument panel, replies, "Judging from the pollution content of the atmosphere, I
believe we have arrived at the latter half of the twentieth century." And
indeed they had. And so have we. And there is plenty of pollution here
to measure.

Today, in the latter years of the twentieth century, pollution is
occurring on a vast and unprecedented scale around the globe. Trends
since World War II have been in two directions: first, toward large releases of certain chemicals, principally from using fossil fuels, that are
now significantly altering natural systems on a global scale, and second,
toward steady increases in the release of innumerable biocidal products
and toxic substances. These shifts from the "sewage and soot" concerns
of the prewar period to vastly more serious concerns pose formidable
challenges for societies, challenges that today's pollution control laws
just begin to address.

The dramatic changes in pollution in this century are best described in terms of four long-term trends.

First is the trend from modest quantities to huge quantities. The
twentieth century has witnessed unprecedented growth in human pop-

JAMES GUSTAVE
SPETH is president of the
Washington-based World
Resources Institute.

ulation and economic activity. World population has increased more than threefold; gross world product by perhaps twentyfold; and fossil fuel use by more than tenfold.

With these huge increases in economic activity and fossil fuel use have come huge changes in the quantities of pollutants released. Between 1900 and 1985, annual sulfur dioxide emissions increased sixfold globally, while nitrogen oxide emissions increased about tenfold, perhaps more. Another gas formed when fossil fuels are burned is carbon dioxide, one of the greenhouse gases implicated in global warming and climate change. Annual global emissions of $CO_2$ have increased tenfold in this century, and a dramatic 25 percent increase in the $CO_2$ content of Earth's atmosphere has occurred.

Second is the trend from gross insults to microtoxicity, from natural products to synthetic ones. Paralleling the dramatic growth in the volume of older pollutants, such as sulfur dioxide, has been the introduction in the post-World War II period of new synthetic chemicals and radioactive substances, many of which are highly toxic in even minute quantities and some of which persist and accumulate in biological systems or in the atmosphere.

One major product of the modern chemicals industry, pesticides, is released into the environment precisely because it is toxic. Projected global pesticide sales for 1990 are $50 billion, a tenfold increase since

1975. Ironically, another major product of the chemicals industry, the chlorofluorocarbons [CFCs], found wide use in part because they are not toxic. Such are the pathways of our ignorance.

Third is the trend from First World to Third World. A myth easily exploded by a visit to many developing countries is that pollution is predominantly a problem of the highly industrialized countries. While it is true that the industrial countries account for the bulk of the pollutants produced today, pollution is a grave problem in developing countries, and many of the most alarming examples of its consequences can be found there.

Cities in Eastern Europe and the Third World are consistently more polluted with $SO_2$ and particulates than most of the cities in highly industrialized countries. The rivers most severely contaminated by bacteria and other pathogens are in developing countries.

Third World populations now rank high in their exposure to toxic chemicals. In a sample of ten industrial and developing countries, three of the four countries with the highest blood lead levels of their populations were Mexico, India, and Peru; for the same ten countries, DDT contamination of human milk was highest in China, India, and Mexico. And what may be the worst industrial accident in history occurred not in New Jersey or West Virginia, but in India.

These first three trends combine, with others, to produce the fourth, the trend from local effects to global effects. When the volumes of pollution were much smaller and the pollutants similar to natural substances, impacts tended to be confined to limited geographic areas near sources. Today, the scale and intensity of pollution make its consequences truly global. For the first time, human impacts have grown to approximate and to affect the natural processes that control the global life-support system.

Nothing better illustrates this broadening of the concern about pollution from a local affair to a global one than air pollution. Local air pollution is improving in some cities in industrial countries, but it is worsening in others, principally cities in developing countries, and is hardly solved anywhere. Meanwhile, global use of fossil fuels, and emissions of traditional pollutants such as sulfur and nitrogen oxides that result from it, continue to climb. Acid rain, ozone, and other consequences of these pollutants are affecting plant and animal life—killing forests and fish, damaging crops, changing the species composition of ecosystems—over vast areas of the globe. Depletion of the stratosphere's ozone layer is a matter of such concern that an international treaty has been negotiated to reduce emissions of chlorofluorocarbons, but the latest measurements indicate the current protocol is already inadequate. And, probably most serious of all, the buildup of infrared trapping "greenhouse" gases in the atmosphere continues. This buildup is largely a consequence of the use of fossil fuels and CFCs, deforestation, and various agricultural activities, and it now threatens societies with far-reaching climate change.

While the regional impacts of a global warming are uncertain and difficult to predict, rainfall and monsoon patterns could shift, upsetting agricultural activities worldwide. Sea level could rise, flooding coastal areas. Ocean currents could shift, altering the climate of many areas and disrupting fisheries. The ranges of plant and animal species could change regionally, endangering protected areas and many species whose habitats are now few and confined. Record heatwaves and other weather anomalies could harm susceptible people, crops, and forests.

These interrelated atmospheric issues probably constitute the most serious pollution threat in history. I say "interrelated" because these atmospheric issues are linked in ways that scientists are still discovering, and the scientists are far ahead of our policy makers. First, they are linked in time. The view is still common today that, initially, we should address local air pollution, then we should turn attention to regional issues like acid rain, and then, at some point in the future, we should address the global issue of greenhouse gases. But the failures of our clean air efforts make urban air quality an issue for today, forcing a 1970s issue from the past into the present. Simultaneously, the realizations that greenhouse gases other than $CO_2$ double the urgency of the problem, and that societies may have *already* committed the planet to a 1.5 to 2.5 degrees C global average warming—these realizations are forcing what was thought to be a "twenty-first century issue" into the present.

These atmospheric issues are also linked in the vast chemical reactor that is the atmosphere, where pollutants react with each other, other substances, and solar energy in a fiendishly complex set of circular interactions. Touch one problem, you may touch them all.

Third, they are linked in their effects on people and on the biota. What are the consequences of multiple stresses—a variety of pollutants, heat waves and climate changes, increased ultraviolet radiation—when realized together? Who knows? We are all still learning.

And these atmospheric issues are linked through the sources of the pollutants involved. CFCs, for example, contribute both to greenhouse warming and ozone layer destruction, but the dominant source of these problems is the use of fossil fuels.

In short, the *time* to address all these atmosphere problems—local, regional, global—is *now.*

The *way* to address all these problems is *together.* And, in the long run, the *key to these problems is energy.*

What can we say about the U.S. role in causing these atmospheric problems? We should take pride in what has been accomplished to date under the Clean Air Act and various U.S. energy laws. But let's not overdo it. The United States still produces about 15 percent of the world's sulfur dioxide emissions, about 25 percent of $NO_x$, and 25 percent of the $CO_2$, and we manufacture about 30 percent of the CFCs. While emissions of criteria (as defined by the Clean Air Act) air pollutants other than $NO_x$ have fallen over the last fifteen years, a period during which real GNP grew about 50 percent, emissions today still exceed two-thirds of 1970 amounts, particulates excepted. In other words, the bulk of the pollution that gave rise to the Clean Air Act in 1970 continues. Similarly, real strides have been made in increasing U.S. energy efficiency: between 1973 and 1985 per capita energy use in the U.S. fell 12 percent while per capita gross domestic product rose 17 percent. Still, the United States today remains a gas guzzler of a nation, consuming a fourth of the world's energy annually and producing only half the GNP per unit of energy input as do countries such as West Germany, Brazil, France, Japan, and Sweden.

Beyond these atmospheric issues are other pollution concerns, and beyond them the challenge of the planet's biological degradation: deforestation, desertification, the loss of biodiversity—in short, the steady process of biological impoverishment. When we take all these challenges together, we see that we are witnessing nothing less than the emergence of a new environmental agenda. This new agenda encompasses the great life-support systems of the planet's biosphere. It is global in scope and international in implication. It is rapidly forcing itself on the attention of policy makers and the public at large.

Almost twenty years ago, U.S. leaders responded vigorously to the environmental concerns emerging then. Today, the new agenda faces us with challenges that are more disturbing and more difficult. It is not enough to say that we must hope that our leaders respond as they did before. We must ensure that they do.

Now into this troubled present comes a message from the future. Not, this time, from Captain Kirk, but more reliably, from the World

Commission on Environment and Development. Consider closely the following passage from the report of the commission, *Our Common Future:*

> The planet is passing through a period of dramatic growth and fundamental change. Our human world of 5 billion must make room in a finite environment for another human world. The population could stabilize at between 8 billion and 14 billion some time next century, according to UN projections. . . . Economic activity has multiplied to create a $13 trillion world economy, and this could grow five- or tenfold in the coming half-century.

Imagine, just as a simple thought experiment, what would happen if greenhouse gases, industrial pollution, and other assaults on the environment rose proportionately with the vast economic growth to which the commission refers. I am not suggesting that this will happen, but thinking this way does highlight the magnitude of the challenge ahead.

In the early 1970s the *CBS Evening News* with Walter Cronkite ran a series of environmental stories entitled, "Can the World Be Saved?" I remember the globe behind this title was firmly grasped by a hand which seemed to come from nowhere. I was never sure whether this hand was crushing our small planet or saving it, but I was sure at least that Cronkite was out to save it. He dramatically presented the much simpler environmental problems of that period to a huge audience, and helped build the powerful environmental consciousness of the day. Today, the question "Can the World Be Saved?" is much more serious and legitimate than it was then.

Societies near and far have set two long-term goals for themselves: improving environmental quality, in part by reducing *current* pollution levels, and achieving a virtual order of magnitude increase in economic activity. Let us not deceive ourselves, or accept blithely the assurances of political leaders who say casually that we can have both. We know from sad experience that we can have economic growth without having environmental protection. But the stakes on the environmental side are much higher now, and they will only grow in the future. I predict that reconciling these two goals will be one of the dominant challenges facing political leaders on all continents in the 1990s and beyond. It will require constant attention at the highest levels of government. It will require strong, effective, smart government.

Environmentalism began on the outside, on the periphery of the economy, saving a bit of landscape here, bottling up some pollution there. It will inevitably spread as creed and code to permeate to the core of the economies of the world. We will all be environmentalists soon.

If these are the challenges before us, what should be done? Let's rephrase Cronkite's question into a somewhat more answerable one: *how* can the world be saved? Certainly, we must strengthen the efforts already begun. The regulatory programs of the industrial countries have yielded definite results over the last two decades, and continuing challenges will require that these programs be enhanced. Monitoring and enforcement capabilities must be strengthened; new types and sources of pollution must be tackled; intermedia effects must be attended to; regional and global approaches to pollution control must become increasingly common; and the overall regulatory process must become more cost-effective, efficient, and streamlined. And much, much more attention needs to be paid to the pollution problems of the developing countries. They can learn from our successes and failures and pioneer new development paths rather than repeat old ones.

Yet something more fundamental will be needed. From its origins in the early 1970s, U.S. air and water pollution legislation has recognized that tighter standards could be applied to "new sources" of pollution, in contrast to existing plants, because new sources present the opportunity to go beyond "end of pipe" removal of waste products and to build in "process changes" that reduce or eliminate the wastes that must otherwise be removed. This concept—source reduction through changing the basic technologies of production and consumption—is fundamental to solving world pollution problems. "Pollution control" is not enough. Societies must work "upstream" to change the products, processes, policies, and pressures that give rise to pollution.

I urged you a moment ago to consider what would happen if pollution increased proportionately with the five- to tenfold expansion in world economic activity projected for the middle of the next century. That would indeed happen if this growth merely replicates over and over today's prevailing technologies, broadly conceived. Seen in this light, reconciling the economic and environmental goals societies have set for themselves will only occur if there is a thoroughgoing technological transformation—a transformation to technologies, high and low, soft and hard, that are solution-oriented because they facilitate economic growth while sharply reducing the pressures on the natural environment. We speak positively of "environmentally sustainable" development. What this means in the context of pollution is technology transformation.

In this limited sense at least, one might say that only technology can save us. That is a hard thing for a congenital Luddite like myself to say, but, in a small victory of nurture over nature, I do now believe it. I do not diminish the importance of lifestyle changes—some go hand-in-hand with technological change—and I await the spread of more voluntary simplicity in our rich society. But growth has its imperatives; for much of the world it is the imperative of meeting basic human needs. And we must not forget it is sustainable economic development— growth that takes the pressure of mass poverty off an eroding resource base—that is an essential component of environmental progress worldwide.

For these reasons, we must think explicitly about society's need to accomplish a technological transformation of unprecedented scope and pace. And we must think as well about the interventions that will be needed to bring it about. Although many emerging technologies offer exciting opportunities, and some are moving us in the right direction, no "hidden hand" is operating to guide technology to reconcile environmental and economic challenges.

The two fundamental processes of this transformation are the process of discovery and the process of application. The first is the realm of science and technology, of research and development. Science and technology must have the financial support and the incentives to provide us with an accurate understanding of Earth's systems and cycles and what our pollution is doing to them; it must deliver to us a new agriculture, one redesigned to be sustainable both economically and ecologically, which stresses low inputs of commercial fertilizers, pesticides, and energy; and it must show us how industry and transportation can be transformed from an era of materials-intensive, high-throughput processes to an era that relies on inputs with low environmental costs, uses materials with great efficiency, generates little or no waste, recycles residuals, and is, hence, more "closed."

To guide and speed the application of solution-oriented technologies will require policy action in the form of both economic incentives and direct regulation. It will require institutional innovation at the national and international levels, particularly to speed the process of international agreement and concerted action. Today, the problems are coming faster than the solutions. We will need a new international law of the environment, environmental diplomats, and the integration of environmental concerns into our trade and other international economic relations.

I have become a believer in the ingenuity of individuals and companies to find efficient solutions and to meet challenging goals, if the incentives are there. We need performance standards and economic rewards and penalties that are powerful, that provide the needed incentives, but that do not micromanage the process of technological innovation. This agency is no stranger to technology-forcing actions. We need more of them. And we should consider economic rewards for those who surpass baseline requirements.

We need to make the market mechanism work for us, not against us. Today, natural resource depletion and pollution are being subsidized on a grand scale around the globe. We have got to get the prices right. We should begin by removing subsidies and then make private companies and governments "internalize the externalities" so that prices reflect the true costs to society, including the costs of pollution. We need an environmentally honest economy.

Let me illustrate these points further by referring to one area where the need for technology transformation is most pressing, the energy sector, and one area where the need for concerted international action is most pressing, the greenhouse effect.

Our energy problems are forgotten but not gone. Energy will return to our political landscape again in the 1990s, driven by a U.S. oil import bill that was $46 billion in 1987 and could reach $80 billion in 1995, and by the grave atmospheric pollution—local, regional, and global—that our use of fossil fuels causes. I talked earlier about the ways that urban air pollution, acid rain, and the greenhouse effect are all linked together, and linked to our energy-use patterns. Addressing our nation's economic, security, and environmental objectives will require a careful process of long-term, integrated energy planning. Put simply, we can no longer safely make air pollution policy and energy policy independently, directed by separate executive agencies with little communication, under laws written and overseen by different congressional committees.

If we and other countries are to meet our economic and environmental challenges, what energy paths should we take? The coming energy transformation, I would argue, must have rapid energy efficiency improvements as its dominant feature, supplemented by increased reliance on renewable energy sources. The potential for energy efficiency gains through technological change is simply enormous. If the efficiency in energy use current in Japan today could be matched in the United States and around the world, total economic output could be doubled globally, and virtually doubled in the United States, without increasing energy use.

Auto efficiency provides a good example of what is possible. Miles per gallon achieved by new cars sold in the United States doubled from 13 mpg to 25 mpg between 1973 and 1985. Ford, Honda, and Suzuki all have cars in production that could double this again to 50 mpg, and Toyota has a prototype family car that could double efficiency again to almost 100 mpg. I am reminded here that there is a huge role for the private sector in the coming technological transformation. Those companies that see the future can profit from it.

One recent global energy analysis, built up from careful studies of energy use in industrial and developing countries, concluded that "the global population could roughly double, that living standards could be improved far beyond satisfying basic needs in developing countries, and that economic growth in industrialized countries could continue, without increasing the level of global energy use in 2020 much above the present level." In this technically and economically feasible future, total energy use goes up only 10 percent between 1980 and 2020 and fossil fuel use grows even less. In such a low-energy, high-efficiency future, the great energy supply debates, such as coal vs. nuclear, which preoccupy us so, lose much of their significance, and pollution problems are knocked down to more manageable proportions.

Large gains in energy efficiency, and the consequent reductions in $CO_2$ emissions, will be essential in addressing what is probably the most serious environmental challenge of all—the global warming that seems to have already begun. I recognize the uncertainties remaining in characterizing the greenhouse effect, but given the risks, I would advocate consideration now of a series of international conventions responsive to the various aspects of the problem.

First, we need to secure swift international approval for the ozone layer protection protocol signed in Montreal last year. We need this for its own sake and to continue the momentum that can get the nations of the world back to the table so that a complete, swift phase-out of CFCs can be negotiated. The phase-out is fully justified on ozone layer grounds alone, but the fact is that a CFC phase-out is the fastest and cheapest way societies can do something major to contain the greenhouse effect.

Second, we need an overall global climate protection convention, the prime goal of which should be to stabilize atmospheric concentrations of greenhouse gases at safe levels. This convention should focus particularly on steps needed to secure reductions in $CO_2$ emissions from fossil fuel use. Two facts stand out in this regard: the United States and the Soviet Union together account for almost half of global $CO_2$ emissions today, and the United States, the USSR, and China together account for about 90 percent of the estimated coal reserves.

Third, the time is ripe for an international agreement to protect the world's tropical forests and to reforest the spreading wasteland areas in many developing countries. The industrial nations have a double stake in halting the now-rapid clearing of the tropical forests. Not only are these forests repositories for about half of the wildlife and genetic wealth of the planet, but $CO_2$ emissions from biotic sources such as deforestation are estimated to be about a fifth of $CO_2$ emissions from fossil fuels. Our stake in the salvation of these forests is sufficiently large that we should be more than willing to help provide financial incentives—incentives that will be necessary if countries of the tropics are to turn their attention to what often appears as a low priority or even a threat to development and sovereignty. I suggest that we go far beyond the debt-for-nature swaps under way today and consider a global bargain as part of this international convention. This bargain would involve the easing and forgiving of international debts in exchange for forest conservation. Of the top seventeen most heavily indebted countries, twelve are destroying their tropical forests at extraordinarily rapid rates, contributing to the world's annual loss of 27 million acres.

And fourth, we need international agreement on the protocol now being developed to limit nitrogen oxide emissions. Unless capped, increasing $NO_x$ emissions will lead to increasing ozone concentrations, and ozone is a greenhouse gas as well as a source of urban and rural air pollution. Many good reasons exist to control $NO_x$ emissions at the international level, and I urge the State Department and EPA to signal U.S. support for the proposed protocol by the fast-approaching July 1 deadline.

Some of you may be wondering: is he going to discuss nuclear power, an *available* nonfossil source of energy? My concern about nuclear power, as things stand today, is that it probably will not, in the end,

provide a major part of the answer to global warming. Its public acceptability is too low and its price is too high. If we try to solve the greenhouse problem by cramming nuclear power down the throats of an
unwilling public and unwilling investors, we will be setting the stage
for prolonged confrontation and stalemate. And what is going to happen
to nuclear power if there are one or two more major accidents like Three
Mile Island and Chernobyl? Moreover, I believe there are safer and
cheaper alternatives for the short run, including the vast potential for
efficiency gains in how we generate and use electricity. For the longer
run, I *would* favor research aimed at reinventing nuclear power in a way
that could gain public and investor confidence; we may need it one day.
My guess, however, is that before such a new nuclear system could be
commercialized in the next century, the price of photovoltaic and other
solar energy systems will be competitive. But who knows? We are all
still learning.

In all these areas, in seeking these treaties and in setting an international example by acting on our own, U.S. leadership and EPA leadership could not be more important. The world is not exactly waiting on
us, but neither will it get very far without us. I hope you will join with
me in urging our presidential candidates to give these issues the time
and thought they deserve. We need to know, beyond the level of gener-
alities, how each candidate would address the emerging environmental
agenda of the 1990s.

Let me conclude with a word about why I am optimistic that the
world can indeed be saved. This address, you have doubtless noted,
reflects a deep appreciation of the importance of economic and technological forces in the modern world. One reason for optimism is that
science and technology are presenting us with answers. We are in the
midst of a revolution in earth science and a revolution in industrial and
agricultural technology; both developments have huge potential in the
areas we have been reviewing.

But if solutions are found, they will come from another realm as
well, from the hopes and fears of people, from their aspirations for their
children and their wonder at the natural world, from their own self-
respect and their dogged insistence that some things that seem very
wrong are just that. People everywhere are offended by pollution. They
sense intuitively that we have pressed beyond limits we should not have
exceeded. They want to clean up the world, make it a better place, be
good trustees of the Earth for future generations. With Thoreau, they

know that heaven is under our feet as well as over our heads. Politicians around the globe are increasingly hearing the demand that things be set right. And that is very good news indeed.

## Questions from the Audience

Q   Mr. Speth, Paul Ehrlich has raised the point that there are 5 billion of us now, and already Earth's capacity to respond to our environmental insults on it is strained. And in another thirty years, there will be twice that number of people. He says that the basic driving force for environmental deterioration is the population explosion, and if we don't handle that, nothing else we do will be of any help. Would you care to comment?

A   We have to make a sharp distinction between two sets of problems. The pollution problems, which I spent most of the time talking about, and the potential for pollution are, I think, much more dramatically affected by the level of overall economic activity than by population growth. Population growth has gone up by a factor of three in this century, but economic activity has increased twentyfold. Population is projected to double at some point in the next century. Economic activity is projected to go up five- to tenfold by the middle of the next century, by some estimates. I think in terms of the pollution issues that we've been going over, that's what you have to watch.

In developing countries, the renewable resource base is being eroded. Deforestation, the denuding of the landscape, the search for fuel wood, the pushing of people into marginal areas, the erosions of the hillsides, these things are affected dramatically by very high rates of population growth and the mass poverty that exists in these countries.

So I think it depends on which issues you are talking about.

Q   You mentioned the tropical deforestation issue. I think it weakens our credibility to advocate conservation there when the old grove forests that are publicly held in this country are being systematically logged right now.

A   Well, I think we should be saving both. If you look in aggregate terms, of course, the industrial countries are not really losing forests, in traditional deforestation terms: that is, except as a consequence of pollution, in Europe in particular, and more recently here. But deforestation is occurring elsewhere. We are losing an area about the size of

Kentucky every year around the globe, and it's principally in the tropical countries.

I don't think we lose our credibility in trying to press for some radical reforms that could slow and eventually halt tropical deforestation. But I agree that we need to be very protective of our own dwindling reserves of old grove forests.

Q Would you speak a little on the presidential campaign, particularly on the need to shift from a local to a global focus, the need for a very fundamental recasting of local and global politics? A lot of people have the impression that the environmental issues are not receiving their due from the political debate.

A I think that is the case. I don't think these issues are getting enough attention, given their seriousness.

I wasn't just whistling Dixie, so to speak, when I predicted that all of these issues would, in the 1990s, come to dominate, and be of top priority on the agendas of the leaders of the major countries. I honestly believe that. I don't think there's any other way for the set of problems that I discussed in my talk to be resolved. And I think it's a great tragedy that the issues are not getting more attention in the campaign.

I would recommend to the Sierra Club, for example, that they stage a major convention of environmental organizations in California sometime during the campaign. Both candidates need to win in California, and the club is very prominent there. They could hold a major convention, and invite the environmental organizations from all over the country, and invite both candidates to come address the group.

I have been very pleasantly surprised with the degree to which these issues—like the ozone layer depletion, the greenhouse effect, tropical deforestation, issues which seem remote to us in our everyday lives—are capturing the attention and the concern of the American people.

All politics is local, as they say. And I don't belittle the difficulties of moving people's attention from the problems in their backyard to the problems of global context. But I have been surprised with how rapidly people are coming to understand and appreciate, and are becoming concerned about, these problems that are not pollution in their backyards or in their fishing streams.

And I suggest that the day will come, if the leaders of our country and other countries don't address these issues, that people are going to be mad, really furious. Because the problems are severe and they affect us all.

Q You mentioned the international environment. Would you comment on an international institutional program that we might expect to see arising, and what might be its best form?

*A*  Yes. This is the cutting-edge question, as far as I'm concerned, because these problems are increasingly international.

The institutions are beginning to respond. But it took a decade or more to get an agreement to protect the ozone layer, and we can't go through these long drawn-out processes. And we don't have the right institutional framework for doing it.

We know that regulation is going to become more international. We'll all be like Europe, where almost all environmental regulation has a continental twist. But I don't know what the right institutional framework is. And I think that's where we need to put a lot of hard thinking.

*Q*  It always seemed to me that the environmental movement has made a basic mistake in allowing itself to be stereotyped over the years as liberal. It seems to me that it's equally valid to protect one person's property from pollution as it is to allow another person's property to cause it. Do you see any way for the environmental movement to avoid, or at least recast, the liberal stereotype? At least neutralize it?

*A*  Well, I think that, in fact, the environmental movement is indeed perceived as being a liberal movement in some circles. But it's also true that if you polled the members of some organizations, like the National Wildlife Federation, you would find that these are not liberals, by and large. I hope that some of the things that I said today got away from this.

The environmental community has become stereotyped, in part, as antitechnology. I think the technologies that we are seeing coming on today, and the ones that we have to push in the future, are essential. I think the growth imperatives are there. What level it would be, no one knows for sure. But if we are going to have that growth, we're going to have to transform the technologies that we're using, and the manufacturing, transportation, and housing. This is going to require a huge commitment from the private sector.

Also in the area of pollution control, I think the environmental community, many parts of it at least, are more prepared today to accept economic incentives as a way of going about its business than ever before.

*Q*  Do you feel that our species has the attention span required to deal with these kinds of issues in the length of time we have left? I recognize the importance of institutions and institutional changes. But in a democratic world I don't think it's possible to have a large institution that's going to control development around the world. And so then you get to the body politic in the United States, Russia, wherever, that seems to be unable to support the ten-, twenty-, thirty-year pull needed for dealing with these kinds of issues. Do you feel that our species is capable of that kind of attention span?

A  I think addressing the greenhouse issue, for example, is going to require cooperation on a scale that we have only seen in wartime. It will be affected strongly by the degree to which the scientists and others were able to convince the people that things like the drought that we are experiencing this summer may be at least exacerbated by global climate change.

If there are events of that type, which clearly could cost billions of dollars, and they become an ever-present set of problems for people, then I think the possibility of keeping people's attention is going to be much greater.

Q  On the subject of technology, do you see biotech as part of the solution? And if so, what are some of the ways that biotech can help, and what are some of the things that we should be watching out for?

A  I do see biotech as part of the solution. I am very excited about the prospects of inoculating corn and other species against various types of pests and thereby reducing the need for synthetic pesticides, for example.

We all know some of the areas where biotech can make a huge contribution. It needs to be regulated strictly. It needs to be watched. I can't believe the industry fell into the trap of not putting out environmental impact statements for years, trying to get out of the requirement and opening itself up to a lot of good scrutiny.

Our institute issued a publication, if you want to pursue it, on the biotech question, on technologies and information technologies. And we're releasing one on recycling and recycling materials to cover waste source reduction. We're looking at those three technologies—I'd like to do others—and the contributions that those technologies can make for solving some of these problems.

Q  You alluded to the problems that can come from subsidizing certain industries. Would you say a bit more about them? And debt-for-conservation swapping?

A  What we have seen in a series of studies, looking at prices of pesticides in developing countries, prices of water, the way the pricing and other factors affect the forest sector and energy, is that developing countries and our country, too, are in some cases subsidizing these items deeply. For example, the cutting of tropical forests. In Brazil, nobody would raise cattle on their own because they would lose a fortune; but because of very low interest rates on loans, tax concessions, land titling and other forms of subsidy, these ranches turn into profitable enterprises. The society as a whole is losing a fortune doing this.

Timber concessions in many countries cost half, or less, of the value of the standing value of the timber. So you get these timber booms, tremendous interest in just getting in there and making a lot of money. That's one of many ways that we're subsidizing pollution, subsidizing resource extraction. These are precious commodities, and they've got precious prices on them. That's got to change. The market is good at some things, but we're not letting it do what it's good at.

On the debt question, I think that some day there will have to be some adjustment in the international debt situation. My guess is that it's going to involve more debt forgiveness, in effect, than the U.S. government is willing to talk about now. Our government, at least.

When that day does come, there will be many people who will ask, "Well, what are we going to get for this?" or "Why are we doing this?" or "Is there something important that can be done in exchange for this?" I think we have an opportunity both to save a great world-class resource, the tropical forests, that we need for lots of reasons and don't want to see disappearing. And it just so happens that some of the most heavily indebted countries, like Brazil, are rich with these resources, and might be willing, if it were done at an international level, using international agencies, to talk about the possibility of a global bargain—debt-for-nature on a grand scale.

Q  What do you see as the role that groups like the Green party in Germany and other countries in Europe, the emerging so-called Green movement in the United States, might be able to play on the international level on all these issues that you've mentioned? Do you see it as a constructive role?

A  Yes. I believe firmly that you have a wide spectrum of folks, here. From people out on the fringes of what the law will let them do, right on through to the most establishment-types of organizations. To me they all have important roles to play. I doubt that we'll ever get a Green party movement in this country, as in Europe. It's just not part of our political make-up, as it is in Europe, to have separate parties on lots of issues.

But somehow we have to succeed in bringing these issues forward in a more visible way in the campaign. I don't know exactly what to do, but it's something I'm going to be thinking about, and something that a lot of you need to be thinking about, too, with all of your different contacts and roles.

[JUNE 21, 1988]

## BIOGRAPHY

In 1982, Gus Speth became president of the newly formed World Resources Institute, a not-for-profit organization devoted to the study of environmental policy issues.

Mr. Speth serves as chairman of the Environmental and Energy Study Institute. He is a member of the board of the Natural Resources Defense Council (of which he was a founder), the Global Tomorrow Coalition, and the Workplace Health Fund. He is a member of the Council on Foreign Relations.

From 1977 to 1981, he served first as a member, then chairman, of the President's Council on Environmental Quality. And from 1981 to 1982, he was professor of law at Georgetown University.

Mr. Speth was a Rhodes scholar, obtained a law degree at Yale, and clerked for Supreme Court Justice Hugo L. Black.

# Should EPA Have
# Cabinet Status?

A few years ago at a meeting of the National Wildlife Federation, we were honored to have Sir Peter Scott, the famed British naturalist, talk to us about the Loch Ness Monster. Sir Peter had done a lot of worrying trying to figure out whether there was indeed a Loch Ness Monster. He was particularly concerned about communicating his findings in an accurate and reasonable way to the scientific community and to the public. To illustrate the need for clear communication, he recounted the following story:

One morning, Sir Peter recalled, he was driving to the Loch on a one-way road. The terrain was steep and hilly, and the one-lane road was made up of a series of abrupt switchbacks, as mountain roads often are. But in this case, there was room for only one car at a time. On the switchbacks, there was space for a car to pull off the road. A driver heading up the hill would pull off and honk his horn. If there was no response to his honk, the upward-bound driver would proceed to the next switchback and repeat the process. If he heard a honk in reply, that meant a car was headed down, and he was to remain in the turnoff until the descending car, which had the right-of-way, was safely past.

Well, one morning he was driving up and did all the things he was supposed to do. He pulled off, honked his horn, and sure enough a honk returned. So he waited patiently, and soon a car came around the turn. It pulled up next to his, and the other driver rolled down the window. Sir

JAY D. HAIR is president and chief executive officer of the National Wildlife Federation.

Peter rolled down his window. The other driver looked Sir Peter in the eye, called out "Pig!" then rolled up his window, and drove off.

Sir Peter said he felt both angry and indignant. Here he had done everything he was supposed to do. He had pulled off, honked, waited patiently, been polite, and now this. He was so angry, he said, that he went roaring around the curve—and collided with a large pig.

That was a breakdown in communication—which occurs too often when discussing environmental matters—and I hope we can steer clear of that hazard here. The people at EPA, I know, often feel a bit bashed. Sometimes you may even feel a bit bashed by my group, the National Wildlife Federation. But I also know, and want to communicate this to you very clearly, we appreciate what you do.

I would like to share with you a few of my thoughts about the challenges and opportunities facing not only the Environmental Protection Agency, but facing the nation and, indeed, the global society, as we move toward the twenty-first century.

We've just finished a unique summer. The summer of 1988 has been the summer of the closed beaches, the summer of record-setting heat waves and global warming. It has served as a warning that we, indeed, have overloaded our atmosphere.

This has been the year that ozone pollution became not a vague measurement, but a very real element of risk to human health.

In many people's eyes, and I've talked to a lot of people around the country, it has been the year the "good life" lost some of its glitter, the year when the environment began fighting back, the year we began to understand the simple truth that environmental protection is more than a quality-of-life issue. It is nothing less than an issue of long-term global survival.

Not so many years ago, the "long term" was viewed in relationship to the year 2000—a long time in the future. Now it's just around the corner. It's a year that's viewed as a demarcation between the old and the new, a beginning not only of the twenty-first century, but of the third millennium. Think of it. How many people have a chance to witness such a grand event?

But more importantly, the leaders of the twenty-first century, the high school graduating class of the year 2000, began first grade this week, in September 1988. What kind of world will these young leaders inherit? Equally important, what kind of leaders will the world inherit? What will these children learn in twelve short years? What have we learned in the past twelve years, to teach them about dealing with an increasingly complex and uncertain future?

Perhaps the most important lesson we have learned is a global one. While we are citizens of specific countries, we are also citizens of the world. That world has been compressed in recent years, compressed by technological revolutions in transportation, communication, and, indeed, in the production of pollution.

As citizens of the world, we are obligated to see the world's abounding contradictions and, in my view, to try to do something about them. We live in a world where humankind has the technical capacity to do so much good and, at the same time, to inflict so much harm. Using modern technology we have walked on the moon, replaced a diseased heart with a fully functioning human one, and stored a million pieces of information on a computer chip smaller than a fingernail.

Yet in this world of technological miracles, as many as 100,000 people, many of them children, starve to death every day. The World Bank has estimated that 800 million people live in conditions of absolute poverty, lives degraded by disease, illiteracy, malnutrition, and squalor.

The technology that has harnessed the energy of rivers also has degraded natural resources, decimated wildlife, and changed forever the wild places of the world. The chemical revolution that has eased the daily chores of those in developed countries also has exposed human beings to potentially dangerous chemicals from the moment of conception to the time of death.

The realities of the world are indeed harsh. It is little wonder, then, that many people stand ready to mislead the public by pretending the world's problems are not really severe; that environmentalists are elitists, alarmists, and antiprogress; that technology can solve most of the problems; that inaction and lack of government involvement present viable solutions; and that the developed world should be allowed to continue its selfish lifestyle. In my view, such is the folly of fools, not of stewards of the world the children of the twenty-first century will inherit.

Dr. Peter Raven, director of the Missouri Botanical Gardens and member of the National Academy of Sciences, has, I believe, made a true observation: "The world that provides our evolutionary and ecological context is in trouble; trouble serious enough to demand our urgent attention. The large-scale problems of overpopulation and overdevelopment are eradicating the lands and organisms that sustain life on the planet. If we can solve these problems, we can lay the foundation for peace and prosperity in the future. By ignoring these issues, drifting passively while attending to what seems more urgent personal priorities, we are courting disaster."

Peter Raven is right. But how do we then reconcile the global contradictions? How do we transform them into opportunities for greater freedom around the world? How do we bring the global community back into harmony with nature without sacrificing recent technological gains, including those that have added to the average human lifespan? And how do we ensure both environmental protection and responsible, sustainable economic development in a world in desperate need of both?

There are no simple answers, but I believe there are five broad imperatives that should guide decision-making in the decades to come.

The first is that society must acknowledge that human health is directly dependent on the health of the global environment. As we deplete our natural resources, as we cause the extinction of species, as we pollute our air and water with toxic chemicals, we are imperiling the quality of all life on Earth. Only when we appreciate that, can we hope to bequeath a sustainable society to the future.

Second, we must recognize that while economic deficits may grab today's headlines, environmental deficits will dominate our future. Any good accounting system can gauge the relationship between assets and liabilities, but what accounting can tell us when our environmental deficit is growing beyond our means to reverse it?

We are indeed overspending. In my view, we are spending our biological capital at breakneck speed without adequately reinvesting in our natural resources portfolio. That overspending can no longer be tolerated, yet it cannot be halted permanently until we develop a comprehensive inventory of the world's wild, living resources. The sad truth is, we don't have any idea how many species of life share this planet with us humans. The numbers range somewhere between 2 million and 30 million species. While we don't know how many species live on Earth, we do know that species are disappearing at a rate perhaps not seen since the loss of dinosaurs 65 million years ago. At the present rate, an average of 100 species may become extinct each day by the turn of the century.

It's tragic that just when we're learning so much about the origins of life we're allowing so much of life's biological diversity to disappear. While we're learning how to improve the quality of life through spectacular advances in biotechnology, we are allowing entire stocks of genetic materials to be eliminated.

In the early 1960s, President Kennedy pledged to put a person on the Moon. By 1969, we accomplished that feat. Wouldn't it be just as worthy for the president today to commit our nation to a comprehensive inventory of the world's living resources by the year 2000? Aside from a world at peace with itself, I know of no better gift we can give the children of the twenty-first century.

The third imperative is a worldwide redefinition of the term "national security." National security must mean more than outright military might. While the realities of the world necessitate military security programs, every country also needs policies that assure the personal security of individual citizens. After all, the long-term threats to human survival do not come so much from military incursions as from global activities that degrade the natural resources on which all our economies and life are based.

Fourth, all elements of society must work cooperatively to find meaningful solutions to today's complex problems. This means a dynamic, purposeful coalition composed not just of environmental groups, but including business leaders, research and education institutions, public officials, writers, philosophers, and, especially, local leaders.

Finally, we must find new and creative ways to develop policies that guide our public and private institutions. We must integrate such varied disciplines as science, engineering, economics, sociology, and law if we are to find solutions to the wide range of complex issues before our society. For too long, we have focused our intellectual energy on single-discipline analysis, ignoring how one discipline is affected by another. We can no longer afford such narrow thinking. Nor can we afford to exempt or exclude any segment of society from responsibility for environmental quality.

In the business community, we must eliminate economic incentives that encourage corporations to cut environmental protection corners in order to improve year-end profits. At the same time, we must provide incentives that encourage the business community to apply its product-development and marketing expertise to the fields of resource conservation and environmental protection.

The crucial question confronting us now is not whether we can change the world, but what kind of world we want. Today, nearly every project even slightly credible becomes possible once we decide what should take place and why. Our national and global problems dictate that we should fashion new ideas, that we implement new plans with new institutions.

In my view, one of the most important steps we in this country must take is to elevate the Environmental Protection Agency to a cabinet-level Department of Environmental Protection. Why? Today, EPA is responsible for a broad range of programs that directly or indirectly affect public health. In fact, no current cabinet office has greater responsibility for, or more directly determines, the quality of life in the United States than does EPA.

The agency now oversees execution of thirteen federal statutes, up from the four that existed when it was formed. The scope of responsibility includes such important issues as safe drinking water, toxic-substance control, clean-air and clean-water regulations, wetlands protection, hazardous-waste disposal, and, of course, the Superfund issues.

Environmental problems have emerged as major public concerns in three distinct phases. The first phase dealt with gross air and water pollution, areas in which progress has been made, but in which residual problems have made victory elusive. The second phase arose from the concern about toxic chemicals, particularly from hazardous-waste dumps that threaten public health. The third phase is now focusing on global environmental problems that may be our most difficult to solve.

Environmental issues are no longer questions about the quality of life, but about the very sustainability of life as we know it. Coping with environmental issues will require a renewed national commitment. We will need to pursue the vigorous enforcement of existing laws. Research and development will have to respond dramatically if we are to understand the risks from an ever-increasing array of environmental concerns. State and local government efforts will have to be strengthened through funding and technical assistance.

Experience has shown that controlling pollution by traditional "end-of-the-pipe" controls is not sufficient. For one thing, end-of-the-pipe controls often only move pollution around. In terms of disposal of solid waste, for instance, everybody wants you to pick it up, and nobody wants you to put it down. Only by using pollution reduction at the source can we fully protect workers, consumers, and natural systems from toxic chemicals and deal responsibly with solid-waste disposal.

Along with source reduction, we must also conserve energy to prevent pollution. Energy production is a major source of many of the most vexing environmental problems, including sulfur oxides, particulate emissions, ozone, acid rain, and, of course, global warming. It will be impossible to cope with this range of problems, particularly global warming, without dramatically increasing society's energy efficiency.

We must also strengthen the institutional means of coping with our environmental problems. State and local governments must be reinforced through federal financial assistance and greater technology transfer. As a major environmental agency of the United States, EPA also must have the status and resources to succeed.

Recently, several proposals have been advanced to make EPA a cabinet-level agency. The National Wildlife Federation enthusiastically supports upgrading EPA to cabinet status and expanding some of its responsibilities as part of the broader commitment to deal aggressively with environmental problems.

The proposals make sense. EPA's budget and personnel level are larger than some current cabinet departments. The United States has been a leader in international environmental efforts, but the EPA administrator is outranked by environmental heads of many foreign governments. On every count, the magnitude of EPA's responsibilities justifies cabinet-level status.

Finally, creation of a cabinet department responds to the persistent public demand that environmental protection be made a top national priority. The American people have again and again signaled their unwavering support for strong environmental legislation and enforcement. In public opinion polls, almost no issue elicits the consistent support that environmental protection does.

In 1985, pollster Lou Harris observed: "In the environmental area, the dynamics of change in recent years has always been in one direction. The American people get tougher and tougher, more adamant and more shocked about the state of environmental cleanup. Majorities in any sound poll conducted on this subject are simply huge and staggering. They parallel nothing less than the belief in free elections and the right to free speech, the right to worship, and the right to private ownership of property." Indeed, public opinion polls in 1986 indicate that support for environmental law is greater today than in the mid-1970s when many environmental laws were enacted.

The Cambridge Report poll in 1986 found 58 percent of respondents favored pursuing environmental quality over economic growth. Only 19 percent favored economic gains over environmental ones, a far smaller percentage than recorded only a decade earlier.

The time has come that environmental concerns must be given frontline visibility among the president's top advisers. The nation's chief environmental officer must have the same access to the Oval Office as do the nation's top military, foreign policy, financial, and educational officers.

There's an old political adage that has been attributed to everyone from Napoleon to the one-time Boston mayor James Curley. That adage is: "There go the people. I must follow, for I am their leader." The people today want a society and a government that work, that recognize their problems, and that invest in sound, responsible ways to resolve them.

We're today preparing for a new century. We need creative new institutional resolve to address the global environmental challenges in the future. As we face those challenges and opportunities, we should take to heart the words of a great conservationist, President Theodore Roosevelt, who said: "Far better it is to dare mighty things, to win glorious triumphs, even though checkered by failure, than to take rank with those poor spirits who neither enjoy much nor suffer much, because they live in the gray twilight that knows not victory nor defeat."

Let's resolve not to live in the gray twilight, but rather to dream big dreams and provide inspired vision for the future. For ours among all generations is literally being given the last chance to protect our environment and to save the best of what remains of our natural world. Nothing less than the long-term sustainability of life on Earth is at stake. Future generations, including those yet unborn, will and should hold us accountable for our actions during our watch. We dare not fail to do our duty.

## Questions from the Audience

Q   What do you see as the number-one environmental problem facing the world today?
A   The number-one challenge is to stabilize the global human population at replacement levels. It's at roughly 5 billion now, and is projected to be around 10 billion before it's stabilized.

Overpopulation drives most of the other environmental problems that we face. It's very frustrating to see the way our country has retreated from assisting in reasonable and responsible human population stabilization programs throughout the world during the last several years.

Our approach to the problem is fairly straightforward. We have a role to play in helping developing countries break the cycle of human misery that they're in now: overpopulation, resource depletion, environmental degradation. We can do that through a variety of ways that are responsible, for example, through foreign aid and assistance with educational programs for birth control.

But it is a serious mistake simply to back away from the problem and our responsibilities because of the right-to-life movement. We don't need to advocate abortion as the solution, but we do need to advocate responsible policies to stabilize the world's human population. Our country can do better, and we should do better.
Q   Would you tell us what contribution you see the United States making to rectifying the problem of global warming?
A   In my view, there are at least three major ways this country can help resolve the problem. One is through international treaties such as the 1987 Montreal protocol on chlorofluorocarbons (CFCs). I think the timetable of the CFC treaty needs to be greatly accelerated.

In my remarks today, I touched on the need for increasing energy efficiency. We simply have to reduce the level of hydrocarbon combustion in this country. Everywhere we see global pollution from burning oil and natural gas. When these reserves are exhausted, there is the huge abundance of other carbon-based sources, coal in particular. We must have more efficient ways of using fossil fuels.

Tropical deforestation is another of the most serious problems we're confronting. The nation has to stop participating in the kinds of development activities sponsored through the multilateral development banks that have encouraged environmentally destructive practices, such as massive deforestation, for so long.

I think we're seeing some changes. But in all of these areas, we are going to require a much higher level of leadership from the president of the United States.

Q   Under your leadership, in what ways do you think the National Wildlife Federation has improved the national and global environment?

A   When I came to Washington in 1981 to head the federation, the first interview I had was with Philip Shabecoff, the national environmental reporter with the *New York Times*. He asked me what my priorities were as president of the organization. I told him the federation would provide leadership to enter an era of "corporate detente." Shabecoff asked if that meant we were caving in to corporate America. Absolutely not, I told him. We're confident enough in our ability to provide sophisticated technical and economic analysis that we can sit down with any corporation or association and talk about the merits of their position and ours. As a research scientist myself, I recognize that the more we can bring sound science into the public decision-making process, the better the public policies we'll produce.

There are other challenges facing the federation. No matter how many laws we have and how well the regulations are drafted and enforced by EPA, the challenge over the next ten to fifteen years is to change the attitude of the free enterprise system from one where environmental costs are internalized to one where they are externalized. Public and environmental health are the sufferers of that old practice.

To tackle this problem, we formed the NWF Corporate Conservation Council with fifteen members. Activities of the council are under a separate budget of the National Wildlife Federation. The council has provided a friendly but rigorous forum. One ground rule: You leave your six-gun at the door when you come in, or you don't play. As far as the federation is concerned, we're willing to learn about the issues facing business. We also perform an educational function for our business members. It's a two-way street.

The council has passed a series of policy statements on wetlands protection, soil erosion, ground-water contamination, and waste reduction.

But so what? If the National Wildlife Federation and our Corporate Conservation Council issue a policy on wetlands protection, what does it really mean? Frankly, I had no idea what it really meant until I started to understand how corporate policy decision-making comes about. Look at the organizations that are members: Du Pont, 3M, USX, Tenneco, Weyerhaeuser, and other major multinational organizations, many with large land holdings.

Many of the wetlands we are trying to protect in this nation are not on public lands, but rather on private lands. When a corporate member signs its name on the line, policies and guidelines for the protection of the wetlands become the marching orders for everybody in that corporation. The orders go throughout the entire world via their management policy guidelines. I had no idea how powerful and important that would be.

I'll give you another example of our current environmental projects. We are developing an outreach program with business schools around the nation. In this, we are engaged in a dialogue with the deans and teaching staffs of business schools. We are trying to emphasize that environmental policies and regulations are as much a part of today's business education as are cash flow and leveraged buyouts. We are developing case studies and other educational materials to make our point. For example, with Du Pont's help, we are developing a case study on how Du Pont, as a major corporation, reached the decision to stop making CFCs, the chemicals that deplete upper-atmosphere ozone. Environmental case studies like this could be distributed through the business-school education system nationwide.

The National Wildlife Federation is active in several areas of this sort, all of which make the point that with basic environmental matters, it's no longer "us" and "them." There is only "us," and if we can't interact responsibly, and can't change behavior, then in the long haul, society will be the major loser.

There is no secret about why the federation has been effective in its relations with business. We're reasonable, we're rigorous, we have good science, and we have the other capabilities to play at the highest levels in that game. We also have excellent litigating capability, which we don't hesitate to use when necessary.

When I came on board the federation in 1981, we had an active litigation docket of about twenty-five cases. Today, there are somewhere around eighty-five. We are very aggressive, but the policy we have pursued is that litigation is the last alternative. In my view, the courts are the conveners of losers, not winners, because when you litigate you've reached the point where you can't resolve your differences. We are actively trying to pursue mediation-to-resolution in some of the very difficult problems we face.

Q   What specific projects do you envision for a new "Department of Environmental Protection," and how would the nation benefit?

A   We haven't done an exhaustive analysis, but let me give you a couple of examples of things that ought to be in a Department of Environmental Protection.

EPA has enormous atmospheric responsibilities. One of the greatest needs is to understand the long-range transport of materials through the air, and the long-term consequences to both environment and human health. The capability of doing this kind of work does not reside at EPA. It resides, instead, at the Department of Commerce.

You have responsibility for coastal-zone management and wetlands protection, yet much of that expertise is not in EPA; it's in Commerce or the Corps of Engineers. There needs to be some consolidation of those programs—particularly regarding research and data gathering—in order for this agency to do what I think people expect it to do.

How would the nation benefit from elevating EPA to cabinet status? Look at the examples of the departments of energy and education. When these important national endeavors were elevated to cabinet status, they were incorporated more directly into the national policy-making function. We must assume there is an improvement in the way the functions are carried out. The heads of the departments of energy and education are sitting at the table with the other cabinet secretaries, and not with their backs against the wall, as the EPA administrator is right now.

Because the environment is not represented directly at the table, others speak up. You get the secretary of the interior suggesting that we all wear hats and sunglasses to avoid the increased ultraviolet radiation from destruction of the ozone layer. The secretary of the interior shouldn't be crafting global environmental policy. In my view, that should be the job of the head of EPA.

Q   If EPA were to gain cabinet status, wouldn't that further politicize its activities? Wouldn't the environment be better served if the agency were to retain its independent status?

A   Sure, there is that risk. Nothing is ever totally positive. A case can be made that with independent status, such as that of the Food and Drug Administration, you may be isolated from the political process. However, EPA is politicized already and always has been.

Your administrator, deputy administrator, and assistant administrators are all political appointees. It's a political world. I think you ought to be equipped with the tools to play on the first team, and with the resources necessary to win. And in my view, a significant part of that is the benefit of cabinet-level status.

More important, however, is whether or not the head of this institution and the president of our nation provide the leadership to make environmental matters important. Giving you a title and a name on the wall of your new building isn't going to do that. You've got to have the resolve. You've got to have the mandate, and you've got to have the leadership. But, symbolically, it would show the nation and the world that we are leaders in environmental protection, as exemplified by representation at the highest level of our government. Substantively and symbolically, that is extremely important.

[SEPTEMBER 1, 1988]

## BIOGRAPHY

Since 1981, Jay D. Hair has headed the National Wildlife Federation, a 5.6 million member conservation and education organization dedicated to informing the public about the environment and ways in which it can be improved.

Dr. Hair serves on the boards of the Global Tomorrow Coalition and Clean Sites, Inc., and is active with a number of other natural resource management and environmental protection committees and forums.

Prior to joining the National Wildlife Federation, Dr. Hair was for several years administrator of the Fisheries and Wildlife Sciences Program at North Carolina State University, and a special assistant to the U.S. Department of the Interior, where he was responsible for coordinating the development of a national fish and wildlife policy.

# A Global View
of Environmental
Problems

Today, rather than give some sort of professorial speech, I would like to say a few things, express a few opinions, and then we can discuss them freely. You can ask me any question, and I will answer with frankness. By the way, it's good to be independent of any government!

I've been asked how I would describe myself, and my answer is always, I don't care about that. I follow my impulses. I have wondered, nevertheless, if the impulse, this tremendous curiosity I have always felt—which is to look through keyholes at what happens in nature— was exceptional or natural. And the more I observe nature, the more I think that the impulse toward exploration is built into almost every organism, including plants.

Plants send feelers, their roots, as far as they can. They have terrible fights for space, as much as humans or animals. I think this drive for exploration is built in every living thing, sometimes from necessity, sometimes from sheer curiosity.

This impulse probably materialized in me at a very young age. I remember that at the age of six I was with my parents near Nice. They had rented, for the summer, an apartment in a small villa where the owner was living on the ground floor. Returning from my swim one day, I brought in objects from the sea, including a beautiful red starfish. I went upstairs and put my starfish on the balcony. I didn't know that the owner, Madame Lepic, had earlier put her bedding outside for airing.

JACQUES-YVES
COUSTEAU is an
explorer, oceanographer,
and founding president of
the Cousteau Society.

And my beautiful starfish fell on her mattress. It was a catastrophe! The starfish left a red imprint on the mattress. Madame Lepic came, vociferating, and my parents were furious. So I waited until things calmed down, and I ran away.

Behind the house was a railway track. Ever since we arrived, I had been fascinated by the passing trains, the big locomotives. On the horizon I was always seeing big clouds of smoke, and I imagined that over there, there had to be a gathering of locomotives that were puffing all these clouds. It had to be a fascinating place.

So, disgusted with my parents and Madame Lepic, I started walking along the train track. When I had gone several miles, evening fell. I had to sleep by the side of the tracks. It was cool. I shivered. I was miserable. The next day I started again, still seeing the smoke in the distance, and I was saying to myself, "I have to go there, I have to go there." But finally I could not go any further, stopped not by fatigue but by thirst. There was no water along the railway track. I was a little bit like a twig in the Sahara Desert. Then the cops arrived and brought me back. But I had, at the same time, begun my career as an explorer, and also I had touched with my senses the necessity of water for survival. Thirst—the absence of water—is the thing that had stopped me.

So time passed, and I spent twenty-seven years of my life as a military officer, which means that I had been prepared for war. When I think of it now, I'm not ashamed, because I learned a lot of things—discipline, for example. Then I was taught to perfect the weapons, torpedoes that destroyed ships; now I am fighting to protect life, while I had been trained to destroy it.

So that was one of my tragedies in the beginning of my career. After that, of course, I did something else much more interesting. Since 1966, first with my two sons and then with Jean-Michel alone, we have been going on our expeditions, always keeping in mind that our work is not only to explore, but also to try to learn lessons about the deterioration of our planet and the damage done to it by human beings.

I first became aware of the damage in 1949. Just a few months after the war, we witnessed the deterioration of the vitality of the Mediterranean. Fishermen were exploding dynamite in order to get food; spear fishermen were beginning to ravage the bottom of the sea, and the results immediately struck us—when I say us, I mean my little team as much as myself. We had to do something to stop the destruction.

I have been confirmed in this, after working for thirty-five years against pollution. I have been confirmed in my belief that the problem is quite complicated. In 1977, *Calypso* started a trip in the Mediterranean, visiting sixteen of the eighteen countries touched by it. The goal was to try to obtain a general picture of pollution in the Mediterranean. We took samples of water, plankton, and sediment. We interrogated fishermen, local authorities, ministers, and chiefs of government. We witnessed the disaster area in Venice at that time.

At the end of our voyage, I gave all my samples to my laboratory in Monaco, and I witnessed the measurements. As the printouts came from the computers, it became more and more apparent that pollution could not account for everything. We saw a drop in vitality that cannot be explained only by DDT, heavy metals, or whatever. There had to be something else. Then suddenly, recalling all that I had seen, I thought, "Yes! Of course!" It was what we, at the time, called "mechanical destruction" of the Mediterranean—what we now call "*saccage*" in French. And I have not yet found the right word in English. *Saccage* means the destruction that an invading army spreads, destroying everything in its path. We are acting like Attila on the Earth today. All this mechanical killing, destroying, dynamite fishing, using nets with mesh too small, draining marshes and lagoons, cutting passes in atolls, and changing the courses of rivers—all these things are not pollution, but they are increasing the effects of pollution. The result is really a synergistic effect between pollution and other forms of destruction.

On top of that, of course, comes the elimination of species. Almost one million species have disappeared since the beginning of the nineteenth century. Forever. That's 8 percent of the total known census of living creatures, exhausted for future generations. Some of those organisms that have disappeared—most are plants—could perhaps have given us medicines or other useful products. But now they will never be of any use.

It is the fluids of life—air and water—that are in danger. As you know, there is, by weight, a lot more water than air, which means that theoretically air is even more vulnerable than water. Up until now, I have given more attention to water than to air; but I'm beginning to change my mind because what is happening today, not only with acid rain but more importantly with the warming of the planet, is mainly damage to the atmosphere. The fate of humankind is intertwined with these problems: pollution, mechanical damage, and heating of the planet, which is another form of pollution. And all of these problems are direct consequences of overpopulation. I can never repeat it enough. The problem of overpopulation was clearly outlined in the first years of the Club of Rome, but for some unexplainable reason, overpopulation has practically disappeared from environmental literature. I don't understand why. Overpopulation has never been more pressing; it has never been more tragic.

When I went to school, the population of the earth was not quite 3 billion. Now there are 5 billion. For the near future, the population of the Earth will increase by one China every ten years. How long can that be carried on?

Yes, it is probably possible, by increasing production, by improving the distribution of resources to the poor nations, to feed 15 billion people in the future. Not very well, but decently. It is probably possible to have 15 billion people survive on Earth. But what kind of life are they going to lead? Are we here to ensure mere survival? Or are we here to protect the quality not only of our own lives, but of the lives of the people who will come after us in the next generations?

When *Calypso* went recently to examine the radioactivity problem on the island of Mururoa, where the French test atomic bombs, we were thinking more of future generations than about us. And when we see the population growing to such an extent, when we see the rich nations become richer and the poor nations become poorer while they grow in population, the number of time bombs that are planted around us—radioactivity, overpopulation, destruction of nonrenewable resources—is such that we're inclined to yell, "Stop it!" We have to do something; we have to put tremendous pressure on our governments to stop these things. Our indignation must be told. It must be broadcast. We have to proclaim it; we have to yell it; we have to show it, not hide it in the corner of ourselves.

There must be public pressure to force the decision-makers to take action. I'm saying this to you because I was there when EPA was created. I was there to see the first triumphant beginning of EPA. The entire world was envying the United States for its creation of EPA. From the beginning, there were environmental laws that are still there, and legal instruments that are at your disposal. They still exist, and they can and should be used. No other country on Earth has anything comparable. None.

So you have the legal tools, but because of political pressure, because of lobbying, you do not make full use of them. We suffer when we see this. I've seen the change in the government. You are suffering from government decisions, from government indifference.

This agency has to remain independent. I'm saying this openly and envying the possibility. We don't have anything like the EPA in France. We have the Ministry of the Environment, which is a slave to government decisions, as they have proven many times. They are not free; they are not independent. Theoretically, you have a degree of independence that is greater than that of any similar organization on Earth. So we are waiting and praying that you use it.

I'm sure that during our dialogue now, real problems will come up, so please ask questions.


## Questions from the Audience

Q  Captain Cousteau, given the limited resources that are available for environmental protection, what do you think are the priority issues toward which we should put those resources?

A  Limited resources? I think you have plenty. I really do. By comparison, at least. But deciding on priorities, that's a very good question.

First, we have to make a clear distinction between strategy and tactics. Fighting pollution is tactics. It has to be done, sure. Fighting mechanical destruction is also tactics. But what is a strategic goal of an organization like yours? That is something that does not belong to me to define. But if you're asking me the question, I can answer it.

I think that our goals, yours and ours at the Cousteau Society, are the same. It is to work in the direction, whether or not we are successful, of preparing a better world for future generations, a better quality of life for those who will come after us. That is, I think, a strategic goal of our organizations. Then the tactical moves have to go in that direction. Any activity that goes in the opposite direction, even partially, must be eliminated. Everything that goes partially toward bettering the quality of life goes along with the strategy that we are implementing.

Q  You suggested that one of the major problems we face is overpopulation. What can we do that is politically realistic to put a cap on population in a democracy?

A  You have already solved the problem of population in America. You are not increasing, really, except by immigration. The same thing is happening throughout Western Europe. The population of France increases by the immigration of North Africans; the population of Germany increases by the immigration of Turks; the population of Great Britain increases by the immigration of Indians, but apart from that, those populations are stable.

So what can you do to induce other countries to do the same? They don't have the same motivations. In Europe, even more so than here, health and education are covered by social security. A European couple makes no provision for health expenses. Everything is paid by the government. They make no provision for education. All education, even at universities, is paid for by the government. So these people can begin to think about their security as being assured. They don't need their children's help to provide for old age. Not so in India, or in any of the developing countries where there is practically no social security, no security at all for the old people. So couples are having as many children as quickly as they can for old-age protection. And how can you criticize that attitude? I don't think you can, for moral reasons. In India they are giving a radio set to couples who don't have children. That really doesn't make any sense to me. The only way to fill the need for a certain degree of security is for the government to provide the security. The more secure people are, the less need they will have for children. And they will have enough children for the continuity of the species, but no more. That's what we should all try to achieve.

There are also religious obstacles. For Catholics, the Pope keeps on saying, "Go on; multiply." I am a Catholic, but the Ayatollah says the same to the Moslems, and the Buddhists say the same, and the Shinto-ists say the same. Why? Because of the competition among religions. The more numbers they have, the stronger they will be in religious competition. The survival of humankind depends on that kind of silly reasoning.

So to answer your question, what can we do, you and I? Nothing. But we can preach for sharing the resources of the world with developing countries, for allowing governments in developing countries to have more money to build up the security of their citizens. Once the citizens are secure, they will do the same as we do. I don't see any other way at the moment. You don't want to castrate people.

Q Some of our problems in atmospheric pollution relate to the burn-ing of fossil fuels, in either electric power plants or automobiles, which leads to generation of nitrogen and sulfur oxides and greenhouse gases. Some of the alternatives in this country don't seem too appealing— nuclear power, for example. Could you share some thoughts on energy production for both industrialized countries and developing countries in terms of atmospheric pollution? What are the choices for the future?

A Most of our sources of energy produce carbon dioxide. It's a fact. All of the cars are spitting out carbon dioxide, and they spit out other things too. So carbon dioxide, $CO_2$, is the number-one byproduct of modern civilization.

As you said, the alternative source of energy, at the moment, has often been considered to be nuclear fuel. Nuclear plants, as we all know, are a tremendous danger. They provide energy without $CO_2$, but at a cost of tremendous heat loss. For the energy produced, a fossil fuel plant loses about 70 percent in heat to the atmosphere. A similar amount is lost by nuclear plants. So what you gain by producing less $CO_2$, you lose by heating the planet more. Besides, nuclear fuel is not going to last for long. We know that. It's only a temporary recourse. One of the solutions that can be considered is fusion, but that's a very compli-cated issue. The choice of the uranium-plutonium system was made only because it produces weapons. There were other avenues for energy production that could have been developed, but they did not produce weapons.

So our mistaken choice was made for military reasons, and the consequences, as always, have boomeranged on us. Not only have we produced weapons that can end the world—the H-bombs—but also we have produced peaceful nuclear plants that are potential bombs. There are Chernobyls in existence. Even in the case of a conventional war, a conventional bomb on one of these plants would make a Chernobyl, at least. Or worse. France, for example, my country, is littered with potential Chernobyls that can be exploded with conventional weapons. It's a tremendous threat to my country. It's something unacceptable to any reasonable being. But there we are. So for the moment we are stuck with soot.

Q Has the deterioration of the Mediterranean been reversed? And what can we learn, either positive or negative, from what the Mediterranean countries have done?

A We have learned a lot of things. To answer your first question first: No, the deterioration has not been reversed. It has been slowed down. That means that the rate at which it deteriorates is lower than it was before. That's the only result we have yet.

As secretary general of the Mediterranean Commission for twenty-two years, I helped to create the Mediterranean pact that was signed several years ago. This pact provides for several billions of dollars to be provided by governments of Mediterranean countries to protect the environment against marine pollution. Practically none of this money has been given yet. So there has been a lot of talking, a lot of papers signed, and nothing done. The only things that have been done are by municipalities and independent parties, but by national governments, nothing at all. That's the lesson we can learn: that we must not put too much trust in those international conferences.

Q This is sort of a religious question. When the astronauts come back from space explorations, they sometimes express feelings about a supreme being, because they're awed by the magnificence of Earth and the universe. You have done a number of undersea explorations, and I wonder about your thoughts on the existence of a supreme being.

A Well. It is a very personal question, but I will answer. I promised that I would answer any question.

Let's forget about my upbringing—I was brought up as a Catholic. My mother and my father were very strict Catholics. Let's forget that. That is a bygone under which I was educated. Then I became a student, and we had our talks and flirted with materialism, with communist ideas, Marxism, fascist ideas—all the nonsense you could listen to at the ages of sixteen, seventeen, and eighteen. Then the religious ideas faded out in me, and I became fairly materialistic for the bulk of my life until I got to be forty or forty-five.

The more I have been acquainted with the process of life, the more I have looked into the new theories of general relativity that describe the universe, into the questions that have been so well posed by Stephen Hawkins in his recent book, *A Brief History of Time: From the Big Bang to the Black Hole*, the more these questions have focused my attention. And beyond all the symbols of religions, beyond all the parables that were created probably by priests to educate people at the time, the farther I go, the more I am persuaded that the universe is oriented. Oriented to what? Nobody will ever know. But there is something behind every single thing. That I believe, yes.

Q Most of the environmental destruction in the world today is done in the less-developed countries. Do you think that EPA or the developed countries in general have a role or a responsibility to help environmental protection in less-developed societies?

A I believe that, from the bylaws of EPA, your first task is to deal with American questions. Am I right? It's too bad, but that's the way it is. So what EPA should be avoiding are national actions that could hurt the rest of the world. For example, the export of toxic waste. That has to be stopped right away. Sending your toxic waste to poor nations is a shocking crime, and it has to be stopped by EPA. That's the kind of international action you can take.

Q Would you comment on the goals and activities of the Greenpeace organization, and the relationship between the French government and Greenpeace, and particularly the destruction of the Greenpeace flagship?

A The goals of Greenpeace are very similar to ours, theoretically. Their methods are not. The methods of the French government are even worse than that. The sinking of the *Rainbow Warrior* was one of the most shocking mistakes and crimes that I know of. It was ridiculous; it was criminal; it is inexcusable.

The methods of Greenpeace do not always have my approval. Their actions appear to be politically oriented even if they are not. I give you the following example: There are a number of nuclear nations—India, China, France, and England are the small ones. The big ones, the ones that really are a threat to the world, are the Russians and the Americans. Do you think that Greenpeace does much in those nations? No. They are aimed at the French. Why?

Sure we are wrong in testing nuclear weapons in Mururoa, but what about America? What about Russia? They test many more weapons. And if there is to be a disarmament, it will come from them or it will not come.

It is not because France will stop testing in Mururoa that Russia will change its policy one iota. We are born French, but we are not slaves to the policy of our country. Not at all. The Cousteau Society doesn't get a cent from my country; we don't want to depend on anything the French government is doing. Nor on your government either. Our position is that we don't want any nuclear weapons on the face of the Earth, but disarmament has to be achieved by the two big nuclear nations first, and then everything will fall in place. We are for total disarmament, or nothing.

We are yelling about that and doing everything we can. I was personally at almost all of the demonstrations. Each time there is a new nuclear site in France, I go to protest. This does not mean that our little country should assume all the evil of the world. No! Evil is in the two big ones.

Q One of the questioners today made the statement that most environmental pollution or degradation is being caused by Third World countries. Do you agree or disagree with that?

A I disagree. By far the bulk of the degradation of the environment is done by developed countries, by us. And on top of it, as I said a moment ago, we have the nerve to send our waste to them. Because they need money, they will accept anything, including that. That is wrong.

It is true that at the Stockholm conference, the representative of Pakistan made the famous statement that environmental care was all right for rich countries, but that developing countries are not interested. I found that same attitude in this country. At the beginning, when we had our involvement days, I met thousands of Americans, and I was surprised that there were very few black people coming to our meetings. One of them told me not to be surprised. He was there because he was one of the favored blacks, but he said, "We have other priorities." So this attitude was real, but it is less and less true here.

In Algeria, I remember very well that twelve years ago they began to install some purification systems for the effluents of industrial plants. They were distributing manuals about ecology in their primary schools; they have done several things of that sort.

More and more, the people in developing countries rebel against destruction of their source of food, which is their soil, their air, their water. So I disagree with that. It was true; it's no longer true.

*Q*   There are two philosophies that often influence decisions that EPA has to make. The first is that the government should put out rules and regulations and tell people they must comply. The second is to educate people about the choices and risks, and to let them decide for themselves. Through their own motivation and knowledge, people would do the right thing. Is one approach better than the other, and does the answer depend on whether you were applying it to an industrialized country as opposed to an undeveloped country?

*A*   I think there is no choice; both must be done. The education of the people is fine, so they will not dump plastic bags in the streets. But a factory will continue sending out mercury and harmful effluents if you don't put out regulations. They will keep on polluting anyway because it's cheaper.

So we do need regulations just as we need red lights at corners of streets. Otherwise there would be a tremendous number of accidents. These regulations should be humane; they should not be dictatorial, but they have to be very severe. Fines today are too small. Many industries prefer to pay the fine and keep on polluting because it's cheaper. As long as this is true, polluters will not be induced to correct their systems. In the ideal country, the big polluters have to be controlled and regulated, and the average citizen has to be educated. There is no conflict between these two concepts. It is essential that they be carried out at the same time.

Now, about regulating the big polluters: I made a suggestion many years ago. Nobody listened, but I'm used to that. But there is a solution that makes a lot of sense to me: Rather than have purification plants at the end of a river where the mixture of pollutants is such that nobody knows how to deal with it, we should depollute at the source. This means many, many purification plants, each one specializing in the toxic product, or the two or three or four toxic products produced by a particular plant.

The cost of these minipurification plants should be borne, in principle, equally by three groups: one-third by the plant; one-third by the community because their health is going to be improved, as a benefit from the purification; and one-third by the federal government because it has to unify the policy of the country. With this approach, the burden on industry would not be so heavy as to induce them to cheat as they do now. So I will recommend this system once more.

*Q*   It seems to be increasingly evident that environmental problems don't recognize political boundaries. Do you see the need for some kind of international, worldwide version of EPA, and do you have any ideas on that?

*A* Yes, it may not be exactly an EPA. You know, there are many people who want to jump over the fence and have a world government. It's much too early for that, but it is obvious that the water system, for example, has to be taken in its entirety. Global regulations and global care are the only solutions for the water system and for the atmosphere. Those two systems are international; they're global, and they have to be treated at the world level. So there could be a higher authority. Nations would have to delegate their environmental authority to that higher authority for control of the water system and the atmosphere. That, I think, would be a very good thing.

The process has been used by Jean Monet in Europe. After the war, Jean Monet created a higher authority for coal and steel. It began with a limited activity. There was a need for coal and steel after the war in Europe, so all the nations said, "Okay, let's work together." And that was the beginning of the European Economic Community. Once the nations tested how well this steel and coal authority worked, they progressively extended the regulations. And in 1992 they're supposed to delegate practically everything.

So I think at the world level, that's the way to go—higher authority on water and air.

*Q* Do you think it's possible that an environmental ethic can actually be instilled into the teachings of the major religions? What better way of changing people's behavior than by teaching from the pulpit?

*A* Yes, but you see, people can do very little for the environment. By behaving well, yes. But take a housewife who buys a product for her washing machine. She goes to the supermarket, and she has a choice among three or four products. None of them is clearly environmentally clean and guaranteed by EPA. At the moment, the choices are made according to advertising and publicity, not according to the environmental quality of the product. So what can the average citizen or average housewife do? They can use unleaded gasoline instead of leaded gasoline; that's done already. But for the household products, for the medical products, there is no control. There is no recommendation based on environmental quality. Yet Canada has started something in that direction. Canada now has a law that a product in general use must bear a seal of appropriate quality for the environment.

I think it's a good idea to make the choice of the average customer more informed. If we are educating the average citizen, at least he or she must be given the possibility of making the right choice. Today citizens don't have that opportunity.

[NOVEMBER 17, 1988]

Jacques Cousteau is well known to Americans through the more than fifty films he has created for television, along with three full-length films (two of which won Oscars). He also has written or collaborated on more than fifty books that have been published in more than a dozen languages.

In 1950, Captain Cousteau acquired a ship that his work would make world-famous: a retired U.S. minesweeper he named the *Calypso*. He transformed the ship into an oceanographic vessel, and the following year used it to test and perfect the first underwater camera equipment for television transmission. In 1959, he introduced the Diving Saucer. This round, highly maneuverable submarine permitted two passengers to observe, take samples, and film at a depth of 350 meters.

Captain Cousteau is one of the few foreign members of America's National Academy of Sciences. He has received honorary doctorates from the University of California at Berkeley, Brandeis University, and Harvard, and the Centennial Award from the National Geographic Society.

Captain Cousteau received his first training in oceanography at the French Naval Academy. In 1936, following a serious flying accident, he began a series of diving experiments. These led in 1943 to the development of the aqualung. During World War II, Captain Cousteau performed antimining missions for the French Resistance, for which he has been named a Commander of the Legion d'Honneur.

# Can We Respond to the Growing Environmental Threat to Civilization?

I would like to outline briefly what I think are the most serious environmental threats to civilization, and then say something about our chances for responding effectively to them. Obviously I am speaking to an audience of people who will be among the major responders.

I have the reputation of being a population nut. I got that reputation because I wrote a book a long time ago called *Population, Resources, and Environment*. But, as some of you may know, when you write a book, you have no control over the title. The publisher controls that. And the publisher decided to call it *The Population Bomb*. In terms of sales, he was undoubtedly correct.

Ecologists are extraordinarily concerned about population. That's not because we think that solving the population problem, and actually shrinking the world's population to a number that is sustainable in the long term, will automatically solve all the rest of the problems of the world. We still could be faced with the threat of war, with environmental deterioration, with racism, with sexism, with economic inequity, and other problems. None of those problems automatically gets sorted out just by solving the population problem. But the critical point is that if we *don't* solve the population problem, no other issue you are concerned with at EPA, or as human beings, is likely to be taken care of in a manner that you would find satisfactory.

Let me give you a few numbers about population that will show why my colleagues and I are so concerned about it.

PAUL EHRLICH, author
of *The Population Bomb*,
is Bing Professor of
Population Studies at
Stanford University.

You can define humanity as having started about 4 million years ago, when the first small-brain hominid stood upright—a little before the time of Lucy. (I think you have to start humanity then, because if you don't count upright, small-brained hominids as being human, then a lot of congressmen wouldn't be included.) It took about 4 million years for the human population to increase from a few hundred individuals to exactly 2 billion on that celebrated date, May 29, 1932—which, no doubt, many of you recognize as the day that I was born.

So 4 million years got us to 2 billion people. When *The Population Bomb* was written in 1968, a brief thirty-six years later, there were 3.5 billion people. Now, in 1988, twenty years after that, we are pushing toward 5.2 billion. More people have been added to the human population since *The Population Bomb* was written, which seems like only yesterday to me, than existed on the planet at the time of the American Civil War. Less than a decade from now, more people will have been added to the planet since *The Bomb* was written than existed when I was born.

So one of the major facts, maybe the major fact on the planet in the last few decades, has been the extraordinary rate of growth of the human population. What makes this so depressing, for those of us who feel that population is a primary driving force in environmental problems, is that there is an enormous lag-time involved in controlling population size. If population is to be controlled humanely by limiting births, rather than allowing nature to increase the death rate, we will have to act very quickly and effectively. Make no mistake about it. I don't have a single colleague who believes the population explosion is not going to come to an end within the next half century. The only question that remains is how.

Will it end because we have made dramatic strides in limiting our birth rate? Or will it be because there are dramatic rises in the death rate, either through the "bang," a large-scale nuclear war, followed by a nuclear winter, or the "whimper," which amounts to just following current environmental trends for a few more decades. That would produce the same results as the nuclear winter.

To get a feel for the momentum built into population growth, consider what could happen in India. Let's take a very optimistic view, and assume that India's total fertility rate (the average number of babies of both sexes born per woman over her lifetime) drops from the current 4.5 to 2.2 over the next thirty-five years. At that rate (and accounting for the babies that die before reaching reproductive age), each woman would be just replacing herself. If, for some reason, this miracle *did* take place over the next thirty-five years or so, India's population would still continue to grow from her 815 million or so today—nobody knows what the exact number is—to somewhere around 2 billion at the end of the next century. That is about the most optimistic scenario you can construct for India. And it means there would be as many people in India at the end of the next century as there were on the planet when I was born.

So, we have a very rapidly growing population, and growth is bound to continue for a long time. But if you talk to the odd economist, or even to the ones who aren't odd, they cannot see why that makes any difference at all. Economists, of course, have all been trained with the standard economics text, which has gross national product being generated with no outside inputs at all. Economists never study physics or biology. They believe in perpetual motion and miracles; they believe that the population can simply grow forever—or, at least, that the limits to growth are so far away that they needn't concern anybody today. Is this a reasonable point of view? Of course not. It is utterly nonsensical.

Let me talk about limits to growth, first by turning to what might be called, by an economist, "the ultimate resource." That is, of course, food. What we are concerned about, remember, is not just the numbers of people. It is their impact on the systems that support us. It is their impact on food resources, on the environment, and so on. When you talk about animals and their environment, the first thing you think of, quite naturally, is food.

We are adding world-record increments to the population now, the highest ever, almost 90 million people a year. That is more than adding the population equivalent of a new United States to the planet every three years. Is our food production keeping up? Curiously enough, as has been predicted for a long time, it is not. Consequently, each year something on the order of 10 million people die of starvation. The peak of food production was in 1985. It has gone downhill in absolute terms ever since. It has been going downhill, per capita, in Africa since 1967. It has been going downhill, per capita, in Latin America since 1983.

The most frightening number that I have heard recently comes from Lester Brown of the Worldwatch Institute. If he is correct (and the preliminary numbers I've seen indicate he is), in 1988, for the first time in its history, the United States consumed more grain that it grew. Now, you have to remember that North America is thought of as the feeding bastion of humanity. Roughly 100 nations are dependent upon North American food exports to keep going. That continued this year because we had large grain stocks. But they are gone now.

The debate now among the *cognoscenti* is this: Should we hope for a drought next summer that might kill a lot of people outright, but would at least get people moving and dealing with some of these global environmental problems? Or should we hope for a wet summer, which would save a lot of lives in the short term, but would undoubtedly cost a lot more in the long term? As you all know, the political system here can operate only if it is getting continual jabs you-know-where. Without another drought, it's almost certain the global warming legislation and related bills now going through Congress will not be passed, or will be gutted and watered down.

Many of us have been looking at the question of the ultimate number of people that can be fed on the planet. You probably have heard that when the anti-birth control encyclical, *Humanae Vitae,* of Pope Paul VI was reaffirmed this year, Pope John Paul II's bishops asserted that the world can theoretically feed 40 billion people.

Well, is it true? The most recent studies of the adequacy of food supplies have been done by a group at Brown University. The numbers have been checked by our group at Stanford, and they are certainly in the right ballpark. You have often heard, no doubt, that we don't have a population problem, only a distribution problem. Well, if you distributed all food equally, and if you didn't feed any grain to animals, and basically everybody moved back to a vegetarian diet, supplemented a little bit by range-fed beef, pork that feeds on garbage, and fish, how many people could be fed?

The answer is about 6 billion.

Right now, we are at the 5.2 billion mark worldwide. That means we don't have a lot of room to maneuver, because we can take care of only 800 million more people—less than a decade's growth—before we hit a limit. That projection is based on 1985 food production, not on this year's production, which is some 10 percent smaller. If we return to the 1985 production level, which should be fairly easy, actually, as food prices go up and people use more inputs, then about 6 billion vegetarians can be fed.

If, however, the average person is to have a South American style diet, where about 15 percent of the calories come from animal sources, then only about 4 billion people can be fed. That means that, right now, about 1.2 billion people would get nothing at all to eat. And if you want to have a healthy North American diet, where about 35 percent of your calories come from animal sources, then you can feed about 2.5 billion people, or less than half of today's population.

The optimists will say, well, somehow we are going to perform miracles, and we are going to grow more food, so we don't have to worry about it. We will just increase the food production as time goes on.

There are, unfortunately, some absolute limits to food production. Nobody is certain what they are. The best study on the subject is by Vitovsik et al., published in 1986 in Bioscience. It simply asked, what proportion of the net primary productivity of the planet, the basic food supply for all animals Homo sapiens and maybe 30 million other species), is now being used, co-opted, or destroyed by humanity on land? The answer is about 40 percent. So if you do away with all other animals on the planet, and give their food to people, you might get through another population doubling and a bit more. You could buy fifty years' time, something like that. Possibly.

But we are dealing with real human beings, not saints who are going to give up grain-fed beef and share everything equally. By any real measure, we are very near the edge on food, without even thinking about things like climate change.

Where do the bishops get their 40 billion figure? They say, theoretically, we could feed 40 billion people. That's correct, if your theory says that we are going to turn all the arable land in the world into a simulation of Iowa, with the same climate as Iowa, and twenty-five Ph.D.'s standing around every experimental hectare during the growing season, with all the inputs you want, and perfect climate. You also assume that none of the 40 billion people will stand on farmland, that the climate will remain the same, and that there will be no acid rain. With all those little assumptions, you might get a number like 40 billion or 60 billion. It depends on whether you assume you can farm the ocean surface, or grow corn underneath a Greenland ice cap. It is theoretically possible.

I would point out, to those of you who are statisticians, that it is theoretically possible to play Russian roulette fifty thousand times in a row, with five out of six chambers loaded, without blowing your brains out. It is theoretically possible that your favorite baseball team will win every game over the next two hundred seasons. All those things are theoretically possible, but only an imbecile would make any plans on the basis of that kind of theory. Yet there are obviously people out there recommending that the entire world should plan on extraordinary good luck.

One of the things that makes that theory so silly, of course, is that the people who promote it do not understand that our entire economic system, our entire civilization, rests on a series of free public service functions of natural ecological systems, and that those "ecosystem services" are beginning to break down. The central question of economics today has been approached by only two or three economists. The question is: How large an economic system can we have and still have it operate safely within the constraints that are set by physics, chemistry, and biology? Meanwhile, "distinguished" economists assume the gross national product will continue to grow at 3 or 4 percent a year forever. They talk ponderously about all this stuff as if the supports of the economic system make no difference at all. But the supports, it turns out, are incredibly important.

One of the principal functions of the ecological systems of the planet is to maintain the gaseous quality of the atmosphere in a state that will keep the climate appropriate for growing crops. And that is one of the ecological services that is now most dramatically breaking down. We've known for many decades that this would happen. At the time I wrote *The Population Bomb*, the question was whether all of the crap we were putting into the atmosphere in the form of dust and other particles was going to cool the earth more rapidly than the carbon dioxide that we're putting into the atmosphere is going to warm it.

In the last twenty years, we've learned a lot more about climatic systems, and it is crystal clear now that the warming is more than overwhelming any cooling. And atmospheric physicists have been surprised that the warming is occurring at a much more rapid rate than had been predicted.

Last summer's drought was one of the major causes of the 1988 decline in food production. Nobody will ever know whether the drought was just a result of normal climatic variability, or whether it is related to the roughly one degree of global warming that has already taken place. Climatic models predict that such droughts will become more frequent. Not every year will be hot and dry, but hot, dry summers will come more frequently. Large hurricanes will also become more common because a hurricane is essentially a device for transfering heat from the tropical regions to temperate and polar regions. Coincidentally, or maybe because of the warming, last year had recordbreaking hurricanes in the Northern Hemisphere.

So things are looking rather ominous on that front. If you talk to the *cognoscenti*—those are the people who understand what we don't know about the climatic system—what scares them is the knowledge that weather is driven by small differences between large numbers. That means there are probably important thresholds that will soon be crossed.

There might be such a threshold, for example, that determines the direction of flow of the Gulf Stream. It could be that the climate changes we are causing will go past the threshold and change the direction of the Gulf Stream. The Stream is part of a planetwide system that goes through both oceans, and it apparently has changed its direction in the past. And if it changes its direction again, things will become very interesting (and *very* cold) in Europe!

The critical thing about global warming is the effect it will have on the worldwide atmospheric system. The system is a heat engine. And when you turn up the heat, you change the circulation patterns. You are going to change the climate around the planet, and you will change it continuously. The climate is not going to go, as some of the sillier Russian scientists think, from State A to State B, where there will be winners and losers. Everybody is going to lose. And they are going to lose primarily because agriculture (particularly at the speed of change predicted) simply will not be able to keep up.

The fools who tell you, "You don't have to worry about it, because the climatic band for growing corn will simply move north into

Canada," miss the point: Where it moves to, there won't be suitable soil on which to grow corn. And although the right soil will eventually develop there, it will take ten thousand or twenty thousand years, and people will find that they starve in less time than that.

So one of the most serious problems we are facing is rapid climate change. And that problem is dramatically tied into our population growth. It is an interesting feedback situation because one of the quickest ways to end population growth is to see to it that our food production continues to fall.

Let me give you a couple of examples. The United States gets about 25 percent of its energy from coal. Coal is the very worst fossil fuel to burn, if you are concerned about carbon dioxide. (I should add, one of the reasons for the surprise about the speed of warming is that people had not realized that methane, chlorofluorocarbons, some of the nitrogen oxides, and other gases—in addition to carbon dioxide—also play roles in greenhouse warming. In fact, many people think methane will overwhelm the carbon dioxide effect early in the next century and will be even more important.) But let's just look at carbon dioxide for the moment. Coal is the worst offender, per unit of energy, in putting carbon dioxide into the atmosphere. Petroleum is less so, and natural gas produces only about 60 percent as much carbon dioxide per unit energy as coal. Yet we get about 25 percent of our energy in this country from coal.

One of the things we should try to do immediately—even though it would be enormously stressful on our economy—is to stop using coal and not replace it with other fossil fuels. That would be a gigantic sacrifice on our part.

Now, let's look at some sacrifices that might have to be made elsewhere. The Chinese have extremely ambitious development plans. Let's suppose that to carry them out, they decide to increase their per capita energy consumption from 7 percent of ours to 14 percent. And suppose they do it, quite logically, by using their abundant supplies of coal (which, by the way, happen to be high in sulfur content). When they do this, the additional injection of carbon dioxide into the atmosphere by the Chinese will more than compensate for our getting rid of coal entirely. Why? Because there are well over a billion people in China. And just that little per capita increase more than makes up for our cutback. And note that this projection assumes that the Chinese halt population growth at 1.1 billion, when it now seems likely that they will increase to at least 1.3 to 1.5 billion.

If the Indians, in the course of their development, should decide to move up to where China is today, to about 7 percent of our per capita energy use, that, too, would overwhelm results of the United States giving up coal, even making superoptimistic assumptions about Indian population growth. If India and China do it simultaneously, then you would have the equivalent of the United States more than doubling its coal use over that period.

Today, most of the problem with the greenhouse warming, and certainly 80 percent of the problem from fossil-fuel use, comes from the rich countries. If you think, as I do, that the poor countries have a right to some level of further development, then you have built into the system an enormous potential for keeping the basic global warming problem accelerating—simply because of existing huge levels of overpopulation and high rates of population growth.

This means that the rich nations such as the United States are going to have to take much more dramatic steps than simply eschewing coal use.

In addition to climate, a number of other ecosystem services are put at risk by the effects of overpopulation. Included in the list is the process of soil generation, which is absolutely critical to agriculture and to forestry. You must also include the disposal of human wastes and the recycling of nutrients, which are essential to agriculture and forestry. And include control of the vast majority of pests that might attack our crops; the running of the hydrologic cycle supplying us with fresh water; flood control; pollination of crops; the maintenance of a vast genetic library, from which we have already drawn the very basis of our civilization, and which the genetic engineers need to get us even more economic benefits. All of these are threatened. You can see the damage being done to many of them on the evening news, although it is never properly interpreted.

Consider the flooding in Bangladesh, which is normally reported as if it were an act of God. What actually happened is that large populations of trees have been wiped out by the increasing numbers of people who are now occupying the Himalayas and who want the trees for firewood. With the trees gone, the soil washes off the slopes and forms chars in the low-lying Brahmaputra and Ganges deltas, where Bangladesh is located. There are 110 million people in Bangladesh, a country the size of Wisconsin. Land is in extraordinarily short supply. So people farm the chars, which are a foot or so above sea level.

When you deforest slopes, whether in the Himalayas or any place else, you disrupt the ecosystem's flood-control services. The soil can no longer absorb rainwater and meter it back evenly over time. Instead, you get alternating droughts and floods. That is what has happened in the rivers that arise in the Himalayas. And so the floods now come down, and Bangladesh goes under water, in large part because of overpopulation in the Himalayas. But overpopulation in Bangladesh means that many people there are living in marginal situations. They can't get to high ground, and so they die.

Similarly, when storms come up the Bay of Bengal, people living in marginal situations in Bangladesh get wiped out. In the early 1970s, 150,000 were killed in a single cyclone; tens of thousands died a couple of years ago; and we don't know how many thousands were killed this year.

The subject is treated in the classical ecological literature; for example, it was discussed extensively by Andrewartha and Birch in their 1952 book, *The Distribution and Abundance of Animals*. When populations get too large, events that might seem unrelated to population size have consequences that are tied directly to population size. For instance, people say that the number of humans does not affect the weather. That is no longer true, but pretend it is. The key point is that the effect of the weather on people is very dependent on their numbers. If there are large numbers, many are forced to live in marginal situations, and they get swept out to sea in cyclones or otherwise suffer from their exposed positions.

Interestingly, the Bangladesh situation is one of the places where national security comes into the picture. The Indians have a dam right upstream from Bangladesh, the Farakka Burrago. When flood waters come pouring down, they do not shut the gates and flood parts of India. They let the water through to flood Bangladesh. Curiously enough, the Bangladeshis are not overwhelmed with gratitude for that. It is one of the many sources of international tension on the Indian subcontinent.

You think of the changing patterns of water use, and you think about the Middle East. The 1967 war in the Middle East was largely fought over water, over serious attempts to divert the headwaters of rivers going into Israel. Israel uses five times the water per capita as her neighbors. But her neighbors have many more "caputs." If things get drier in the Middle East, as they well may, the soil may become wet with another, even more precious, fluid. Around the world, more and more international tension is being associated with resource and environmental problems.

I could go on with a litany, but I don't want to concentrate on this. I just want to point out that virtually every problem we consider to be environmental is connected, either directly or indirectly, to one degree or another, with population growth and overpopulation.

The thing of importance here is not absolute numbers of people, *per se*, but rather the state of their resources and that of their environment. The impact of a population on its environment is nicely described with a simple, three-part, multiplicative equation John Holdren and I published many years ago. It involves the number of people, P; their level of affluence, A, defined by measures of consumption; and the environmental damage caused by the technologies, T, used to provide each unit of consumption. Then the impact, I, can be represented by $I = P \times A \times T$. If you want to protect the environment, so as to keep the magnitude of I down, you obviously have to operate on all three of these factors. If you ignore any one of them, and allow it to grow too far, then you are just going to be out of luck.

That, I think, is my number one take-home message. If you design a plan for dealing with global warming that does not have a large content of population control, you are wasting your time. No matter how clever you are with technology, or how much affluence is reduced, the growth of the population will easily overwhelm it.

As a general example, suppose that around the world we worked hard to change everybody's behavior and achieved the absolute miracle of reducing the Affluence times Technology $(A \times T)$ component by 10 percent. Everybody reduced their affluence by some measure, and we got so efficient with our technologies that we managed to reduce the per capita environmental impact of *Homo sapiens* by 10 percent. I imagine that would take many, many years and a lot of struggle, but assume it is done instantly. The gain would be overwhelmed in six or seven years of population growth, because that is how fast the population grows by 10 percent. If you managed to halve the environmental impact of our technologies and left everything else alone, then in fifty years you would be back where you started, because the population will have doubled in roughly fifty years, depending on what assumptions you use.

It isn't that any of us thinks that too much affluence, poor distribution, and environmentally malign technologies aren't important. But we do know those things are amenable to relatively quick fixes, if the political and social will to do so can be generated. What is not amenable to a relatively quick fix, and *should not* be fixed quickly, is population growth.

It would be quite undesirable for society to go to zero children for ten years. That would screw up the economy tremendously. All the baby food manufacturers would go extinct, the grade school teachers would take up other professions. And then all of a sudden you would have kids coming through again.

An interesting (and difficult) demographic question is how low a reproduction rate is reasonable? How far below a net reproductive rate of one can we go and still avoid the disruption of dramatic changes in age composition, in which groups of people go through the age structure in pulses? The possibility of social disruption must be balanced against the rapid destruction of life-support systems. And if we do *not* get our birthrate down very fast, to the point of shrinkage, humanity is going to be in even deeper trouble.

But the main factor in the three-part equation is the population element, P. It is a problem that requires a start as rapidly as possible, because of the enormous lag-time involved in stopping growth. The other two elements are very important also, but the lag-times are not so formidable there.

It is important to understand that, right now, the globe as a whole is overpopulated, and not only by subjective aesthetic standards. There are objective standards by which we can determine that the planet as a whole is overpopulated. And the overpopulation is almost certainly worse in the United States than in any place in the world.

The only way society has been able to support 5.2 billion people is by doing something none of us would do in the course of our everyday lives: We have been living on our capital. That number of people cannot possibly be supported on "income." We are able to support 5.2 billion only by using up what is essentially the one-time bonanza that *Homo sapiens* inherited with the planet.

You think immediately about consumption of fossil fuels, and that is part of it. Although things like coal and oil shales are going to be around for a long time, in historical (to say nothing of evolutionary) terms fossil fuels are disappearing in the blink of an eye. The same is true of other high-grade mineral resources. But they are a minor part of the problem.

A critical part of the one-time bonanza we are using up so fast is the high-grade soils on which the prosperity of the United States is built. Americans acquired some of the richest soils in the world, and we have exploited them very well. But they are disappearing.

Soils are eroding away elsewhere even more rapidly. In places like Haiti, you see that the soil is gone. If you fly over the Caribbean, just look at the colors of the rivers where they hit the ocean, and you have the whole story of what is happening to Caribbean countries.

Soils are an absolutely critical part of our equation. As Lester Brown has said, and he is absolutely right, civilization might survive the depletion of petroleum, but it will never survive depletion of topsoils at the current rate.

A second critical part of our inheritance is our underground water. We are depleting the Ogallala aquifer, the biggest aquifer underneath the United States, at feet per year, when it is recharged at fractions of an inch per year. And we are doing it, by the way, on the basis of that wonderful economic humbug, the idea that there is an infinity of resources. You can read the stuff that people wrote when they started to mine the Ogallala: "When we exhaust this aquifer, there always can be other water projects." The overdraft on the Ogallala is equivalent to the flow of the Colorado River. So all those nice, circular irrigation patterns you see when you fly to San Francisco are going to disappear, along with the farmers who are doing the irrigating. This will happen even without global warming and drought.

We are getting rid of our underground water—fifty times as much of it under the United States as falls on the country annually—not just by overdraft but by paving over recharge areas and by toxification.

And of course, related again to symptoms of our living on capital, are the plastic-laden garbage scows now floating around the oceans trying to find places to unload. Our coasts are places where you can practice sewage swimming, a sport that originated in Europe. You may not know it, but in the early 1970s, people would walk along the beaches at Nice and spray perfume on them to cut down the fecal smell. Now you can have that smell at the beaches of New Jersey or New York. But U.S. knowhow has entered into it. We now put our medical wastes out there too, so you can get an injection as you swim along, to protect you from the bacteria that are in the feces.

We are destroying not just the soils and not just the water of the planet. We are also getting rid of the other species of organisms that share our planet, which are probably the most important part of our inheritance—some 30 million different species, and billions of genetically distinct populations. This is a supply from which not only have we drawn the very basis of our civilization, and a great many enormous economic benefits, but also the working parts of the ecological systems that keep the biosphere running properly.

One of the major contributors to global warming is the cutting down of forests, particularly in the tropics, and their burning. That takes carbon that was sequestered in wood and puts it into the atmosphere. The trees are no longer around to suck the carbon back out in the process of photosynthesis. And as we exterminate those tree populations, we are exterminating ourselves.

Now, let me make a brief summary of the population component in all of this, although it is an oversimplification: Rapid population growth in poor countries is a major factor in keeping those countries poor. Instead of being able to take capital and put it back into increasing the well-being of each individual, those countries have to put the capital back into just taking care of new arrivals. There are many other dimensions, but in simplest terms, rapid population growth among the poor helps keep them poor.

At the same time, overpopulation in the rich countries is destroying the planet. Overpopulation in the rich countries is wrecking the life-support systems of the planet and destroying its resources. In my view, that is as serious a global problem as rapid population growth in the poor countries, and perhaps a much more serious one. The problems of the world are not that poor Indians do not know how to use condoms. It is mostly that rich Americans, and the like, want to continue to live the way we are living at the cost of our children's and our grandchildren's futures.

So now to turn to the issue of what we are going to do about it, and why aren't we doing more.

Recently a demographer I know refused to use a paper about population in a collection he was editing because the paper included the word "crisis." There was no crisis, he said. One of the questions you want to ask of people like that is, just what would it take for us to have a population crisis?

Here we are. We have the largest annual increment to our population in history: 90 million people are being added to the world every year. We are within a few years of crashing through the theoretical limits of the number of people that can be fed, if everybody turns into vegetarian saints. The life-support systems of the planet are running down, posing an enormous threat to humanity's ability to produce even the amount of food that is produced today. And it is going to take, at an absolute minimum, under very optimistic assumptions, something on the order of 100 years to halt human population growth, if it is done humanely by limiting births, rather than by a gigantic rise in deaths. As one physicist said—and I think he is optimistic—before 2020, a billion people may die from global warming alone. It is clear that anybody who is working against contraception and limiting births is simply voting in favor of many more people dying prematurely.

So, why don't people recognize this as a crisis? Why don't people want to deal with it? That is what I want to turn to for the next part of my talk.

Unfortunately, in spite of what some people think, we are the product of billions of years of evolution. So, when you ask people to take action on population issues, you are asking them to work against all of their biological evolutionary history and part of their cultural evolutionary history. Let me tell you what I mean.

The name of the game in evolution has always been to out-reproduce your neighbors. When you ask people to practice contraception, you are actually asking them to turn their back on winning, in evolutionary terms. Natural selection simply means differential reproduction. Some organisms with certain genetic characteristics reproduce more than others, and the ones that reproduce more are the ones whose characteristics are represented in future generations.

One of the cheery signs is that large numbers of people on this planet do go against their biological evolutionary history and do practice contraception, do limit the size of their families. Fortunately, we also have a body of cultural evolution that has led us to understand, from the point of view of the health of our civilization and our children, that it is better to have fewer children rather than more. This shows that cultural evolution can work against the grain of biological evolution.

But not everybody is willing to work against the grain on this particular issue, and that is a big barrier, quite clearly. People have said to me, "If we practice contraception, we are lowering ourselves to the level of the animals." I find that an amusing view. I always ask them which particular animals they have recently seen using contraception. Almost by definition, the only single thing that people do that no other animal does, is to practice contraception. It is a widespread behavior in human beings. Other animals use tools. Bees and wasps use tools. Chimpanzees use tools. Chimpanzees are capable of quite conceptual thoughts, problem solving, and so on. But no chimp has ever been seen to grab a condom and use it properly. So condom use is one of our most human characteristics, and that is cheering.

Perhaps the most important reason we have not come to grips with a lot of humanity's long-term global problems is, again, evolutionary. It involves both our cultural evolution and our biological evolution. Until very, very recently, there was no reason for us to evolve any capacity even to detect these trends.

The average person thinks he sees the world as it really is. In fact, we perceive maybe 1 billionth of the possible stimuli we could perceive. EPA's job would be infinitely easier, for example, if people had some parts of the nervous systems of dogs. A lot of your problems deal with chemical pollution of one sort or another, but humans are not good chemosensors. We have lousy chemosensory capability compared to many animals. If we could detect that thin film of pesticides on the apple, as we could if we were really good chemosensors, we would feel a lot differently towards FIFRA [the Federal Insecticide, Fungicide, and Rodenticide Act, a major law covering pesticides].

We are sight animals. Why? Because for one very important period in our evolutionary history, we lived in trees. If you have ever done any climbing around in trees, you can actually do this experiment. Try shutting your eyes and sniffing where the next branch is before you jump. Guess who produced more offspring, the branch sniffers or the ones who saw where the branch was!

Our evolutionary history has given us a very small and constrained view of the world, almost a caricature of the world. And it also prevents us from detecting gradually changing trends. If the climate started to change on an *Australopithecus*, it could migrate or die. It was not causing the climate to change, and it could not do anything about the climate change. Until very recently, there simply was no reason for human beings to acquire the ability to detect gradual changes. Psychologist Robert Ornstein and I have written a book, *New World, New Mind* (Doubleday, 1989), that explains all this in detail.

We actually seem to have characteristics that force us to suppress change in our environment that takes place over decades. The best example I can give you is a personal one that probably everyone here has experienced: You have a friend you have known for a decade or more, and you think of that friend as basically unchanging—until you find a picture of you and him or her twenty years ago at a party. Then you think, my gosh, could we really have looked like that?

We suppress the gradual changes that go on around us. We pay a lot of attention to starts of trends, and then habituate. Let me give you an example of that. I can remember how terrified I was when the first atomic bomb went off. I can remember waking up in a sweat in 1946 when there was a thunderstorm, thinking an A-bomb had been dropped on New York. At that time, there were maybe ten 15-kiloton bombs in the world.

Since then, we have built up to the level where we have enough weaponry, just in the strategic arsenals of the United States and the Soviet Union, to destroy a Hiroshima once every second, nonstop, for two weeks. Yet my terror has in no way increased proportionately to that. When something has started, you pay a lot of attention to the start, but you don't pay attention to what goes on gradually afterwards. It's the same with many of our environmental problems.

The first time people become aware of what is going on in population growth, they get afraid. But then the fear tends to fade out, because on the time scale of their lives, population growth seems to be going on gradually.

So one of our big problems is that we evolved quick reflexes. If the branch we are standing on starts to crack, we pay attention immediately. If a car swerves out of the other lane and comes towards us, we have the reflexes to deal with it. That is because when a bear appeared in the door of the cave, we either fought or ran. We didn't sit there and say, "Now, what is the probability of there being another bear outside? How often does this occur? Is this a new trend? Were there as many bears fifteen years ago as there are today?"

No, we didn't evolve that way. We didn't evolve the slow reflexes that we need to get scared about a little squiggly line on a graph attached to an instrument that measures how much carbon dioxide there is in the air over an observatory on the Mauna Loa volcano because, first of all, we can't perceive carbon dioxide directly. It is less than 1 percent of the content of the atmosphere. It's tasteless and colorless. And we don't pay attention to little squiggly lines, anyway.

If I were to make a recommendation to people at EPA about what they might do about these incredible global problems, besides what they already are doing, it would be this: Always keep in mind, in everything you do, that we are all forced, one way or another, to act locally. We are not forced enough to think globally. But any issue you are dealing with is going to be exacerbated by such things as population growth, by the idea that we always have to be more affluent, by the preposterous idea that economic growth can go on much longer. Those big issues are out there fighting you every time you try to clean up a mess anywhere, or try to make the world environmentally more sane.

Now, everybody can't deal with the big issues. In fact, none of us can deal with the big issues, in a sense. What all of us can do, though, is to make sure in our talks, in our reports, in the preambles to laws and regulations, in every place possible, to push the "global problem" message at the politicians. For instance, we should say: "Yes, we should get rid of coal burning as fast as possible. We are going to deal with how we might do that in Report X. But also, while we are trying to stop burning coal, we must remember that if we don't do something to control the population in the United States, moving away from coal is not going to make any difference. Reading Report X would be a waste of time. And we no longer have any time to waste." I believe that this is a most important message.

A second important message is this: One of the principal duties of EPA, whether statutory or not, is to inform the public as much as possible about these issues.

In one area, economics, people have gradually been trained to look at trends and squiggly lines. That is because they are perpetually reported to us. What is the only kind of chart you ever see on television? The last thirty days of the stock prices, right? Or a chart showing what has happened to the value of the dollar, or to the GNP, or to inflation. We have grown accustomed to looking at relatively long-term economic trends signaled to us by squiggly lines.

One of the things I think EPA ought to do is start sending around to radio stations, TV stations, and newspapers the equivalent of those squiggly lines for how much carbon dioxide there is in the atmosphere, or how much methane there is going to be. Methane is tied intimately with population growth, because a lot of it comes from the guts of cattle and from rice paddies and from ponded water in cut-down tropical forests. What is going to happen to the methane? What are the national, regional, and global demographic trends?

People say that isn't news. Well, the stock market isn't news either. It goes up and down. The predictions of the economists about it are always wrong. But the economists manage to stay in the newspapers and on TV even though they don't have the first clue about how the world works, and even though they are never right even about narrow aspects of the economic system.

By contrast, the predictions of biologists and environmentalists have pretty much been right-on, yet those aren't presented daily in the newspapers. There is no little box on the front page that gives the environmental index, the way there is for the stock index. It seems to me the government could do a lot in this direction, particularly since the electronic media operate under government license and are supposed to be responsible. That is another place where I think EPA could do a lot of good.

But I think the main message for people working in an organization like this is something I find in my own life all the time. It is very easy to get yourself totally absorbed in the problem that you are working on at the time, as a scientist or administrator, and lose the big picture. Even though my wife Ann and I have taken as one of our main jobs trying to keep track of the big picture, it is not all that easy. It is, again, not built into our genes. The immediate keeps forcing itself on us all the time. It takes real effort to keep pushing yourself out and saying, "Yes, this is a very important problem I am working on, but if we do not solve X, Y, and Z, my solution here is not going to make any difference." So we have to keep looking at the big picture. Try to force yourselves to do that.

I am delighted to have had an opportunity to be with you. It is nice to be addressing a group that is trying to solve these problems. Too many people are not.

## Questions from the Audience

Q   After Paul Ehrlich has been appointed the first secretary of population affairs by President Bush, the president will call him in and say, "Okay, Mr. Secretary, I know we have to educate people about squiggly lines; and I know we have to burn less coal; and I am going to get my secretary of commerce and secretary of education to work on that. But I have a real, immediate problem here: In a democracy where crisis is always looming, what can I, as president, do about population; something with a strong political impact?"

A   Most of you are a lot younger than I am. But let me give a bit of historical perspective on what I think is one of the biggest problems we have in our country. I am guessing that all of you have personal ideas on this subject, and I acknowledge there is no scientific content in the following statement whatsoever.

We have really been short of leaders. I keep thinking back to when I was a kid and FDR was president. I was born in 1932. He came to office in early 1933, and right through the war he was the leader. In a sense, it was sort of a dictatorship, because there was no change in leadership.

But he was a leader. When he talked on radio, everybody sat down and listened. And he talked articulately. It was absolutely the antithesis of what we saw in the recent presidential campaign. I am a Republican, a conservative Republican in the sense that I do not think destroying our resources for the fun and profit of this generation is a good idea. I think the Reagan administration was undoubtedly the worst in the history of the country, not because President Reagan was any more incompetent or stupid than some of our past presidents, but because those earlier bumblers did not have the capability of destroying the world by ignoring global problems as Reagan has managed to do.

What we need is a president—Bush could do it—who will get up there and say:

"I don't care whether you re-elect me. What you have to do is read my lips. There are too many Americans. In this country, economic growth is much more the disease than the cure. If there is going to be any hope for the rest of the world, we in this country are going to have to get off the growth kick and move towards shrinkage. Saving the rest of the world is absolutely critical to saving our own children.

"We are going to have to have not a Council of Economic Advisors, but a Council of *Environmental* and Economic Advisors. Economics is incredibly important because a lot of the issues of how you change society to deal with environmental problems immediately become economic problems. But ecology is even more important than economics; without functioning ecosystems, there would be no economy at all."

"As your president," he should tell us, "I am going to keep hammering you on this whether you like it or not, because this is important for the United States. You elected me president. We have a government that is republican, in the basic sense of the word. You don't send people to Washington and then look over their shoulders via the media and have them make every decision on the basis of what a few yahoos back home think. The reason you send people to Washington is, presumably, because you feel they are outstanding individuals with real decision-making capabilities. Some period later—two, four, six years—you decide whether they did a good job. If you think the country is in better shape, then you re-elect them. And if not, you send other representatives to make decisions." End of my presidential statement.

Decisions should not be made by the people back home. They should be made by the president and other elected officials, who by now should be pretty well persuaded by what all the scientists are telling him: That we're in deep doo-doo, and we have to do something about it.

And if the president doesn't get re-elected, tough. Who would want to be president of the United States for more than one term anyway? It's not all that charming a job, as far as I can see.

If you want to see what a leader is, rightly or wrongly, look at Gorbachev. If you think we have problems with bureaucracy in this country—we have it bad enough at Stanford—go to the Soviet Union.

I had my first trip there this year. It was appalling. We were at a Pugwash meeting. I could actually see the old KGB elements fighting the new Gorbachev elements. And you know, there could even be lives at stake. It is a little different there. But here is a guy, Gorbachev, who is really reversing course in a much tenser, tighter, and more hideous situation than anybody faces in our country. What we need is a leader with his kind of guts and his kind of outlook.

What is the budget of EPA now—$5.2 billion? That is ten, count them, ten Stealth bombers. I am a pilot. Once the USAF had the B-58 Hustler, a plane designed to fly into mountainsides because it's unstable and depends on computer stabilization. It did a beautiful job. I think every last Hustler flew into a mountainside. Then there was the B-1, $258 million a crack. It flies into mountainsides for the same reason, beautifully. The Stealth obviously is also computer-stabilized. It will be about $600 million a crack. And it has no conceivable military use.

Two or three MIRVed missiles from one Soviet submarine or from a U.S. missile submarine could destroy the other society permanently if they could distribute their warheads appropriately. The level of overkill available already is so astonishing that the thought of spending $600 million a crack on Stealth airplanes is absolutely bananas. For ten of them, you could replicate EPA. And I think that would probably be very helpful.

There was a time when the EPA was rated the most efficient and best agency in the government. It may still be. I haven't seen the numbers recently. But we obviously need to greatly enhance EPA's capabilities and stature. Head of the EPA should be one of the highest-ranking cabinet offices. It should be right up there with the Department of Defense. DOD should be joined, in a sense, with EPA because the environmental security of the United States is much more threatened than its national security is.

If we are going to solve our environmental problems, we have to have a reallocation of resources. It isn't our financial resources alone that are going into nonsense like the Stealth. It is also the intellectual resources. More than half the scientists in the world are reputed to work for the military, one way or another. There also are huge environmental problems created by the simple act of preparing for a war we know would be the end of civilization if we fought it.

We were talking about leadership. Gorbachev understands the human predicament very clearly. I think the message gets to him so much more clearly because Russia is "in the tubes." When you look around there, and go into what passes for a food market, you see six boxes of dried fish.

I was a guest of the Soviet Academy. They tried to show us the best of everything. And let me tell you, even when you see the best of everything, things are very marginal in Russia. They are in such trouble economically that Gorbachev has clearly seen that the system cannot go on the way it is now. I am sure he is sincere about the things he has said. Whether or not he will beat out the conservatives, who would love to see him disappear, is another question.

Q   What do you think of the morality of China's approach to the population problem?

A   Well, I have argued about this a lot for a long time. There are a number of difficult moral dilemmas in population or immigration policy in general.

My view on this has always been focused more on the United States than on China. I have always said if we wait until the politicians wake up and understand how serious the population problem is, we will get cures that are very horrendous. I still believe that to be true.

I think the Chinese have been way out front on this and have been trying to deal with the population problem in ways that are not horrendous. It's very interesting that there has been so much right-wing criticism of China's population policy on the basis of the abuses that have occurred. There have been forced abortions. There is a great deal of pressure put on women to have abortions and not to get pregnant again. There has been some infanticide of first-born female children, because the Chinese value sons. I can't imagine this, myself. I like women much better than men, but that is my own personal bias. I have a granddaughter. I'm delighted. But sons mean a lot in Chinese culture.

The reason we know about it is the Chinese have been open about it. Their literature has been full of it. They have not tried to conceal it, and they have tried to correct it. I think it is as moral a program as a country of 1.1 billion people, largely undeveloped, speaking a whole series of languages, could possibly put together; with the possible exception that they should have thought more demographically. They might have been better off to introduce a birth-spacing mode—to delay childbearing, rather than limiting it to just one. There is some thought now of revising the program in that direction.

This is a problem not unlike one we face here. Suppose you were to come up with a slogan and a program that is easily enforced—either by peer pressure or by the government—something to the effect of, "Stop at Two," and everybody obeyed. Then you would probably get family size down, I would guess, to about 1.5 children, which is where it should be, instead of about 1.8.

A more rational way would be to say we want an average of 1.5. Which means that some people who don't really want to have children should be encouraged not to have any, and some people who are especially good at parenting ought to have three or four. You can get the same result that way, but it would be more difficult in terms of propaganda, pressure, evaluation, and so on.

I think the Chinese, considering their constraints, have shown that a lot of progress can be made. The sad thing is that the system is starting to erode, because the new entrepreneurial situation has made children appear more economically valuable again. So the birth rate is actually going back up in China. They may well climb to 1.3 or 1.5 billion or beyond before growth stops.

So these are difficult questions. They are moral questions, not scientific. And I have given you a personal opinion.

Q Do we have to depend on disasters and scare tactics to make a difference in population growth and critical environmental matters?

A It depends on what level. For decades we couldn't get any action telling people that the atmosphere was going to change, that the climate was going to change and clobber agriculture. Then we had last summer's drought. All of a sudden there was lots of hot weather, at a time when we've been talking a lot about warming, and then you start getting action.

You can trigger action that way. But it would be better to make sure that nobody grows up in the country without having certain basic ideas taught to them from the time they are in the first grade.

Then you wouldn't have people saying we can grow forever, and so on, because they would have learned otherwise. It is again a personal point of view. Periodically, I receive requests that go like this: "I know an economist who says we can have an infinite population. Would you go on the radio and debate him?"

Now, I don't think there is any member of the National Academy of Sciences in physics who is called up by a TV station and told, "Joe Blow says the world is actually flat. Would you go on TV and debate him?" Or someone who says that actually the sun is going around Earth. Would you go on TV and debate him?

In the course of normal education in this country, you find out that the world isn't flat and that actually Earth goes around the sun. TV and radio people and newspaper people, having been raised in that culture, are able to do first-level sorting. Obviously, we don't in this society consider every idea of equal value and every position worth debating on television. But the journalistic sorting you get on some issues is of better quality than others. And the sorting we get on population/resource/environment issues is horrendously bad. You can get all the way through Stanford University, which a lot of people think is a first-rate university, without discovering where your food comes from. Most of our students think it materializes overnight in supermarkets. Our average student doesn't know how many people there are in the world, doesn't know what the growth rate is, doesn't know how an ecosystem works. We had a big debate on whether Cicero or Malcom X should be taught in the Western Civilization course. It tore the campus apart. Most of the professors involved in the debate are clueless as to how the world works.

So until we start changing that sort of milieu, we are going to be stuck with counting on catastrophes to trigger action. And they do tend to create temporary progress.

In other words, it's not that we haven't slowly been moving in the right direction. After all, EPA is a relatively new institution. The environment has become institutionalized in the U.S. government. In spite of the last eight years of disaster, the environment is institutionalized in our society. So we are moving in the right direction.

The trouble is that we are moving much more slowly than the problems we are trying to deal with. While disasters work as temporary stimuli, we have to find ways to keep public attention focused on these problems all the time. That is what I had in mind when I spoke of trying to get the papers to deal with environmental matters, of trying to raise the subject to at least the level that economics occupies in people's minds. The environment means much more to people's future than economics.

Q   What do you think about the viewpoint that economics and the environment are so closely tied together they are almost like two sides of the same coin?

A   Oh, yes. Economics and environmental problems are in essence the same thing. Ecologists and economists should be the world's greatest allies rather than enemies. The words "ecology" and "economy" come from the same source: *oikos*, the Greek word meaning house. Economics is housekeeping in the usual sense of the word and ecology is nature's housekeeping. Ecologists and economists use many of the same sorts of mathematical models, in fact.

Slowly but surely, small groups of younger economists and people like Herman Daly are trying to bring economics into the battle. But there is still a long way to go. I urge you to encourage economists to become more aware of what is going on in the world. It is not a matter of putting them down, it is a matter of getting them in. It's getting input-output models to minimize the environmental damage being done by the economic system.

There are all kinds of ecological modeling that economists should be doing in the normal course of their work, and if they don't start doing it pretty soon, ecologists are simply going to move in and do it for them. A lot of my theoretically oriented colleagues are getting interested in these questions. So it is a good place for the two disciplines to come together. If you can encourage the economists to join us, go for it.

Q   How do you get environmental education into the lower grades?

A   When EPA has the budget of DOD, you can give grants to schools to support that. One of the things I've discovered over the years, working sometimes on government money, is that the action tends to go where the money is. It may not be the system we like, but that's the way the world works.

For example, if grants were available for hiring somebody to design an environmental curriculum in each school system, and there were other awards for support of environmental education in school systems, then I think such education would become more widespread. Things are already improving. Certainly, kids nowadays learn more about "ecology," in quotes, than they did thirty years ago. By a long shot. If we had a hundred years to spare, I would be the world's biggest optimist, because if you take something of a historical view, the change we've seen in the last twenty years in this country, even with the eight Reagan years of going backwards, has been absolutely spectacular. In social change, one does not ordinarily expect a monotonic move in the right direction. The thing that is so horrendous is that the scale of our problems is going up so much more steeply.

Certainly there are some things central government shouldn't be involved in. But stimulating this sort of education is a very good place for government to be, particularly since what ought to be taught is more or less universal. A curriculum could be designed by the EPA with the collaboration of educators and scientists from around the country.

At Stanford's Center for Conservation Biology, we have a little group that looks specifically at questions of conserving biodiversity and keeping the ecosystems running. We have a high-school curriculum now being tested in schools in the San Francisco Bay area. With any luck, if we get it perfected, it will spread at the high-school level. And that is where I am convinced change must be initiated. It is not that the universities will not gradually change; universities are only somewhat more conservative than the Roman Catholic church.

Actually, there's a big difference. Perhaps you saw the *Washington Post* article where the Pope said *Humanae Vitae* is reaffirmed, and the bishops said you can feed 40 billion people here on Earth. Then the article went on to report that 80 percent of Catholics don't believe a word of this. People often say to me, "Isn't this really a Catholic problem?" Nonsense. The average Catholic performs reproductively just like other people in the same country of the same economic status, regardless of religion. Actually the Church has changed more than universities have, because the average professor at Stanford still thinks the university is a great place and is doing everything right. So the Church is actually ahead of us in terms of change.

Q  If we should think globally but act locally, what should our position be on the trade deficits?

A  The trade deficit, the whole question of international trade, is closely related to what we've been discussing, but it's also more widely misunderstood than almost any other. If you go back and read the old-time economists, they thought that tariffs were not a good idea. The premise was that Englishmen would want to stay in England and produce their woolen goods, and the French would want to stay in France and produce their wine. You had a system where the English could sell wool to the French without high tariffs, and the French could sell wine to England, and everything would be great.

The thing economists didn't think about, and has now come to pass, changing the whole game, is that capital is what's moving around now. The Englishman will take his capital, and instead of making woolen clothes in England, will hire people in Malaysia to make clothes out of wool from Australia. Mobile capital makes the Reaganesque position on international trade absolutely nonsensical and dangerous.

What this is leading to is a single worldwide labor pool with the costs of labor going continuously down. Because now, not only is capital fleeing the United States to avoid high labor costs—going to Taiwan, going to Mexico, or to Malaysia—but it's now fleeing Malaysia and going to Kasmir. It's fleeing Japan and going to Nepal, and so on.

This is going to drive down the rewards of labor around the planet. One of the reasons America is a rich country is that our workers have been well paid. But the current trend, coupled with the international trade situation, could lead to a world more and more made up of poor people with a few rich. That's not going to be a good world for any of us to live in.

So the international trade situation is much more complicated than people would think. It is tied into the population problem because one of the critical elements is labor. Labor is not in short supply on a global scale. It is locally in short supply, but not on a global scale. Capital is well aware of that, which accounts for the international capital setup.

I don't know what the answer is, but this is precisely the kind of question that large numbers of economists should be examining in great detail. That's one of the places where economists and ecologists ought to be working together.

Q  What are your thoughts on the theory that the planet is a self-regulating organism?

A  What about Gaia? This is an idea put forth by Jim Lovelock and Lynn Margulis: Earth is essentially a self-regulating organism that keeps making conditions more pleasant for life. The living part of the planet changes the physical part of a planet, and keeps on changing it, to make conditions better for the living part.

I just attended a big conference on this, and I think the general view of most of my colleagues would go something like this: There *is* a weak version of the Gaia hypothesis—namely, that living organisms have had an enormous effect on the physical characteristics of the planet. That is correct.

For example, there was no oxygen in the atmosphere until there were living organisms that produced it. That in itself created a very dramatic change in the physical characteristics of the planet, particularly since the ozone layer came from the oxygen. Life wasn't able to come out on land until we had an ozone shield because of the UVB [ultraviolet B] radiation. We're now moving back to the situation where life won't be able to do very well on land as we destroy the ozone layer. Some of you may remember the days when roadhouses had toilet seats that were underneath ultraviolet sterilizers. Well, that's the direction we're moving, living on one of those toilet seats under an ultraviolet sterilizer.

So the weak form of the hypothesis is correct. The strong form, that somehow miraculously the planet will be kept habitable for life because organisms are making it better all the time—all of us feel that is utterly incorrect.

There are some negative feedback loops that help. Early on, life was anaerobic. Under those circumstances, why didn't the planet adjust itself to provide ideal conditions for anaerobic organisms? As oxygen was put into the atmosphere, they had to retreat to living in places like termite rectums. I don't think, if you were a bunch of anaerobes sitting around in a termite rectum, you would be saying to each other, "Wow, isn't it great? The planet has adjusted itself to make it wonderful for us to survive."

The point is, there is no mechanism by which Earth can evolve to keep conditions ideal for life in the long term. The analogy falls apart because biological systems evolve. But, Gaia enthusiasts argue, how about ant nests? The climate inside ant nests is beautifully regulated. And the ants have helped make that climate. Isn't that an analog for Gaia?

Of course it isn't, because there have been billions of ant nests—an ant colony is basically a biological individual—that didn't regulate their temperatures so well, and they lost out. It was a selectional process in which the well-regulated nests persisted and reproduced, and the not-well-regulated nests didn't.

There is no equivalent history of Earth, of billions of Earths from which we are selected to favor ones that were providing a favorable environment for life.

So there is not much content for EPA in this. The notion that you can count on the automatic Gaia-like regulation of the planet solving our problems is a very dangerous one.

The population problem, on the other hand, is a central problem that could be automatically solved for us. But I don't think many of us would like the solution.

[DECEMBER 14, 1988]

Paul Ehrlich, a biologist who has specialized in population biology, is Bing Professor of Population Studies at Stanford University. In policy research related to human ecology, he frequently collaborates with his wife, Dr. Anne Ehrlich.

Dr. Ehrlich is the author or coauthor of more than five hundred scientific papers and articles in the popular press, as well as thirty books. *The Population Bomb*, perhaps the best known of these, has been the subject of serious consideration and debate ever since it appeared in 1968. It has recently been replaced by a new book, coauthored with Anne Ehrlich, *The Population Explosion*.

Dr. Ehrlich is honorary president of Zero Population Growth, Inc., and past president of the Conservation Society. He is a fellow of the American Association for the Advancement of Science, a member of the United States National Academy of Sciences, and president of the American Institute of Biological Sciences.

# Environmental
# Problems in
# the Tropics

I would like to present a rather personal view of the destruction of tropical forests, and of the environmental problems resulting from that destruction. And I'd like to do this by sharing with you some important and interesting details about tropical biology.

Tropical biology is unique. It differs from the biologies of other geographical regions most notably, I believe, in its incredible complexity. The tropics are the center of the most diverse groups of plants and animals to be found anywhere on Earth. Species diversity there is several orders of magnitude greater than it is in temperate regions. And the interrelationships between plants and animals, plants and plants, and animals and animals are more complicated there than they are in any other environment or habitat.

It's on that complexity that the real problems of tropical environments are based. So also are the real problems of saving them, of doing something about the future.

Let me first try to put things into perspective. There is no question but that we are now causing major environmental perturbations with global consequences. Our species has had an "unnatural" effect ever since we became ecologically distinct from the rest of the animal kingdom. That happened when we invented agriculture and started massive changes in natural systems. Environmental problems caused by human activities are not new. They are not a phenomenon restricted to the twentieth century. Only the scale and pace of change is now different.

MICHAEL H. ROBINSON, an animal behaviorist and tropical biologist, is director of the Smithsonian Institution's National Zoological Park in Washington, D.C.

As an example of effects human beings have had on the environment in the past, I can cite something from David Attenborough's (1987) fine book on the Mediterranean civilization, *The First Eden*, which was based on the TV program. Attenborough shows a galley, the El Real, which took part in the last great battle between the Ottoman Empire, in the south, and the Christian north. This was a sea battle in the Mediterranean in 1571, the battle of Lepanto. The Ottoman Empire was decisively defeated, and the movement of the Muslims into Europe was ended.

But El Real was just one ship out of more than 250 that were involved in that battle. And, this is the crucial point, just one of those ships took over 650 trees to build. Perhaps you've never thought of the deforestation effects of building navies.

To get oak for building parts of the El Real, they had to go all the way to Spain. Goats, charcoal production, and shipbuilding had totally deforested large areas of the Mediterranean coast. The climate of the region had changed from one which could support a large population, in the days of Carthage, to a xeric habitat. But even when Plato was alive, two thousand years earlier, the soil was already disappearing, and there was extensive deforestation because of the amount of wood used for fuel, and the effects of goat pasturage. So you see, human beings have been messing up the environment, changing its climate radically, from a very early time.

Our species started in a narrow area of East Africa, and it took a long time to occupy the rest of the world. Our species slowly and progressively extended its range. Australia, the Antipodes, and the New World came very late in our spread. At the time that happened, the human population was very small. It stayed at around 5 million for an enormous period of time, then accelerated to the present population level in a relative twinkling of history's eye.

But even when our population was comparatively small, in the sixteenth century for instance, we messed up the environment and changed it radically. Now, with our population in the billions, we're changing it at a rate for which there isn't really an adequate adjective in the English language. We are changing things on the same scale as some of the major geological catastrophes in the past. Nemesis, the so-called death star that some have suggested as the agent of the great extinction at the end of the Mesozoic era, would have had an effect comparable to the one we are now having on life on Earth.

That's pretty awesome. So where do the tropics fit in? The answer partly depends on one of the most interesting biological ideas of the last hundred years, the new assessment of the number of species of animals on Earth made by Terry Erwin. At a time when every country was known, and every country was explored, Erwin's work has recently upped our estimate of the number of animal species by a factor of ten to twenty.

Erwin, an entomologist at the National Museum of Natural History, sampled the canopy of tropical rain forests for insect species, and he came up with this new estimate of how many species there are. The rain forest canopy was, until very recently, the last place on Earth that really hadn't been explored. The problem is how to sample it, one to two hundred feet above the ground. Erwin did it by firing a line into the canopy, hoisting up a fogging machine and fogging the canopy with a quick-acting insecticide. He laid plastic sheets on the forest floor, and the sheets caught the stuff that dropped down. Eventually the collection was taken back to the laboratory and sampled. This work led to a new estimate of between 15 and 30 million species of insects, instead of the 1.5 million that everyone had thought before.

This is an estimate based on certain assumptions, and Erwin is often criticized for making assumptions that aren't yet tested. But he thinks that his is a conservative estimate, and I agree with him. If he's anywhere near right, then there are many, many more animals on Earth than we believed even recently, and they are overwhelmingly located in

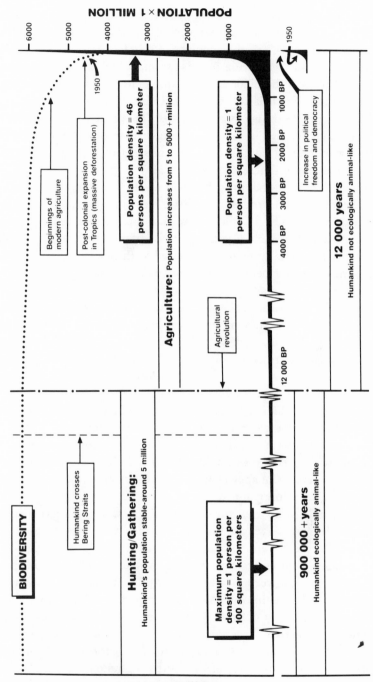

the tropics. Whereas we once thought that 60 percent of all animal species on Earth were in the tropics, the figure is now closer to 99 percent. And most are in the canopies of rain forests.

My personal idealization of what tropical biology is about focuses on Pieter Brueghel the Elder. I'm thinking of his famous painting, *Children's Games*, which is full of small-scale activity, with hundreds of figures doing little things, playing games. There are no panoramic vistas, but rather detailed interactions. Likewise, tropical biology is epitomized by incredibly complex interactions between large numbers of animals and plants. These are going on all the time.

If you lived with that Brueghel, you would find something new in it every day of your life. You'd find a little bit of action in the corner that you had never noticed. "Look at that man there on the roof, he's doing this, that, and the other." If you live in the tropics for twenty years, as I did, you're continually being confronted with new, wonderfully complex games that are being played between animals. The best way to illustrate this is with a few case histories.

Consider, for example, *Bradypus*, the three-toed sloth, a marvelous creature. It's a gentle, slow-moving, leaf-eating animal. It turns out to be an ecosystem in itself. Each of its hairs is grooved and contains at least three species of microscopic plants growing there. That helps camouflage the beast. Evolution has tailored the hairs on the sloth's back to provide a refuge for algae.

But sloth moths are an altogether different story. Early on in the 1960s, when I first went to Panama, nobody knew why sloths had moths. Sloth moths are a particular species, always found on the sloth's fur, as many as fifteen to twenty moths on an individual sloth. What are they doing there? The answer was worked out by two scientists—Jeff Waage and Gene Montgomery.

The whole story ties the moths to the sloth's digestive habits. Sloths eat leaves. Leaves are extremely difficult to digest because they contain cellulose, for which mammals have no digestive enzyme. Some animals chew their cud to help break down cellulose. Sloths keep it in the intestines for a week at a time. During that time, the gut bacteria break down the cellulose. As a consequence of prolonged food-retention, sloths only defecate once a week. And when they do, they descend from the tree, dig a hole with their tail, and defecate—and that is the moment the sloth moth has been waiting for. That glorious moment! The sloth moth flies off the sloth, alights on this fecal mass of processed leaves and lays its eggs. The whole climax of the moth's life is keyed to finding a resource for the next generation of moths—the leaf remains are sloth moth baby food. That is an intricate association. A moth that was once free-living, flitting from flower to flower, has now become a habitual passenger of the sloth, always waiting for the host's defecation.

Another marvelous adaptation is that of the frog-eating bat, *Trachops*, which eats male frogs and nothing else. There are bats that eat insects. There are bats that eat nectar. There are bats that eat fruit. But a frog-eating bat is an unusual kind of evolutionary adaptation. It finds the frogs by listening to the mating calls of males. And it can tell the difference between a mating call of an edible frog and a poisonous frog. You can prove that by putting the bat in a large flight cage and playing frog calls to it from loudspeakers. It will swoop on the loudspeakers playing the calls of edible frogs, and distinguish between them and calls of poisonous frogs. That's a wonderful piece of evolutionary fine tuning.

The other side of the story is equally exciting. My friend Stanley Rand, a herpetologist, studied frog calls from the point of view of the frog. And his story fits into the bat story. He studied a frog called *Physalaemus pustulosus*, a frog with a very complex, two-part call, a "whine" and a "chuck." If there is one male in the pond, then it just goes, "whine, chuck." If there are two males in the same pond, then each adds a second chuck, "whine, chuck, chuck." And, if there are three or more, then they add a third element to the call, "whine, chuck, chuck, chuck." With lots of frogs you get a real chorus. I came from the University of Wales, where choral singing is part of our tradition. These things singing outside my house in Panama at night sounded like a Welsh choir, slightly out of tune.

The males call to attract females. And Mike Ryan was able to prove, by playbacks of tapes of frog calls, that the most complex call is the most attractive. So, if you really want to get a female, you go, "whine, chuck, chuck, chuck," not, "whine, chuck." And yet a frog alone sings the simplest, least effective song. Why? Perhaps so as not to attract something else, less desirable than a female frog. Eureka! Ten years later, Merlin Tuttle discovered what a complex song does attract, beside the ladies: a great predatory frog-eating bat! You sing a simpler song because it is more difficult for a bat to locate you.

That's a neat story. There are very few things for a scientist more satisfying than making an interesting prediction, and having somebody else prove it later. It's almost as good as winning a domestic argument.

Here's another story of subtle complexity, this one worked out by my friend, Neal Smith, also in Panama. A bird called an Oropendola builds a meter-high basketwork nest with a hole in the side. It's a beautiful woven nest that takes a long time to build. The birds nest in colonies, and are parasitized by cowbirds, which lay their eggs in the host nest. The cowbirds behave like the European cuckoo. They use another species to raise their young.

Very early on, Neal found that some colonies of Oropendolas throw out the cowbird's egg, and some colonies keep them. He called them discriminators and nondiscriminators. Why should some discriminate against a parasite and others accept the parasite? It's an exciting question.

The methods used to solve that problem give you some idea of the ingenuity of tropical biologists. One way to find out what's happening in nests 60 feet off the ground is to lift the nest down and look inside. Then you must put it back up, because if you leave the nest on the ground then you spoil the whole experiment.

One early solution was to stand on a 12-foot ladder holding a 50-foot aluminum pole. You use the pole to lift the nest down to look inside, see what's going on, and then put it back where it came from so that the bird will carry on incubating. How do you put the nest back? It's not easy. Initially, Neal put contact adhesive on the nest and on the branch, and brought the two together. You can imagine how very difficult it is to bring two contact adhesive surfaces together without sticking the pole to the ladder and everything else.

The next solution was wonderfully ingenious. He stapled a rat trap to the nest. It was one of those rat traps that snap. He set it open, pushed the thing back against the tree, and whomp, it would just hang on there. Great stuff. Then there was the final solution. The U.S. Air Force lent him a cherry-picker, and he was able to look into the nests from the bird's level without removing them from their natural attachment.

Neal looked at more than five thousand nests over a period of nearly eight years. The story gets very complicated, and I must cut out most of the steps in the logical deduction process. Remember, the discriminators throw out the cowbird egg, nondiscriminators don't. There was another difference. The discriminators always live in colonies in trees that have bees' and wasps' nests in them. The nondiscriminators live in trees that have no such nests.

The next piece of evidence concerns a murderer. A fly, called the botfly, lays its eggs on an Oropendola chick, and the maggots eat away at the baby bird. (The botfly also affects human beings in the tropics; if you can't shower daily, as most peasants are not able to do, the eggs will hatch and the larvae burrow into your skin.)

These insects kill baby birds. But things are not so bad if you have a cowbird in your nest. It is programmed to hatch before your own chick, so that it can out-compete your baby. And it hatches with its eyes open. Evolution has provided for that so that it can out-eat your baby. It also programs it, inadvertently, to be a fly killer. When a fly flies in, it is eaten by the cuckoo, and therefore your baby is safe from fly parasitization.

If the tree has wasps' or bees' nest in it, however, the wasps and bees deal with the botflies and eat them before they can get anywhere near the chicks. You don't need to have an alien child in your nursery. But if you can't have a tree with wasps and bees, then you raise an alien that keeps your chicks free from parasitization. This is a beautiful story that took a lot of piecing together, and a nice example of what happens in the complex tropics.

My last story is a tale of two spiders. It was worked out by my student Fritz Vollrath. It concerns a large, tarantula-like spider found in Panama called a diplurid. Fritz found diplurids living together with tiny spiders from a totally different family, the family Symphytognathidae. What did each of these little spiders do for a living? It would wait for the host spider to finish off its prey, sitting on its head like a crown. And when the host had digested its prey, converting it into a liquid, a kind of bouillon d'insecte, the little symphytognathid would climb down the face of the host, lower its otherwise useless jaws into the soup, and slurp it up. It is a parasite that depends on the host to liquify its food. It is such a crazy specialization that nobody even had a name for the relationship. In scientific language we called it Dipsoparasitism, and got away with it.

So, those are some really intimate and complicated associations between animals. There are equally complex ones between plants and animals. There are ants that defend plants against leaf-eating insects, and all kinds of other marvelous things. That's what tropical biology is about: intimate, complex relationships on a micro-scale, with thousands and millions of species.

Having sketched some details of what is at stake, I would like to set the scene of what is now happening to the rain forests, why it is happening, and what we might do about it.

Tropical forests are being destroyed at an alarming rate. Estimates from around the world differ substantially, and there's a lot of controversy about which ones to believe. But most authorities agree that worldwide, 50 percent have vanished since the beginning of this century. Good data from satellite imagery show that in Central America, over 55 percent have gone.

The causes of the destruction vary from country to country and region to region. In Central America, slash and burn agriculture accounts for 70 percent of the loss, timber extraction for 15 percent, and cattle ranching for 15 percent.

In many areas fuel wood extraction is a significant factor. In Sri Lanka four years ago I saw, in a major national park, stacks of fuelwood every 300 feet along the main road through the park. They were being picked up by trucks out of Colombo and taken back there for fuel for factories, brickworks, domestic cooking, and the like. In one part of Sri Lanka, people were mining live coral from the sea at one side of the road and converting it into lime with firewood from the tropical forests on the other side. Worldwide, a billion and a half people get more than 90 percent of their energy from fuelwood. It's a tremendous drain. You all have heard the projection for Africa and the fuelwood shortage there. They can't afford alternative fuels for cooking. But this exerts enormous pressure on the environment.

What can we do about it? From my viewpoint, there seem to be two possibilities. We can stop the destruction with some kind of moratorium, or we can look after the worst cases in some kind of environmental triage.

A proposal to halt the destruction has been made by Ira Rubinoff. His idea is that Third World countries should be subsidized for preserving forests. The subsidy should be derived from a levy on the developed countries, just as the OPEC levy protects the oil producers. You pay so many dollars per hectare preserved, in hard currency. If that were done, the people in the Third World countries could use the hard currency to buy the agricultural surpluses of the developed world.

You've heard of debt-swapping and all the rest of it. If we bought time, what could we do with the time? We could look at schemes for breeding endangered species.

Ex situ breeding schemes are symbolic and stimulating, but they really do not form a substitute for preserving habitats. With perhaps 30 million species of insects alone, there's no way we can save what is in tropical forests by ex situ preservation. It's like saying to somebody, "The National Gallery is on fire. You can rush in there and save one painting." What you should do is try to save the gallery. For the environment, that means saving habitats.

Zoos and botanic gardens can play important roles in this effort. I think that zoos are crucial to inculcate in people a respect for tropical flora and fauna. It could give them a sense of the wonder and beauty of it all, and the glory that goes with the tropical rain forest, moving them to do something about the destruction. Television works for that kind of thing, to a very limited extent. If you see a tropical animal on a television screen, it is diminished to some small, two-dimensional image. If you can go and really see a Golden Lion Tamarin leaping about the trees at Rock Creek, or a toucan, or any of those glorious animals up close, I think you would be moved to take some kind of action about it. That's where I see the future of zoos, as a vast education experience for our urban population.

I'd like to see zoos progress from being zoological parks, where just animals are kept, into biological parks where we can bring together the whole of the living world—where plants are not a just backdrop to animals, not only something pretty to set animals against, but living things as exciting and important as animals. In the BioPark we can show the interactions between plants and animals, the really beautifully fine-tailored interactions, as in pollination.

I want to produce a pollination exhibit at the National Zoo, where we'll have all the splendid flowering plants and butterflies and hummingbirds and other pollinators. I'll call it my "Hall of Floral Sex," because flowers are the sex organs of plants. They evolved not for our eyes, but rather they're attuned to the insect eye and the eye of the hummingbird. They're there to attract pollinators to do this job, and they've make use of some of the most intricately beautiful mechanisms in the living world. When a bee pokes its tongue down the tube of some orchids, the male parts grasp onto the bee's tongue and cling there. And when the bee extracts its tongue, the male part of the flower is stuck to the tongue at just the right height. When the bee pokes down the next orchid, the male part of the orchid brushes against the female parts and transfers the pollen. Darwin worked that out a hundred years ago.

All this is magnificent stuff that we could show to kids. We could build model flowers, in which they could crawl and see how the whole mechanism works. You know, your kid crawling down a big model orchid flower with candy at the bottom instead of nectar. I think that if kids could do that kind of thing, they would get some reverence for what we are destroying, and want to do something about it.

Let me sum this all up. The tropical forest ecosystem is probably the most intricate co-adapted system on Earth. It's being destroyed. In it are treasures that we will never be able to appreciate, unless we save them.

People often ask me why we should save rain forests. Perhaps a good answer is: Because of the tropical frog that Michael Zazlov at NIH studied. That frog is probably the source of a whole new family of antibiotics. The tropics are where the battle between species is at its most intense, where there are more bacteria attacking more organisms, and more fungi, and more parasites. It is there that the defensive systems of animals against parasites, against funguses, against diseases, against insects, have reached their apex. If there is any place on Earth to look for broad spectrum antibiotics, fungicides, insecticides, it's the tropics. We are liable to lose all that, unless we act.

But, even more importantly, we're more likely to lose all the beauty and glory that has taken millions of years to perfect. If you destroyed my favorite Brueghel, to me that would be sacrilege of the worst possible kind, because it's such a beautiful painting. But there are people all over Vienna who've painted copies of it. You could get a copy of that Brueghel that would deceive 99 out of every 100 people. But, if you destroyed that Golden Lion Tamarin, there isn't a copyist anywhere that could bring it back.

It is in your hands, and our hands, and I hope together we can do something before it's too late.

## Questions from the Audience:

Q It seems that there are a lot of socioeconomic implications to some of the efforts to save the rain forests. How do you go about reorienting people's priorities, or teaching them to use their resources wisely?
A That's a complex problem. One of the worst things we do is to go into a country and, in a very patronizing way, say to a person, "You should not cut down the forests. Think of posterity. Think of the aesthetic effects," and that kind of stuff. The guy probably has five or six kids, all of whom have big bellies through malnutrition, and he's living

in a little palm hut. Before we can call on him to save the forests, we must provide him with a decent alternative source of living.

At the Smithsonian in Panama, we developed a program called "Alternatives to Destruction," in which we investigated possible ways of using the rain forests as sources of hard currency income, without destroying them. What happens now is that various government agencies support food self-sufficiency all over the developing world. They cut down trees to raise crops, which could be grown much more efficiently in other parts of the world where there's a greater depth of soil, and a climate more congenial for the basic staples.

Our "Alternatives to Destruction" program in Panama looked for things that grow in tropical forests and that can be cropped. One idea, which the Washington press treated with great disdain, was to ranch iguanas, which are large lizards. In Panama, iguanas are regarded as a delicacy. And iguanas eat the leaves in the canopy of the rain forest. So they convert the primary productivity of the forest into meat. Now, you can't send cows into the canopy to graze, but you can send up iguanas. If you cut the forest down and replace it by grass, the amount of grass that grows there is not equivalent in productivity to the amount of leaves on the trees.

So ranching iguanas makes sense. And iguanas, strangely enough, convert leaf into meat with an ecological conversion efficiency equal to that of sheep. It's a slower process, but calorie for calorie it produces as much. We can produce artificial nests for female iguanas that get 95 percent hatching success. That's to be compared with about 5 percent in the wild. We can even introduce them to small farms, where the farmer can release them around his house, and they can crop the trees nearby. It's a good scheme and it's working.

Even nicer, there is a rodent in Panama called the paca, a nocturnal animal about as big as a small dog, which is the most delicious meat that you could ever hope to try. Everybody that finds something new to eat says, "Oh, it tastes just like chicken." Well, paca puts chicken to shame. The paca is nocturnal, and nocturnal animals don't have to run to escape their predators. They don't get lean and hungry like Cassius. They get fat. The paca is a perfect food animal. It eats things that cattle and conventional domestic animals can't eat, because it has huge gnawing incisors. A cow will break its teeth off on a palm nut, but a paca can eat nuts and fruits that fall from the canopy. We've been doing a paca domestication program.

The Incas domesticated the guinea pig, and 18,000 metric tons of meat are produced every year in Peru from guinea pigs that people here keep in shoeboxes under their beds. The paca is a much larger and meatier animal.

In Asia there's a marvelous animal called the "bearded pig" which eats nuts and fruit from the forest. Herds of up to half a million bearded pigs range all over Borneo, and they don't even get tied to the seasonality of the forest, because when they've eaten all the fruits in one area, they migrate to another area. Unlike the paca, they're not accepted as meat, because there's a large Muslim population there. But that's just one of those minor snags.

Q   Whenever I see that growth of population that you've cited, I can't help but feel helpless, and despondent for our children and our grandchildren. Can we do anything in time?

A   I'm not sure we're going to do it in time. I just can't see that we can do it in time.

Every time I go back to Panama in the dry season, there's more smoke, more burning, more destruction. The whole west bank of the canal was subject to a $15 million aid program to plant cashews to preserve the area. But after two years of waiting for the cashews to grow up and bear fruit, the peasants who had been subsidized to grow them decided they couldn't wait that long. They cut down the cashews and grew corn.

It's happening all over New Guinea, which is a biologist's paradise. One of the most exciting countries on Earth is being deforested very rapidly.

Tom Lovejoy said at the 1989 AAAS meeting that we have ten years to decide the fate of the tropics. After that, the situation is irreversible. I think he's right. We've had biodiversity conferences. We've had meetings. We've had resolutions. We've had lots of talk, and nothing is happening. But, we continue trying. Maybe the greenhouse effect of last summer is finally going to shock people into wanting to do something.

Q   Don't you feel that the population explosion is the basic problem underlying all environmental problems?

A   There's absolutely no question that it's a major problem. It's a mistake to concentrate only on population, though. In Brazil, for instance, there is a greater acreage of cleared land per head of population than in the United States. You might say that if they could make that land as productive as our land, they could cope with the population problem. But, as Jefferson pointed out, it's often easier to clear new land than to invest in good husbandry to take the existing land up to a reasonably productive level.

It's the National Zoo's hundredth birthday on March 2. One of the things one can do when one is celebrating a centennial is to look back a hundred years, and look forward a hundred years. I've been able to do that in print, ahead of everybody else who will be doing it in 1999. I have a ten-year march on them.

What's happened in the last hundred years is remarkable. What could happen in the next hundred years is that we might finally break through on photosynthesis research. And, instead of having to grow food, we might finally be able to synthesize it in vitro from carbon dioxide and water. If we ever do that, then we could forget about clearing forests, and make all the world back into a green and pleasant land, and bury our cities underground, and have the United States wall-to-wall buffalo and passenger pigeons, and prairies, and recreational areas.

It's not entirely impossible that we might be able to duplicate photosynthesis. Would anyone have predicted in 1889 that we would have created radio and penicillin, that we would have flown to the moon, that we would have done all the marvelous positive things that this last century has brought? One has to maintain hope.

[FEBRUARY 14, 1989]

---

BIOGRAPHY

Since May 1984, Dr. Michael H. Robinson has been director of the Smithsonian Institution's National Zoological Park in Washington, D.C. Prior to that, he had been deputy director of the Smithsonian's Panama-based Tropical Research Institute. Dr. Robinson is an animal behaviorist and tropical biologist who has published extensively on predator-prey interactions, the evolution of adaptations, courtship and mating behavior, and freshwater biology. His favorite animals are cats, of any and all kinds.

Dr. Robinson is a fellow of the Linnean Society of London, the Zoological Society of London, the Royal Entomological Society of London, and the Institute of Biology. He is former director of the American Arachnological Society.

---

# The Battle
# for the Planet

## A Status Report

Each year at Worldwatch Institute we do a *State of the World* report. In effect, we give Earth an annual physical, checking its vital signs.

The results of these physicals—we've given the planet six of them now—are not reassuring. Each of the vital signs shows continuing deterioration from year to year. Each year the forests are shrinking; the deserts are expanding; the topsoil layer is thinning on a lot of our cropland. The ozone layer in the upper stratosphere is being depleted. The number of plant and animal species on Earth is diminishing, and the greenhouse gases are building in a very predictable way.

The key question is, How will these changes affect us? We know that we cannot continue to damage our life-support systems without eventually paying a heavy price. But how will we be affected? What will the price be?

Is there likely to be a buildup of carcinogens in the environment so severe that it increases the incidence of cancer, dramatically raising death rates? Or will the rising concentration of greenhouse gases make some regions of the planet so hot that they become uninhabitable, forcing massive human migrations? Will depletion of the ozone layer that protects us from ultraviolet radiation lead to serious health problems—a rising incidence of skin cancer, eye damage, including earlier cataract formation, and the suppression of human immune systems? Could there be a rise in sea level that would force a relocation of the hundreds

LESTER BROWN, called by the *Washington Post* "one of the world's most influential thinkers," is the founder and president of the Worldwatch Institute, and principal author of the annual *State of the World Report.*

of millions who live only a few feet above current sea level? Or will it be something that we cannot now even anticipate?

The answer is that without decisive action, all of these things will probably happen, though some will affect us more and sooner than others. We know from geographic analyses of epidemiological data that there are cancer hotspots in some industrial regions, but the increased number of cancer cases in the United States that is attributable to toxic chemicals is still minuscule compared with the 390,000 deaths per year attributed by the surgeon general to cigarette smoking. The chemical age is still young; it may take time for the full health effects of exposure to toxic chemicals to become evident.

If the buildup in greenhouse gases continues and temperatures rise as projected, some regions could become uninhabitable. A glimpse of such a future was seen last summer in the Yangtze Valley of Central China where temperatures rose above 100 degrees Fahrenheit for several consecutive days. One manifestation of heat stress was the dramatic rise in heat stroke victims. In the central China cities of Shanghai, Nanjing, and Wuhan, hundreds died and local hospitals were overrun with heat stroke victims.

When will the consequences of the global changes that we have set in motion be felt? Will we pay the price or will our children? Or, as with the irreversible loss of biological diversity, will it be all generations to come? Some of the global changes, such as rising sea level and ozone depletion, are not likely to have serious social consequences until we are at least a few decades further down the road. Others may cause dislocation in the next few years.

Amidst all the uncertainty, food scarcity is emerging as the most profound and immediate consequence of global change, one that is already affecting the welfare of hundreds of millions of people. All the principal changes in Earth's physical condition that are coming about—shrinking forests, deteriorating rangelands, soil erosion, desert expansion, acid rain, stratospheric ozone depletion, the buildup of greenhouse gases, the loss of biological diversity, and the dwindling per capita supplies of cropland and fresh water—are having a negative effect on the food prospect.

The first concrete economic indication of broadbased environmental deterioration now seems likely to be rising food prices. They have the potential to disrupt economies and, over time, governments. People in some parts of the world are already reeling from the effects.

In Africa, with the fastest population growth of any continent on record, a combination of deforestation, overgrazing, soil erosion, and desertification have contributed to a lowering of per capita grain production some 17 percent from the historical peak in the late 1960s. The fall from an annual output of 155 kilograms per person in the late 1960s to 129 kilograms in the late 1980s converted the continent into a grain-importing region, fueled the region's mounting external debt, and left millions of Africans hungry and physically weakened, drained of their vitality and productivity. In Latin America, rapid population growth and environmental degradation have contributed to a 7 percent fall in per capita grain production from the peak reached in 1981.

For the world, grain production per person climbed an impressive 40 percent between 1950 and 1984. Since 1984, it has fallen each year, dropping a record 13 percent during this four-year span (figure 1). Four-fifths of the 13 percent production decline was offset by reducing world carryover stocks of grain from the equivalent of a record 101 days of world consumption in 1987 to about 60 days in 1989, not much more than "pipeline" supplies. The remaining one-fifth was absorbed by the 3 percent decline in world grain consumption per person that resulted from rising prices.

In describing this recent four-year period, I don't mean to imply that the combination of population growth and environmental deterioration is solely responsible. Depressed world prices for farm commodities, ill-

Figure 1

World Grain Production/Per Capita
1950–88

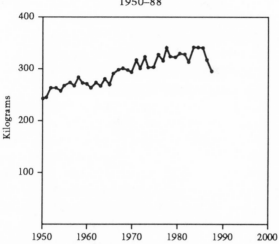

Source: U.S. Department of Agriculture.

conceived farm policies, adverse weather, and even climate change may
have contributed. Nor do I want to imply that this four-year stretch is a
new trend, but it does mean that it is becoming more difficult to systematically raise food production per person than it was prior to 1984.

For many years, reports on deforestation have used the 11-million
hectare annual loss of tropical forests, which was based on a 1980 Food
and Agriculture Organization (FAO) survey. But when the Brazilian government, using information provided by satellites, reported that 8 million hectares of its Amazon rain forest were burned off in 1987, mostly
to clear land for ranching and farming, it became clear that the Amazon
is being destroyed far faster than previously thought.

The causes of deforestation vary, but land clearance for agriculture,
as in Brazil, is the leading source of deforestation worldwide. In densely
populated countries, such as India and Ethiopia, firewood gathering is
more often responsible. An FAO study estimated that in 1980 some 1.2
billion of the world's people were meeting their firewood needs only by
cutting wood faster than nature could replace it. In 1982, India's remaining forest land could sustain an annual harvest of only 39 million tons of
wood, far below the estimated fuelwood demand of 133 million tons.
The gap of 94 million tons was closed either by overcutting, thus com-

promising future firewood production, or by burning cow dung and crop residues, compromising future food production.

In Africa, the degree of imbalance between firewood demand and the unsustainable harvests of wood varies widely. For example, in both semiarid Mauritania and mountainous Rwanda firewood demand is ten times the sustainable yield of the remaining forests. In Kenya, the ratio is five to one. In Ethiopia, Tanzania, and Nigeria, demand is two and a half times the sustainable yield. And in the Sudan, it is roughly double.

Regardless of the reason for the tree cover losses, the consequences are usually the same. Soil organic matter declines, reducing the moisture storage capacity of the soil. Rainfall runoff increases. Percolation and aquifer recharge decrease. Soil erosion accelerates.

Deforestation directly alters local hydrological cycles by increasing runoff and, perhaps less obviously, by affecting the recycling of rainfall inland. The former is now strikingly evident in the Indian subcontinent, where deforestation of the Himalayan watersheds is increasing rainfall runoff, leading to increasingly severe flooding. The data in table I indicate that the area subject to annual flooding in India has expanded dramatically, more than doubling since 1960.

Accelerated runoff as a result of deforestation was evident in early September 1988, when two-thirds of Bangladesh was under water for several days. The 1988 flood, the worst on record, left 25 million of the country's 110 million people homeless, adding to the growing ranks of "environmental refugees."

Eneas Salati and Peter Vose have analyzed the effect of deforestation on the recycling of rainfall inland in the central Amazon (table 2). In a healthy stand of rain forest, they point out that about three-fourths of

TABLE I

*Area Subject to Flooding in India*
*as Deforestation Progresses*

|      | Million Hectares |
| ---- | ---------------- |
| 1960 | 19               |
| 1970 | 23               |
| 1980 | 49               |
| 1984 | 59               |

*Source*: Centre for Science and Environment, New Delhi, India.

TABLE 2

*Water Balance in Amazonian*
*Watershed Near Manaus, Brazil*

| Path of Rainfall | Proportion of Rainfall (percent) |
|---|---|
| Evaporation of rainfall intercepted by vegetation and from forested soil | 26 |
| Transpiration from vegetation | 48 |
| Total evapotranspiration | — |
| Stream runoff | 74 |
| Total rainfall | 26 |
| | 100 |

*Source*: Eneas Salati and Peter B. Vose, "Amazon Basin: A System in Equilibrium," *Science*, July 13, 1984.

rainfall is evaporated either directly from the soil and from the surface of leaves, or from transpiration by plants, and roughly one-fourth runs off into streams, returning to the ocean. Such high levels of cloud recharge have led ecologists to refer to tropical rain forests as "rain machines."

After deforestation, this ratio is roughly reversed, suggesting that as deforestation of the Amazon continues, the vigorous recycling of water inland from the Atlantic will weaken, leading to lower rainfall and a drying out of the western Amazon. Moisture left in the air when the westward-moving air masses are directed southward by the Andes into southern Brazil and the Chaco/Paraguay river regions becomes part of the rainfall cycle in major farming areas. If this is reduced, Salati and Vose believe it "might affect climatic patterns in agriculture in south central Brazil." In effect, efforts to expand beef production in the central Amazon could indirectly reduce rainfall and food production in the country's agricultural heartland to the south.

Although it has been the subject of little research, a similar situation exists in western Africa, where the interior region depends on rainfall that is recycled inland via the coastal rain forests. Although there is little or no research on deforestation and the recycling of rainfall into the continental interior, it is hard to see how the flow of moisture inland would not have been reduced by the extensive deforestation of the coastal tier of countries, stretching from Senegal through Nigeria. We do know that the isohyets [lines on a map indicating areas with equal rainfall] have shifted steadily southward in the Sahelian region over the last three decades. Thousands of villages all across the southern edge of the Sahel have been abandoned in recent years. The number of Mauritanians living in Senegal and Mali may now exceed those remaining in Mauritania. Even the survival of some ancient cities, such as Timbuktu, is in question. The drying out and desertification of the Sahelian region is probably the largest source of environmental refugees in the world today.

In addition to adversely affecting the hydrological cycle, deforestation can disrupt nutrient cycles as well, reducing the land's biological productivity. Drawing on field data from Ethiopia, World Bank ecologist Kenneth Newcombe reports that when land is without trees, mineral nutrients are no longer recycled from deep soil layers. As this nutrient cycle is breached, soil fertility begins to decline. As trees disappear, villagers begin to burn crop residues and animal dung for fuel. This in turn interrupts two more nutrient cycles: removing crop residues and diverting dung from fields degrades soil structure and leaves the land more vulnerable to erosion.

Eventually cow dung and crop residues become the main fuel source. Data gathered on household fuel use in the central Indian state of Madhya Pradesh show this energy transition is well underway. Cow dung has edged out firewood as the principal household fuel, with the use of crop residues not far behind (table 3). As this flow of nutrients from the land into villages and towns continues, it drains the soil of its fertility, leaving farmers vulnerable to crop failure during even routine dry seasons.

If this process continues over an extended period, with no nutrient replenishment, land productivity will decline to the point where families can no longer produce enough food for themselves or their livestock, let alone for markets. A mass exodus from rural areas begins, often triggered by drought that could formerly have been tolerated.

As deforestation directly and indirectly reduces soil organic matter and moisture storage, it can lead to a new kind of drought—one that results not from reduced rainfall but from the reduced ability of the soil

TABLE 3

*Household Fuel Consumption in*
*the Indian State of Madhya Pradesh*

| Fuel | Quantity (million tons) |
|------|------------------------|
| Cow dung | 9.64 |
| Firewood | 9.47 |
| Crop residues | 6.93 |

*Source*: Centre for Science and Environment, *The State of India's Environment, 1984–85* (New Delhi, 1985).

to store moisture. This was among the concerns that led to the convening in India of a national seminar in May 1986 entitled "Control of Drought, Desertification and Famine." Attended by nearly a hundred professionals, the conference was concerned that the "temporary phenomenon of meteorological drought in India has tended to be converted into the permanent and pervasive phenomenon of desertification, undermining biological productivity of soil over large parts of the country." In a radio address to the nation, Prime Minister Rajiv Gandhi recognized the link with deforestation: "Continuing deforestation has brought us face-to-face with a major ecological and economic crisis. The trend must be halted."

Many of the costs of deforestation do not show up in national economic accounts. As nearby forests dwindle and disappear, women and children travel further and work harder to meet minimal firewood needs. Eventually, as in some villages in the Andes and the Sahel, firewood scarcity reduces people to one hot meal per day. Deforestation can not only adversely affect food production, but it can deprive people of the fuel to cook what food they do produce.

Although the data for grassland degradation are even more sketchy than for forest clearing, the trends are no less real. A United Nations study charting the mounting pressures on grasslands in nine countries in southern Africa shows that the capacity to sustain livestock populations is diminishing. This problem is noticeable throughout Africa, where livestock numbers have expanded nearly as fast as the human population. In 1950, Africa had 238 million people and 272 million livestock. By 1987, the continent's human population had increased to 601 million, and its livestock numbers to 604 million.

Because little grain is available for feeding them, the continent's 183 million cattle, 197 million sheep, and 163 million goats are supported almost entirely by grazing and browsing. Everywhere outside the tsetse fly belt, livestock are vital to the economy. But in many countries, herds and flocks are destroying the grassland resource that sustains them. The U.N. report on the nine countries in southern Africa observes that "for some countries, and major areas of others, present herds exceed the carrying capacity from 50 to 100 percent. This has led to a deterioration of the soil—thereby lowering the carrying capacity even more—and to severe soil erosion in an accelerating cycle of degradation."

Overgrazing gradually changes the character of rangeland vegetation and its capacity to support livestock. As degradation of rangeland continues, its capacity to carry cattle diminishes, leaving it to goats and sheep, which can browse the remaining woody plants. This shift in the composition of Africa's livestock herd has been particularly evident since 1970 (table 4).

As grazing and wood-gathering increase in semiarid regions, the rapidly reproducing annual grasses replace perennial grasses and woody perennial shrubs. The loss of trees, such as the acacias in the Sahel, means less forage in the dry season, a time when the protein-rich acacia pods formerly fed livestock. Annual grasses that dominate the land-

TABLE 4

*Changes in Africa's Livestock
Populations 1950–70 and 1970–87*

| Average Annual Change | 1950–70 | 1970–87 |
| --- | --- | --- |
| | (percent) | |
| Cattle | +2.15 | +0.82 |
| Sheep | +1.67 | +1.64 |
| Goats | +1.67 | +1.88 |

*Source*: U.N. Food and Agriculture Organization, *Production Yearbook* (Rome: various years).

scape are far more sensitive to stress than perennials and may not germinate at all in dry years.

Fodder needs of livestock populations in nearly all Third World countries now exceed the sustainable yield of grasslands and other forage resources. In India, the demand for livestock fodder by the year 2000 is expected to reach 700 million tons, while the supply will total just 540 million tons. The National Land Use and Wastelands Development Council reports that in states with the most serious land degradation, such as Rajasthan and Karnataka, fodder supplies satisfied only 50 to 80 percent of needs, leaving large numbers of emaciated cattle. When drought occurs, hundreds of thousands of cattle die. In recent years, local governments in India have established fodder relief camps for cattle threatened with starvation, much as food relief camps are established for starving human populations.

Overgrazing is by definition a short-term phenomenon. Deteriorating grasslands that cannot sustain livestock populations cannot sustain the human populations that depend on them. Countless thousands of those who made a living from grazing their flocks and herds as recently as a decade or two ago now populate food relief camps in Africa or the squatter settlements that surround almost every major city in Africa and in the northern reaches of the Indian subcontinent.

Soil erosion is a natural process, one that began as the first soil was formed when Earth was still young. Because new soil is being continuously formed from parent materials, erosion becomes an economic threat only when it exceeds the new rate of soil formation, which is typically estimated at 2 to 5 tons per acre per year.

As the demand for food has risen in recent decades, so have the pressures on Earth's soils. In the face of this continuing world demand for grain and the associated relentless increase in pressures on land, soil erosion is accelerating as the world's farmers are pressed into plowing highly erodible land and as traditional rotation systems that maintain a stable soil base are beginning to break down.

Throughout the Third World, increasing population pressure and the accelerating loss of topsoil seem to go hand in hand. Soil scientists S. A. El-Swaify and E. W. Dangler have observed that it is in precisely those regions with high population density that "farming of marginal hilly lands is a hazardous necessity. Ironically, it is also in those very regions where the greatest need exists to protect the rapidly diminishing or degrading resources." It is this vicious cycle, set in motion by the growing demands for human food, feed, fiber, and firewood, that makes mounting an effective response particularly difficult.

In other parts of the world, traditional cropping rotations that included nitrogen-fixing legumes permitted farmers to cultivate rolling land without losing excessive amounts of topsoil. Typical of these regions is the midwestern United States, where farmers traditionally used long-term rotations of hay, wheat, and corn. By alternating row crops, which are most susceptible to erosion, with cover crops, like hay, soil erosion was kept below the natural rate of new soil formation. As world demand for food soared after World War II, however, and as the cost of nitrogen fertilizer fell, farmers abandoned these rotations in favor of continuous row cropping.

An estimated one-third of the world's cropland is now losing topsoil at a rate that is undermining its long-term productivity. At the Institute, we estimate the worldwide loss of topsoil from cropland, in excess of new soil formation, at 24 billion tons per year, roughly the amount of topsoil on Australia's wheatland.

When most of the topsoil is lost on land where the underlying formation consists of rock or where the productivity of the subsoil is too low to make cultivation economical, it is abandoned. More commonly, however, land continues to be plowed even though most of the topsoil has been lost and even though the plow layer contains a mixture of topsoil and subsoil, with the latter dominating. Other things being equal, the real cost of food production on such land is far higher than on land where the topsoil layer remains intact.

Leon Lyles, an agricultural engineer with the U.S. Department of Agriculture, has provided perhaps the most comprehensive collection of research results of the effect of soil erosion on land productivity. Drawing on the work of U.S. soil scientists, both within and outside government, Lyles compared fourteen independent studies, mostly undertaken in the Corn Belt states, to summarize the effects of a loss of one inch of topsoil on corn yields. His survey found that such a loss reduced yields from 3 to 6.1 bushels per acre (see table 5). These fourteen studies showed that the loss of an inch of topsoil reduced corn yields on eighteen sites by an average of 6 percent.

Results for wheat, drawing on twelve studies, showed a similar relationship between soil erosion and land productivity. The loss of an inch of topsoil reduced wheat yields by 0.5 to 2.0 bushels per acre. In percentage terms, the loss of an inch of topsoil reduced wheat yields an average of 6 percent, exactly the same as for corn.

TABLE 5

*Effect of Topsoil Loss on Corn Yields*

| Location | Yield Reduction per inch of Topsoil Lost (bushels/acre) | (percent) | Soil Description |
|---|---|---|---|
| East Central, Illinois | 3.7 | 6.5 | Swygert silt loam |
| Fowler, Indiana | 4.0 | 4.3 | Fowler, Brookston, and Parr silt loams |
| Clarinda, Iowa | 4.0 | 5.1 | Marshall silt loam |
| Greenfield, Iowa | 3.1 | 6.3 | Shelby silt loam |
| Shenandoah, Iowa | 6.1 | 5.1 | Marshall silt loam |
| Bethany, Missouri | 4.0 | 6.0 | Shelby and Grundy silt loams |
| Columbus, Ohio | 3.0 | 6.0 | Celina silt loam |
| Wooster, Ohio | 4.8 | 8.0 | Canfield silt loam |

Sources: Various reports cited in Leon Lyles, "Possible Effects of Wind Erosion on Soil Productivity," *Journal of Soil and Water Conservation,* November/December 1975.

Although there are few reliable data on the effect of soil erosion on land productivity for most countries, some insights into the relationship can be derived from these U.S. studies. Given the consistency of the decline in productivity across a wide range of soil types and crops, it would not be unreasonable to assume that a similar relationship between soil erosion and land productivity exists in other countries. Research on west African soils shows that a loss of 3.9 inches of topsoil, roughly half of an undisturbed topsoil layer, cuts corn yields by 52 percent. Yields of cowpeas, a leguminous crop, are reduced by 38 percent.

Because of the shortsighted way that one-third to one-half of the world's cropland is being managed, the soils on these lands have been converted from a renewable to a nonrenewable resource. Although the loss of topsoil does not show up in the national economic accounts or resource inventories of most countries, it is nonetheless a serious loss. Each year the world's farmers are trying to feed 88 million more people, but with 24 billion fewer tons of topsoil than the year before.

Grave though the loss of topsoil may be, it is a quiet crisis, one that is not widely perceived. Unlike earthquakes, volcanic eruptions, and other natural disasters, this human-made disaster is unfolding gradually. And it is unrecognized since the intensification of cropping patterns and the plowing of marginal lands that leads to excessive erosion over the long run can lead to production gains in the short run, thus creating the illusion of progress and a false sense of food security.

Although soil erosion is a physical process, it has numerous economic consequences affecting land productivity, economic growth, income distribution, food sufficiency, and long-term external debt. Ultimately it affects people. When soils are depleted and soils are poorly nourished, people are often undernourished as well. What is at stake is not merely the degradation of soil, but the degradation of life itself.

One of the most serious consequences of continuing population growth is the worldwide shrinkage in cropland per person. Between 1950 and 1981, the world grain area increased some 24 percent, reaching an all-time high (see figure 2). Since then it has fallen some 6 percent. That the world's cropland area would expand when the world demand for food was growing rapidly is not surprising. What is surprising—and worrying—is the recent decline. This is due partly to the systematic retirement of highly erodible land under conservation programs in the United States; partly to the abandonment of eroded land, as in the Soviet Union, partly to the growing conversion of land to nonfarm uses,

Figure 2

World Harvested Area of Grain
1950–88

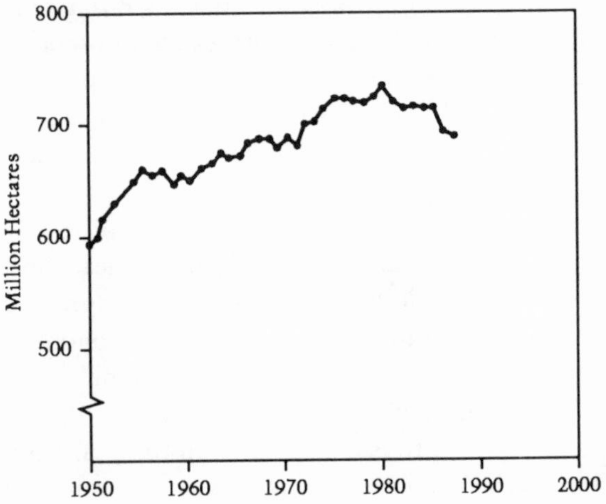

Source: U.S. Department of Agriculture.

a trend most evident in densely populated Asia; and partly to cropland set aside to control production, as in the United States.

After the second surge in world grain prices between 1972 and 1973, farmers throughout the world responded to record prices by plowing more land. In the United States, they not only returned idled cropland to use, they also plowed millions of acres of highly erodible land. Between 1972 and 1976, the U.S. area in grain climbed some 24 percent, but soil erosion apparently increased even faster. By 1977, American farmers were losing an estimated 6 tons of topsoil for every ton of grain they produced.

The United States is now in the fourth year of a five-year program to convert at least 40 million acres of highly erodible cropland to either grassland or woodland before it loses most of its topsoil and becomes wasteland. As of today, some 28 million acres have been converted under ten-year contracts.

The Soviet Union, lacking such a program, has abandoned roughly a million hectares of grain land each year since 1977, leading to a 13 percent shrinkage in area. Abandonment on this scale suggests that inherent fertility may be falling on a far larger area, helping explain why the Soviets now lead the world in fertilizer consumption, using twice as much to produce a ton of grain as does the United States.

The conversion of cropland to nonfarm uses is also shrinking the cropland area. In China, one result of the past decade's welcome prosperity is that literally millions of villages are either expanding their existing dwellings or building new ones. And an industrial sector expanding more than 12 percent annually since 1980 means the construction of thousands of new factories each year. Since most of China's 1.1 billion people are concentrated in its rich farming regions, new homes and factories are often built on cropland. This loss, combined with the shifts to more profitable crops, has reduced China's grain growing area 9 percent since 1976.

One country that can increase its cropland area somewhat in the short run is the United States. As recently as 1987, it was idling 50 million acres of cropland to control production. About half of this is being returned to production in 1989. The remainder could be returned to use in 1990. This will be substantially offset by the 40 million acres of highly erodible cropland, mentioned earlier, that is being withdrawn from production.

There are a few countries that are still steadily expanding their cultivated area. Brazil, for example, has nearly tripled its cultivated area since midcentury, with most of the growth coming in the south and southeast outside the Amazonian basin. Although the expansion has slowed during the 1980s, further growth is in prospect over the remaining part of this century and beyond (see table 6).

This modest short-term gain in the United States and the longer-term prospective gain in Brazil and elsewhere will expand the cropland base. It is unlikely, however, that these gains will offset the losses under way elsewhere. The prospect for the rest of this century is for no meaningful net addition to the world's cropland base.

Between 1950 and 1989, the world grain area per person declined from 0.23 hectares to 0.14 hectares, a shrinkage of 39 percent. Assuming that the projected growth in population materializes with no net gain in world cropland over the next two decades, grain area per person will fall to 0.10 hectares per person by 2010, a further drop of 29 percent. Given the scarcity of new cropland, after midcentury many countries worked to raise land productivity by expanding the irrigated area. Between 1950 and 1980, the world irrigated area expanded from 94 million hectares to 236 million hectares, a 2.5-fold gain that closely paralleled the growth in food output. After 1980, however, growth slowed dramatically (table 7).

Unfortunately, not all the irrigation expansion during the preceding three decades was sustainable. In recent years, the world's two leading food producers, the United States and China, have experienced un-

TABLE 6

*World Grain Land, 1950–80, with Projections to 2010*

| Year | Total Grain Land (million hectares) | Per Capita Grain Land (hectares) | Change by Decade (percent) |
|------|------|------|------|
| 1950 | 593 | .23 | |
| 1960 | 651 | .21 | −8 |
| 1970 | 673 | .18 | −14 |
| 1980 | 724 | .16 | −11 |
| 1990 | 720 | .14 | −12 |
| 2000 | 720 | .12 | −14 |
| 2010 | 720 | .10 | −17 |

TABLE 7

*World Gross Irrigated Area, Total and Per Capita, 1950–80,*
*with Projections to 2000*

| Year | Total Irrigated Cropland (million hectares) | Per Capita Irrigated Cropland (hectares) | Per Capita Change by Decade (percent) |
|------|----------|----------|----------|
| 1950 | 94  | 0.037 |     |
| 1960 | 136 | 0.045 | +22 |
| 1970 | 188 | 0.051 | +13 |
| 1980 | 236 | 0.053 | +4  |
| 1990 | 259 | 0.049 | −8  |
| 2000 | 279 | 0.045 | −8  |

*Sources:* Data for 1950–80 adapted or derived from W. Robert Rangeley, Washington, D.C., private communication, June 1989, and from U.N. Food and Agriculture Organization, *FAO Production Yearbook 1988* (unpublished printout) (Rome: 1989); projections for 1990 and 2000 are Worldwatch Institute estimates; per capita figures derived from population data (based on data from U.S. Bureau of the Census) in Francis Urban and Philip Rose, *World Population by Country and Region, 1950–86, and Projections to 2000* (Washington, D.C.: U.S. Department of Agriculture, Economic Research Service, 1988).

planned declines in irrigated area. The U.S. irrigated area, which peaked in 1978, has shrunk some 7 percent since then, reversing several decades of growth. In addition to falling water tables, depressed commodity prices and rising pumping costs have contributed to the shrinkage.

Further declines are in prospect. In 1986, the USDA reported that more than one-fourth of the 21 million hectares of irrigated cropland was being watered by pulling down water tables, with the drop ranging from 6 inches to 4 feet per year. They were falling either because the pumping exceeded aquifer recharge or because the water was from the largely nonrenewable Ogallala aquifer. Although water mining is an option in the short run, in the long run withdrawals cannot exceed aquifer recharge.

In China, where the expansion peaked in 1978, irrigated area had shrunk 2 percent by 1987. Under parts of the North China plain, in the region surrounding Beijing and Tianjin, the water table is dropping by 1 to 2 meters a year, as industrial, residential, and agricultural users compete for dwindling supplies of water.

In the Soviet Union, the excessive use of water for irrigation takes the form of diminished river flows rather than falling water tables. Roughly a third of the Soviet Union's irrigated cropland is centered around the Aral Sea in Central Asia. Irrigation diversions from the Syr-Darya and Amu-Darya, the two great rivers of the region that sustain the landlocked sea, have led to a 40 percent shrinkage in its area since 1960. Soviet scientists fear a major ecological catastrophe is unfolding as the sea slowly disappears. The dry bottom is now becoming desert, the site of sandstorms that may drop on the surrounding fields up to half a ton per hectare of a sand-salt mix, damaging the crops that water once destined for the sea is used to grow.

Competition between the countryside and cities for fresh water supplies is intensifying in many countries. Faced with absolute limits on the amount of fresh water available in the southern Great Plains and the southwestern United States, cities unable to afford new projects are buying irrigation water rights from farmers. In the competition between agricultural, residential, and industrial water users, it is agriculture that invariably surrenders water.

Irrigation systems are deteriorating in some countries. United Nations' analysts estimate that close to 40 percent of the world's irrigated area is suffering from varying degrees of water-logging and salinity. In many cases, this condition can be reversed, providing the capital is available for the installation of underground drainage systems. In other situations, however, the salt content of the water being used for irrigation is so high that there may not be any practical way of dealing with it, meaning that the irrigated land will eventually be abandoned.

There are still many opportunities for expanding the irrigated area, but given the losses that are occurring in some countries, the world is not likely to reestablish a trend of rapid, sustained growth in irrigated area like that from 1950 to 1980. In retrospect, this growth will probably be unique. Any future gains in irrigated area may depend as much on gains in water use efficiency as on new supplies.

Between 1950 and 1980, world irrigated area expanded 2.6-fold, while population increased scarcely 1.7-fold, raising the amount of irrigation water used per person by 56 percent. This increase helped offset the effects of the shrinking cropland per person. But between 1980 and 1990, we estimate the irrigated area will increase by only 16 million hectares, far less rapidly than population, leading to a reduction in irrigated area per person of 11 percent. During the 1980s, for the first time since midcentury, the world is experiencing a shrinkage both in irrigation water and in cropland per person.

From the beginning of agriculture until around 1950, most of the growth in world food output came from expanding the cultivated area. As the frontiers disappeared around midcentury, farmers shifted to raising land productivity. Between 1950 and 1981, a period during which the cropland area expanded only modestly, roughly four-fifths of the growth in world food output came from raising productivity. During the seven years since 1981, a period when the world cropland area declined, all growth in output has come from land productivity gains. In effect, we now have ten thousand years of experience in increasing food supplies primarily by expanding cultivated area and four decades by raising land productivity.

Between 1950 and 1984, the world's farmers raised their grain yield per hectare from 1.1 tons to 2.3 tons, a remarkable feat. Four technologies—chemical fertilizer, irrigation, high-yielding dwarf wheats and rices, and hybrid corn—accounted for most of the increase. Growth in fertilizer use has led the way. From 1950 through 1984, fertilizer use climbed from 14 million to 125 million tons, a gain of more than 11 percent per year. Since then, growth in fertilizer use has slowed dramatically as the growth in irrigated area has slowed, as the yield response to fertilizer use has diminished, as commodity prices have weakened, and as Third World debt has soared. In addition, many financially pressed governments have reduced fertilizer subsidies. From 1984 to 1988, usage went from 125 million to 135 million tons, an annual rise of only 2 percent.

Over the past generation, the world's farmers have successfully substituted fertilizer for land (figure 3). In per capita terms, world fertilizer use quintupled between 1950 and 1984, going from 5 kilograms to 26 and offsetting a one-third decline in grain area per person. As varieties are improved, the response to fertilizer use continues to rise, albeit slowly in recent years.

Eventually the rise of grain yield per hectare, like the growth of any biological process in a finite environment, will conform to the standard S-shaped growth curve. So, too, will the response to inputs, such as fertilizer, that are responsible for the rise. The fertilizer use curve shown in figure 3 appears to be conforming to the S shape.

The ultimate constraints on the rise of crop yields will be imposed by the upper limit of photosynthetic efficiency. Evidence that photo-

Figure 3

World Fertilizer Use and
Grain Area Per Capita, 1950–88

Source: U.S. Department of Agriculture.

synthetic constraints may be emerging can be seen in the diminishing returns on fertilizer use. Whereas twenty years ago, the application of each additional ton of fertilizer in the U.S. Corn Belt added 15 or 20 tons to the grain harvest, today it may add only 5 to 10 tons. In analyzing recent agricultural trends in Indonesia, agricultural economists Duane Chapman and Randy Barker of Cornell University note that "while 1 kilogram of fertilizer nutrients probably led to a yield increase of 10 kilograms of unmilled rice in 1972, this ratio has fallen to about 1 to 5 at present."

If the response to additional fertilizer use is diminishing, what other technologies can continue to boost world food output in the way that the tenfold increase in fertilizer use has since midcentury? Unfortunately, no identifiable technologies are waiting in the wings that will lead to the quantum jumps in world food output, produced by the four outlined above.

There has been an overall loss of momentum in the growth in world food output. Although there are still many opportunities for expanding food output in all countries, it is becoming more difficult for some to maintain the rapid expansion in output that the growth of their population demands.

Of all the global changes we have set in motion, climate change is potentially the most disruptive. Already suffering from slower growth in food output, the world is now confronted with the prospect of hotter summers. Farmers who have always had to deal with the vagaries of weather must now also contend with the uncertainty of worldwide climate change.

The drought- and heat-damaged U.S. grain harvest in 1988, which fell below consumption probably for the first time in history, dramatically illustrates how hotter summers may affect agriculture over the longer term in the United States and elsewhere. Grain production dropped to 196 million tons, well below the estimated 206 million tons of consumption (table 8). This shortfall was filled by drawing down stocks. U.S. commitments to export close to 100 million tons during the 1988–89 marketing year may be satisfied by exporting much of the remaining U.S. grain reserve. With a normal harvest, the United States

TABLE 8

*U.S. Grain Production and Exportable Surplus by Crop Year, 1980–88*

| | (million metric tons) | | |
| Year | Production | Consumption | Exportable Surplus from Current Crop |
|---|---|---|---|
| 1980 | 268 | 171 | +97 |
| 1981 | 328 | 179 | +149 |
| 1982 | 331 | 194 | +137 |
| 1983 | 206 | 182 | +24 |
| 1984 | 313 | 197 | +116 |
| 1985 | 345 | 201 | +144 |
| 1986 | 314 | 217 | +97 |
| 1987 | 277 | 215 | +62 |
| 1988 | 196 | 206 | −10 |

*Sources*: U.S. Department of Agriculture, Economic Research Service, *World Grain Harvested Area, Production, and Yield 1950–87*, (unpublished printout) (Washington, DC: 1988); USDA, Foreign Agricultural Service, *World Grain Situation and Outlook*, August 1988.

typically harvests 300 million tons of grain, consuming 200 million tons and exporting roughly 100 million tons.

As noted earlier, climate change will not affect all countries in the same way. The projected rises by 2030 to 2050 of 1.5 to 4.5 degrees Celsius (3 to 8 degrees Fahrenheit) are global averages, but temperatures are expected to increase much more in the middle and higher latitudes and more over land than over the oceans. They are projected to change little near the equator, while in the higher latitudes rises could easily be twice that projected for Earth as a whole. This uneven distribution will affect world agriculture disproportionately, since most food is produced on the land masses in the middle and higher latitudes of the northern hemisphere.

Here I will limit the discussion of how the global warming will affect the food prospect to the situation of North America. Though they remain sketchy, meteorological models suggest that two of the world's major food-producing regions—the North American agricultural heartland and a large area of central Asia—are likely to experience a decline in soil moisture during the summer growing season as a result of higher temperatures and increased evaporation. If the warming progresses as the models indicate, some of the land in the U.S. western Great Plains that now produces wheat would revert to rangeland. The western Corn Belt would become semiarid, with wheat or other drought-tolerant grains that yield 40 bushels per acre replacing corn that yields over 100 bushels.

On the plus side, as temperatures increase the winter wheat belt will migrate northward, allowing winter strains that yield 40 bushels per acre to replace spring wheat yielding 30 bushels. A longer growing season would also permit a northward extension of spring wheat production in areas such as Canada's Alberta Province, thus increasing that nation's cultivated area. On balance, though, higher temperatures and increased summer dryness will reduce the North American grain harvest, largely because of their negative impact on the all-important corn crop.

Drought, which afflicted most of the United States during the summer of 1988, is essentially defined as dryness. For farmers, drought conditions can result from lower than normal rainfall, higher than normal temperatures, or both. When higher temperatures accompany below-normal rainfall, as they did during the summer of 1988, crop yields can fall precipitously. Extreme heat can also interfere with the pollination of some crops. Corn pollination can easily be impaired by uncommonly high temperatures during the ten-day period in July when fertilization occurs.

A rise in average temperatures will also increase the probability of extreme short-term heat waves. If these occur at critical times—such as the corn pollination period—they can reduce crop yields far more than the relatively modest average temperature increase of a few degrees might indicate.

This vulnerability of corn, which accounts for two-thirds of the U.S. grain harvest and one eighth of the world's, can cause wide year-to-year swings in the world grain crop. An examination of U.S. corn yields since 1950 shows five sharply reduced harvests over the last thirty-eight years (figure 4). The only pronounced drops before the 1980s came in 1970, from an outbreak of corn blight, and in 1974, when a wet spring and late planting combined with an early frost to destroy a part of the crop in the northern Corn Belt before it matured.

Three harvests since 1950 have been sharply reduced by drought, all in the 1980s. Each drop has been worse than the last. Compared with the preceding year, the 1980 corn yield per acre was down by 17 percent, that in 1983 was down by 28 percent, and that in 1988 by a staggering 34 percent.

Figure 4

U. S. Corn Yield per Hectare
1950–88

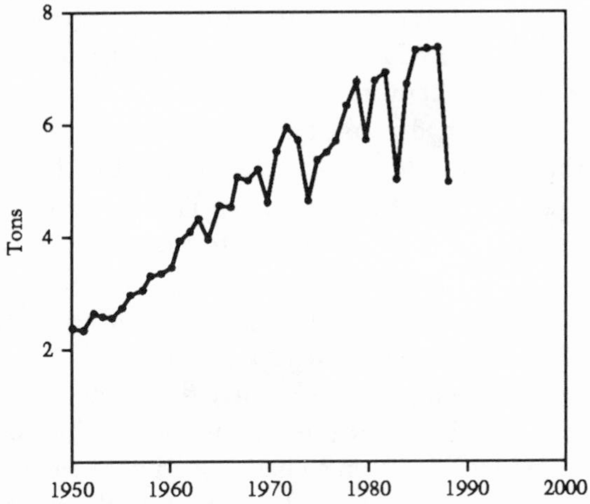

Source: U.S. Department of Agriculture.

These three reduced harvests each occurred during one of the five warmest years of the last century: 1980, 1983, and 1988. There may well be a cause-and-effect relationship, but there is no way at this time to conclusively link the drought-depressed U.S. harvests with a global warming, since annual weather variability is so much greater than the rise in average global temperatures measured during the 1980s. We do know that the conditions experienced in the Corn Belt during the summer of 1988 were similar to those described by the meteorological models as the buildup of greenhouse gases continues. Although it is a scary thought, if the drought and heat of 1988 is a sample of the hotter summers to come, then the days of the North American breadbasket could be numbered.

What are the likely consequences of the recent slower growth in world food output and the global warming? Two widely asked questions define the two most common food scenarios. One is, What will the food situation be like if the world's weather this summer is "normal"? The other is, What if the United States experiences a severely drought-reduced harvest this summer, similar to that in 1988?

The answer to the first question is that even with normal weather, it may not be possible to rebuild depleted world grain stocks. This would mean that farmers are now having trouble keeping up with population growth and that for the foreseeable future the world will be living more or less hand-to-mouth, trying to make it from one harvest to the next.

The answer to the second question, which applies to future years as well if we cannot rebuild stocks, is that grain exports from North America would slow to a trickle. The world would face a food emergency. Never during the half century since America emerged as the world's breadbasket has it not had a large quantity of grain to export (table 9). By September, there would be a frantic scramble for the comparatively meager exportable supplies of grain from France, Argentina, and Australia. There is no precedent by which to assess the impact of such a situation on grain prices. They could easily double, sending shock waves throughout the global economy that could destabilize national governments in low-income countries.

All available evidence indicates that the ranks of the hungry are expanding during the late 1980s, reversing the trend of recent decades. Uncertainties and stresses from a changing climate are now being overlaid upon an already tightening food situation. In the absence of a major commitment by governments to slow population growth and strength-

TABLE 9

*World Grain Trade, 1950–88*

| Region | (million metric tons) | | | | |
|---|---|---|---|---|---|
| | 1950[1] | 1960 | 1970 | 1980 | 1988[2] |
| North America | +23 | +39 | +56 | +131 | +119 |
| Latin America | +1 | o | +4 | −10 | −11 |
| Western Europe | −22 | −25 | −30 | −16 | +22 |
| Eastern Europe and Soviet Union | o | o | o | −46 | −27 |
| Africa | o | −2 | −5 | −15 | −28 |
| Asia | −6 | −17 | −37 | −63 | −89 |
| Australia and New Zealand | +3 | +6 | +12 | +19 | +14 |

[1] Plus sign indicates net exports; minus sign, net imports.
[2] Preliminary.
*Sources*: U.N. Food and Agriculture Organization, *Production Yearbook* (Rome: various years); U.S. Department of Agriculture, Foreign Agricultural Service, *World Rice Reference Tables* and *World Wheat and Coarse Grains Reference Tables* (unpublished printouts) (Washington, D.C.: June 1988).

en agriculture, food insecurity and the social instability associated with it will dominate the political landscape in many countries for years to come.

As noted earlier, per capita grain production is now declining in two regions of the world. In Africa it has fallen 17 percent over the last two decades, and in Latin America it has fallen 7 percent from its all-time high in 1981. This sustained decline in grain output per person, which is likely to continue in these two regions, could spread to other regions during the 1990s.

In real terms, world grain prices were at an all-time low in early 1987, having fallen slowly, albeit irregularly, for many decades. But in a one-year span between July 1987 and July 1988, world grain prices went up by roughly one-half, where they have since remained. As of March of this year, wheat prices were up from July 1987 by 62 percent, rice prices by 34 percent, and corn prices by 56 percent (table 10).

Rising grain prices combined with falling incomes in many heavily indebted Third World countries pose a dilemma. Higher prices are

TABLE 10

## World Grain Prices, March 1989 Compared with July 1987

|  | July 1987 | March 1989 | Change |
|---|---|---|---|
|  | (dollars) | | (percent) |
| Wheat (dollars/bu.) | 2.85 | 4.63 | +62 |
| Rice (dollars/ton) | 212 | 284 | +34 |
| Corn (dollars/bu.) | 1.94 | 3.02 | +56 |

Source: International Monetary Fund, International Financial Statistics (Washington, D.C.).

needed to stimulate output and encourage additional investment by farmers. But on the demand side of the equation, the world's poor cannot cope with higher prices. Perhaps a billion or more of the world's people are already spending 70 percent of their income on food. If the price of grain rises dramatically, they will be unable to adjust. They will be forced to tighten their belts, but they do not have any notches left.

The social effect of higher grain prices is much greater in developing countries than in industrial ones. In the United States, for example, a $1 loaf of bread contains roughly 5 cents worth of wheat. If the price of wheat doubles, the price of the loaf would increase only to $1.05. In developing countries, however, where wheat is purchased in the market and ground into flour at home, a doubling of wholesale grain prices translates into a doubling of bread prices. For those who already spend most of their income on food, such a rise can drive consumption below the survival level.

Even before the recent grain price rises, the social effects of agricultural adversity were becoming highly visible throughout Africa. In mid-1988, the World Bank, using data through March 1986, reported that "both the proportion and the total number of Africans with deficient diets have climbed and will continue to rise unless special action is taken."

In Africa, the number of "food insecure" people, defined by the bank as those not having enough food for normal health and physical activity, now totals over 100 million. Some 14.7 million Ethiopians, one-third of the country, are undernourished. Nigeria is close behind, with 13.7 million undernourished people. The countries with 40 percent or more of their populations suffering from chronic food insecurity are Chad, Mozambique, Somalia, Uganda, Zaire, and Zambia. The bank summarized the findings of its 1988 study by noting that "Africa's food situation is not only serious, it is deteriorating."

In its 1988 report, "The Global State of Hunger and Malnutrition," the U.N.'s World Food Council states that the number of malnourished preschoolers in Peru increased from 42 percent to 68 percent between 1980 and 1983. Infant deaths have risen in Brazil during the 1980s. If recent trends in population growth, land degradation, and growth in external debt continue, Latin America's decline in food production per person will almost certainly continue into the 1990s, increasing the number of malnourished people. The council summarized its world-wide findings by noting that "earlier progress in fighting hunger, malnutrition and poverty has come to a halt or is being reversed in many parts of the world."

When domestic food production is inadequate, the ability of countries to import becomes the key to food adequacy. During the late 1980s, low-income grain-deficit countries must contend not only with an increase in grain prices, but also in many cases with unmanageable external debt, which severely limits their expenditures on food imports. The World Bank nutrition survey of Africa was based on data through 1986; since then, conditions have deteriorated further as world grain prices have climbed.

Time and space constraints have limited this assessment to global changes that will affect food production in the near term. Others, such as rising sea level and stratospheric ozone depletion, will exert a greater influence over the longer term. Increasing ultraviolet radiation is of particular concern because it could adversely effect both the oceanic food chain and the yield of the more sensitive crops, such as soybeans, the world's leading protein crop.

Nearly all the global changes that I have summarized are affecting the food prospect negatively. I have outlined the effect of many of these changes, including soil erosion, deforestation, increased rainfall runoff, decreased recycling of rainfall inland, waterlogging and salting of irrigation systems, falling water tables, grassland degradation, and shrinking cropland area and irrigation water supplies per person. In many countries, these negative influences on agriculture are now overriding the contribution of new investment and the adoption of more productive technologies designed to raise food per capita production.

The disturbing conclusion of this analysis is that the year 1984 may be a faultline separating two distinct eras in the world food economy.

Between 1950 and 1984, the world was able to systematically raise grain production per person, lifting it some 40 percent, or more than 1 percent per year. In the new era, dating from 1984, we may not be able to count on systematic worldwide gains in per capita food output without a massive reordering of priorities. Indeed, it could take many years merely to regain the 13 percent loss in per capita grain production since 1984.

In the new era, the food prospect may depend as much on the ability of energy policy makers to trim carbon emissions as on the ability of agricultural policy makers to stimulate food output. For if energy policy makers do not act quickly, they could leave farmers with an impossible task of trying to feed 86 million more people per year in the midst of potentially convulsive climate change.

And in the new circumstances, where expansion of food output is more difficult, achieving an acceptable balance between food and people may depend more on family planners than on farmers. The issue is not whether population growth will eventually slow; it will. The only question is whether it will slow because we quickly move toward smaller families or because we let hunger and rising death rates check population growth, as they now are doing in some countries in Africa.

The gap between what we need to do to protect our environmental support systems and what we are doing is widening. Unless we redefine security, recognizing that the principal threats to our future come less from the relationship of nation to nation and more from the deteriorating relationship between ourselves and the natural systems and resources on which we depend, then the human prospect as we enter the twenty-first century could be a bleak one. If we do not act quickly, there is a risk that environmental deterioration and social disintegration could begin to feed on each other.

## Questions from the Audience

Q   It is generally acknowledged that fossil fuels such as coal and petroleum are major contributors to the greenhouse effect. What would you like to see happen regarding the use of fossil fuels versus nuclear energy?

A   The most sensible thing to do, it seems to me, is to adopt the least-cost strategy for reducing the fossil fuel carbon emissions that comprise the bulk of greenhouse gases. There are long lists of investments that can be made toward that end, mostly in improved energy efficiency, some in using renewable energy sources.

To reduce carbon emissions, we have two or three decades of heavy investment ahead of us. This is still less costly than equivalent energy generated by nuclear power. Nuclear power also involves the potential for nuclear weapons. I'd like to see us move toward a non-nuclear world.

Q  To what extent does the potential of a northern shift in the growing season offset the overwarming effects?

A  There are near-term and long-term answers to that question. In the near term, I think there would be a substantial lag in the willingness of the Canadian government, say, to create infrastructure in the northernmost parts of the country, and of Canadian farmers to move in and invest in those new lands that might climatically become cultivable. It would take some years. Just as a matter of prudence, one would need to know that, in fact, the warming was real and that it was warm enough to move farms, say, 200 miles farther north. There would be a time lag.

In the long term, agriculture in the world has evolved in response to a particular climatic regime. Climate has changed very little since agriculture came on the scene ten thousand or so years ago. As a result, agriculture is keyed to the existing climate system. If climate begins to change, a lot of adjustments will have to be made. A lot of investments will have to be made. More irrigation here, more drainage there, and so on.

Another problem is that the soils in the northern reaches, for the most part, are not particularly good. The soils in northern Canada are fairly thin. There is only one corn belt in the world, and it's in the midwestern United States. It's a remarkable piece of real estate, and one reason we are the breadbasket of the world. If we lose that because it dries out, or becomes too hot to sustain corn production, and we have to go to small grains or something else, then we and the world will have lost a major asset.

There is a good chance the interior of the major continents, Asia and North America, will dry out, get hotter and dryer. Both happen to be important food-producing regions.

So, although there are agricultural pluses associated with the warming, my sense is that the minuses would greatly outweigh them in both the short run and the long run.

Q  You have spoken of the food crises perhaps galvanizing a helpful response. Isn't there at least as great a danger that it would simply accelerate the most dangerous threats, like deforestation and excessive pumping of world waters?

A  I believe the answer is yes, but it could go either way. The risk is that environmental deterioration, economic decline and social disintegration could begin to feed on each other. If environmental deterioration feeds on social disintegration, and conversely, then I think we're in trouble. People would become so preoccupied with short-term survival, it would be impossible for political leaders to take any actions that have long-term benefits. That, I think, is a real risk.

Q  These are all clearly transnational problems. Given the state of the world and the tendency of nations to defend their national sovereignty, do you think as a species we're advanced far enough to surrender some of these concepts of sovereignty and shift to greater cooperation among nations? Is there a solution to this problem?

A  We have to hope so. It is the big challenge of the next decade, and we think we've only got a decade to get things turned around. If all these trends I've been describing are still going on at the end of the next decade, then I think the social disintegration and environmental deterioration will be feeding on each other on a growing scale.

It's going to take a shift in the way we think about things. Historically, the closest equivalent would be the way we redefined the role of a victorious country after a war, as we did in the late 1940s. Traditionally, it had always been that if you win a war, you plunder. But we turned that around, and actually helped rebuild the countries that had lost the war. That was a major shift in thinking.

The question is, are we now at a point where we could quite literally redefine security? Can we recognize that today's real threats to the human prospect may not be so much the country-to-country conflicts, but the relationship between mankind, now numbering 5.2 billion, and the natural systems on which we all depend? It may not be the man-to-man but the man-to-nature relationship that now is threatening our future. If we can grasp that, and if we have some political leaders who can help translate it into policies and into international initiatives, then we have a chance.

One wonders where the Churchills and the Roosevelts will come from. It may be that Gorbachev is one of the national political leaders with the ability to move us in the right direction. At this point, however, one would have to conclude that Gorbachev is much better in conceptualizing and recognizing the need for changes, but has not been terribly successful yet in implementing changes. The implementation side, at least in his own society, has posed serious problems for him. Implementing economic reform, for example.

Perhaps the world needs someone like Gro Harlem Brundtland, the prime minister of Norway. She is playing an important role in helping reshape international thinking so that we might recognize that environmental deterioration may be the real threat now to the human future. We have to hope that such leaders will emerge at key places in the world, and will bring about the change in thinking called for by the changing times.

Q  You paint an apocalyptic picture, a return to the Dark Ages, but haven't people always muddled through? We did come through the Dust Bowl era and the Great Depression, when things were considerably worse worldwide than they are today.

A  Perhaps there is a similarity to the Dust Bowl and Great Depression era, but it is very remote. People in the world today are so dependent on cooperative, international efforts, economically and otherwise. Even in the Great Depression, most people in cities still had relatives on the farm, and many could get back to the farm and find some security. In a world where close to half the world's people are living in cities, that's no longer possible. So I don't think it would be a muddling through situation. We're either going to make it or we are not. The "not" side is pretty grim.

Q  What do you see concerning water conservation and water distribution issues?

A  Investments in water efficiency are still lagging in most of the world. And if there are to be any increases in the irrigated area in the years ahead, much of it must come from using water more efficiently.

In the United States, we need to move away from the essentially free water given many farmers in the West. Users should pay something like a market price for the water. That would cut out a great deal of waste. There are steps in that direction. But that's a big jump we ought to take quickly. It is simply an institutional weakness in our system.

Today we are as profligate with water as we were with oil before the big oil price hike. When the price of food goes up—this year, three years from now, whenever it is—and it's a big jump, then we'll get some serious rethinking about water and how to increase water efficiency. Water efficiency in agriculture will become an important indicator, as energy efficiency is for the economy today.

Q  Integrated pest management—the practice of reducing reliance on chemical pesticides—is highly regarded by EPA and many environmentalists. Do you see the practice falling by the wayside as we strive to increase worldwide food production, or are there elements of integrated pest management we can reasonably retain?

A   One almost has to look at individual situations to answer that. There are some cases where heavy reliance on chemical pest controls have simply reached the point where it's not working anymore. Insect resistance is such that there is very little control. That is a production effect.

A year ago in Indonesia, for example, they banned thirty-six of the major pesticides used on rice, particularly those to control the brown leaf hopper. They were using so much pesticide they were destroying all sorts of natural predators and upsetting natural balances. The pesticides simply weren't working, and they had to change. So, if one of the trends associated with use of chemical pest controls is falling production, then integrated pest management obviously would have a positive production effect.

Here's an interesting question: To what extent will the effort to make agriculture more sustainable around the world—that is, to assure longer term production—lead to reduced output in the short term? That is a question which, empirically, has not been seriously addressed.

I do think we get a little romantic sometimes. For example, we talk about doing away with chemical fertilizer. This country is exporting 100 million tons of grain a year. In that grain are several million tons of nutrients, pure nutrients: nitrogen, phosphate, potash, et cetera. If you are living in a interdependent world where there are hundreds of millions of people depending on that grain moving out of this country, then you have to be able to replace those nutrients in this country. There's no way of doing it organically on a large enough scale, so we are forced to use chemical fertilizer.

Look at China. China went probably as far as a country could in using all possible organic material for fertilizer. China discovered there was a limit to how many people they could support that way, and they had to turn to chemical fertilizers to keep moving production upward.

It's an important question, and I'm sure it is going to get more attention as food supplies tighten, and the concern about some of the consequences of increased use of pesticides grows.

Q   You have suggested that Malthus was right; that population does tend to increase faster than the means of subsistence. What magnitude of effort is needed on the family planning front to solve this problem?

A   It would probably require a greater change in human behavior in a shorter period of time than we've ever experienced at the global level.

But some individual countries —very large ones—have been successful in family planning, so we know it can be done. In the last chapter of *State of the World '89*, we propose two things on the population problem. One: As a general policy, the secretary general of the U.N. and the president of the World Bank should advocate the two-child family as an upper limit. This will be a worldwide goal, not something to be enforced. Two: Given, the food situation, and the fact that population growth is exacerbating almost all the global problems we face, from soil erosion to the buildup of greenhouse gases, we should try to cut world population growth in half between now and the end of the century. That means going from the current rate of about 1.7 percent per year to, say, .8 or .9 percent.

As I mentioned, two countries have actually done better than that. Between 1949 and 1956, Japan cut its population growth rate more than half. After the war, with their empire gone, they realized they had to live with the resources on the islands. That forced a dramatic shift in mindset about what the ideal family size in Japan would be.

The other country that cut its population growth rate in half was China. China did it between 1970 and 1976, a major achievement. They're having trouble now holding the line, as you know.

But the fact that these two countries, both substantial in size, have done this suggests that other countries, if they get serious, may also be able to do it. It's going to be tough. It would be a lot tougher, though, to have to accept the alternative, which is slower population growth caused by rising death rates.

Q   You've been very informative about some of the environmental and economic conditions we face. But what ideas do you have about choosing policies? What might we start thinking about that can help us out of this dilemma?

A   The kinds of things that need to be done, the key issues, are in the areas of energy policy and population policy.

Certainly, concerning energy policy, this country is in a position to play an important role by example. I would like to see us begin to systematically develop a U.S. program designed to contribute to a global carbon stabilization effort. The EPA might well provide leadership on this.

Unfortunately, for the last year or two, most of the leadership has been coming from Congress. There are at least three major climate stabilization bills on the Hill now. All three were there last year, and they've been reintroduced in the current session. That legislation should be coming from the administration. It's always awkward when

Congress tries to lead on these major issues, and that's what's happening at the moment.

On the population front: As a country, we must begin to recognize the population threat for what it is—a trend that can certainly undermine civilization as we know it. It has already begun to, in some parts of the world. Then we need to speak out on the subject.

Q   What *is* the current world trend in population?

A   The growth in world population was just under 2 percent per year around 1970. It's edged down very slowly since then. It's now about 1.7 percent. But the edging down has been so slow, that the annual increment is continuing to increase. In other words, in 1970 we were adding about 70 million people a year. We're now adding about 88 million people a year.

So the overall trend has not been encouraging. Although a few countries have done very well, the world as a whole has not.

Q   Do you see a need in this country to change the structure or relationship of state and federal institutions that control our natural resources and environment matters?

A   What is most needed now is leadership, not changes in institutions or agencies of governments. In the kind of political system we have, we heavily depend on the head of state for leadership, and if we don't we get it, then it's very difficult.

If we're going to turn things around—given the enormous amount of change that's required in such a short period of time—it's going to take a lot of information to underpin and guide that change.

We don't have time to train a generation of teachers, who would train a generation of students, who a generation later will become decision makers. That's not an option any more. The changes have to come within a matter of years among those of us who are already making decisions. The media are going to have to play an important role in raising the level of public understanding of issues to the point where the public will support an effective policy response.

In this vein I would cite one simple example, namely, the January 2, 1989 issue of *Time* magazine—the "Planet of the Year" issue. If you saw it, you'll remember they had thirty-two pages devoted, in effect, to the state of the planet. At the end of each section; climate, waste, population, et cetera, they had a list of recommendations on the important steps that needed to be taken worldwide.

*Time's* handling of the subject represents a major departure for news magazines, and the media generally. Senior management at *Time* decided they could no longer simply report on the problems, but had to become involved in helping formulate a response. Certainly, that's a little dangerous journalistically, particularly if the subject is not a relatively neutral one, such as the environment, but I think it's a risk that we now have to take.

*Time*'s thirty-two-page section was not news analysis, it was a giant editorial. They didn't just assign a half-dozen writers to produce it. They convened a conference of about thirty people from around the world who work on these issues—people like me from various countries. For two days we worked on the issues in a very intensive way, with their senior reporters and editors. That became the basis for the special issue, and gave it some credibility.

Of all the institutional gaps that exist, I think the one between what the media are now doing and what they will need to do is perhaps one of the greatest.

I am indebted to my colleague John Young, for his assistance with research and analysis, and to Sandra Postel and Chris Flavin, for their review and constructive suggestions.

[MAY 16, 1989]

---

BIOGRAPHY

Lester Brown is the founder and president of the Worldwatch Institute. The institute is an independent, not-for-profit research organization established to alert decision-makers and the general public to emerging global trends in the availability and management of human and natural resources. The institute publishes an annual *State of the World Report* in fourteen languages.

Mr. Brown is a member of the U.S. committee for UNICEF, the Planning Committee for New Directions, and is on the boards of directors of the Overseas Development Council and numerous associations and professional societies. He has authored or coauthored *By Bread Alone, Building a Sustainable Society*, and eight other books.

In 1986, Mr. Brown was honored with a MacArthur Foundation award. In 1989 he won the Sasakawa Environment Prize.

From 1959 to 1969, he worked for the U.S. Department of Agriculture, becoming administrator of the International Agriculture Department Service. In 1969 he was appointed a senior fellow with the Overseas Development Council, a position he held until he founded the Worldwatch Institute in 1974.

---

# The End of the Beginning

During twenty years in leadership positions in protecting the environment at local, state, national, and international levels, I have developed a healthy respect for EPA. I consider your institution one of the most important in our country. I recognize the members of your staff as dedicated, conscientious, competent, hard-working, underpaid public servants. And I consider your administrator, Bill Reilly, an outstanding leader with the training, experience, global perspective, and demonstrated commitment necessary for his super-important assignment. Thank you for what you are doing, and thanks for the opportunity to speak to you about your mission, and my mission, to save the biosphere.

I do not wish to belabor you with a discussion of the specifics of the many programs and technologies with which you are involved. You are much more knowledgeable and qualified than I to cope with them. It is my objective, rather, to consider the basic causes of the problems that you are assigned, and societal forces at work that complicate your assignment.

The world is facing a mounting environmental crisis—caused by *Homo sapiens'* cumulative assaults on the biosphere—a testimony of our sorry stewardship of planet Earth. The crisis stems from a converging of many growing threats to plant, animal, and human life. You know what they are, but let me enumerate some of them: the building up of greenhouse gases in the atmosphere, altering the climate; forests cut ten times, or more, faster than they are replaced; hazardous wastes

RUSSELL PETERSON, founding chairman of the Global Tomorrow Coalition, is president emeritus of the National Audubon Society.

recycled through drinking-water faucets; radioactive wastes added daily to huge, unsafe stockpiles; the extinction of plants and animals, narrowing Earth's crucial biological diversity; chlorofluorocarbons destroying the ozone layer; oil befouling coastal resources; dumps requiring hundreds of billions of dollars to clean up; wetlands and crop lands disappearing as cities and deserts expand; wastes closing beaches; smog deteriorating urban life; consumption of natural resources by affluent nations growing exponentially; over one billion people in absolute poverty scouring the countryside for fuel and food.

Clearly our security, nationally and globally, is being lost.

The problems I listed are the *symptoms* of the environmental disease that plagues our planet. The *cause* is exponential growth both in the number of humans and in our use of natural resources. The world population has more than doubled since World War II, and is now growing in absolute numbers faster than ever before—approximately 90 million more per year. The world economy has grown more than fivefold since World War II, and is projected to grow at least fivefold over the next half century. The cumulative impact on the biosphere of these two combined forces—ever more people using ever more resources—provides an awesome challenge to world leadership and a super threat to the quality of life of future generations.

Not only have we world citizens been spending and wasting and despoiling our descendants' natural inheritance, we have been saddling them with huge debts. Here in the United States we have, especially in the past eight years, spent far beyond our income, drying up the investment funds required to cope with the cumulating predicament. A prime cause of this financial problem is the maintenance—even though we are at peace—of a military machine that is thousands of times more powerful and destructive than any that ever existed before—even in wartime. While at peace, this machine has run rampant over the environment, becoming the worst polluter in our country, dumping nuclear and other poisonous wastes at thousands of sites.

Of much greater significance to the environment is the work of the military machines of the U.S., the USSR, Britain, France and China, and their industrial, political, and scientific cohorts in creating, producing, and deploying nuclear weapons—the common enemy of all life. The nuclear ordnance on one U.S Trident II submarine, for example, could ignite enough cities and oil tank fields to produce sufficient smoke to block out sunlight, lowering temperatures and devastating agriculture and plant and animal life over wide areas of the world. Many scientists have come to believe in the potential for this nuclear global cooling and its catastrophic biological consequences.

The tens of thousands of nuclear warheads deployed around the world by today's five nuclear powers, and the hundreds of thousands of troops trained to use them, make a catastrophe due to equipment failure, human error, or unauthorized firing, disturbingly possible. The accidents caused by humans at Three Mile Island and Chernobyl, the shooting down by mistake of a commercial airliner by a modern sophisticated warship, an oil tanker straying out of a ten-mile-wide channel to hit a well-known reef, illustrate the potential for human error to frustrate the most carefully designed safety programs. Until the day when nuclear weapons might be banned globally, environmentalists should work to lower the number of nuclear weapons to some small fraction, say 5 percent, of today's inventory, and provide multiple safeguards against inadvertent use of the remainder.

All the threats the global environment I have discussed have been recognized for decades by many people of vision, the so-called doomsayers. Here is what Albert Einstein wrote in 1947:

> We are shrunk into one community with a common fate. . . . Everyone is aware of that situation, but only a few act accordingly. Most people go on living their everyday life; half frightened, half indifferent, they behold a ghostly tragi-comedy that is being performed on the

international stage. But on that stage, on which the actors under the flood-lights play their ordained parts, our fate of tomorrow, life or death of the nations, is being decided.

Major obstacles to the world's facing up to the impending crisis have been the preoccupation of the people with the near term, and their excessive dedication to material progress. Decision makers are primarily concerned with improving this quarter's financial statement, getting reelected next election, gaining tenure, or obtaining funding.

What is needed are more people, and especially leaders, who think comprehensively and globally, who weigh the impact of today's decisions on the quality of life of future generations, and who gain job satisfaction primarily from contributing to the welfare of others. It is urgent that more people practice what President John F. Kennedy advised: "Ask not what your country can do for you, but what you can do for your country." For my purpose today, let me paraphrase it this way: "Ask not what your biosphere can do for you, but what you can do for your biosphere."

Toward this end, I believe that each of us should adopt a responsible Earth ethic, such as to accept the moral duty and obligation as a citizen of the world to protect the biosphere by learning of the interdependence of all life, the atmosphere, waters and soils. We must further society's assessment of the long-term impacts on the biosphere of actions before they're undertaken, so as to be able to make responsible choices among alternative futures. To further such an ethic, we must emphasize more extensive and effective teaching about the whole. In light of our current understanding of the implications to all walks of life of the global interdependence of things, no one whose training is solely in a traditional discipline can justifiably claim to be adequately educated.

One earlier champion of seeing things whole was the renowned biologist, Aldo Leopold, born 102 years ago. He put it this way: "All the sciences and arts are taught as though they were separate. They are separate only in the classroom. Step out on the campus and they are immediately fused."

What are required are securely funded colleges of integrated studies that award bachelor's, master's, and Ph.D. degrees in integrated studies. Such institutions, through rigorous undergraduate and graduate training, could produce professional generalists who think comprehensively, globally and long-term; who understand the interdependence of all things; who integrate the technical, economic, social, environmental, and political variables involved; and who assess the long-term impacts and feedbacks of their decisions. This is the training required for the most important jobs in our society. Yet no institution provides it.

There is no place in the federal government where consideration of the whole is carried out, where the goals, problems, resources, opportunities, and alternative actions are considered from a global and long-term perspective with a concern for quality of life of future generations. The Council on Environmental Quality (CEQ) was set up to contribute to such an integrated perspective, but the Reagan administration scuttled it, converting it from the environmental conscience of the executive branch to an apologist for the antienvironmental actions of the Reagan administration. What we need now is to combine CEQ, the Council of Economic Advisors, and the National Security Council into a new entity, a council of holistic advisors.

Certainly the world's movers and shakers need to give more attention routinely to the longer-range impact of their decisions. For example, society needs more of a say in the type of technology that is used to satisfy its needs. We cannot leave the choice of technology strictly to consideration of the financial return to be gained by those who invest in it.

We in the United States and other Western nations are proud of our free enterprise, market-oriented economies, and rightly so. The record clearly shows how the countless market decisions of millions of us day after day, functioning as Adam Smith's "invisible hand," have steered a course to the great benefit of most of us. But the record also shows that such a system can be corrupted by the decisions of a powerful few, acting in their own self-interest and/or in ignorance or denial of the long-term or global consequences of their decisions. In light of current understanding, Adam Smith would probably have called this force the "invisible foot." It will kick us in the future if we ignore the long-term and global consequences of our present actions.

To avoid being kicked by the invisible foot, we need government intervention. This is clearly the case in protecting the environment. The market will not do it.

For example, the dumping of hazardous wastes over past decades permitted the selling in the marketplace of better things for better living at lower costs. But now it appears that it will take fifty years and hundreds of billions of dollars, charged to future production and future taxpayers, to clean up the inherited mess. It is difficult to believe that any competent institution assigned to provide our nations with some foresight capability would not have foreseen several decades ago, in the light of the explosive growth of the chemical industry, the need for controls to ensure a safe and practical means of disposing of the thousands of new chemicals being created annually. In so doing, they would also have provided the insight to ensure that the users of the new chemicals paid the price to cover the costs of their appropriate disposal, rather than passing such costs onto future generations. Given such sound economic considerations, some hazardous chemicals would have lost out to other materials in the competitive marketplace.

Currently, we continue to exhibit similar but more serious negligence as we fail to bring our nation's foresight to bear on the nuclear waste problem. Even though nuclear energy has been with us for only a short time, we have already accumulated a frightening array of wastes, including mountains of uranium mill-tailings, billions of cubic feet of low-level waste, deadly high-level wastes now held at dozens of locations around the country, and abandoned radioactive buildings and facilities that stand under guard—all awaiting the nation's decision to spend as much to dispose of them as it did to build them. Recent disclosures show that our government's lack of foresight in handling wastes at its nuclear weapons facilities was especially outrageous.

The development of nuclear energy in the 1960s was projected in the myopia of the specialists involved at that time to provide electricity "too cheap to meter." But in 1985 one of the world's leading business magazines, Forbes, reported, "The failure of the U.S. nuclear power program ranks as the largest managerial disaster in business history, a disaster on a monumental scale." The management had ignored many of the safety and environmental problems, and when government forced them to face up to some of these problems, the costs became excessive.

The increasing evidence that low-frequency electromagnetic radiation may be a serious threat to life provides another example of how those closest to the problem and responsible for it denied its existence, and for fifteen years downplayed and belittled disturbing findings of investigator after investigator. This is a problem that called for a major in-depth study that a courageous impartial guardian of the public interest, such as EPA, should provide. EPA needs to be given the resources to do such jobs.

The genetic engineering of plants and bacteria is a new field that calls for EPA's careful oversight and control. The initial reports of developments in this field are highly optimistic, accentuating the positive. This is typical of new developments unless they have some obvious major flaws. Products with unrecognized negatives will sail ahead in the euphoria of this new science. Strong pressure will be applied by scientists and by industry to overcome the "nay-saying of the regulatory bureaucrats." I believe that government should presume all such new creations guilty until proven innocent. This, no doubt, will slow up development, and may well call for extending patent rights to provide for such delay.

Many of the uses foreseen for genetically engineered bacteria are in environmental control processes, and thus a special potential benefit to EPA's mission. In those cases, EPA will especially need to be aware of the invisible foot.

The fear that governmental planning and regulations to protect the environment are harmful to a market-oriented economy is misplaced. Government regulations and a market economy complement each other. Neither can do the job alone. Fortunately, many leaders in the business community now recognize this.

Also fortunately, today the people of the world are getting the environmental message. Polls show that an ever-higher percentage are concerned about their environment. In the United States in June of 1989, according to a *New York Times*/CBS News poll, 80 percent of the people agreed that "protecting the environment is so important that requirements and standards cannot be too high, and continuing environmental improvements must be made, regardless of cost."

A survey by the conference board of the leaders of several hundred major companies found that they ranked environmental problems as the top priority issue for business in the next five years. Business now recognizes that environmental degradation is detrimental to everyone's bottom line.

The recent quickening in international environmental conferences, treaties, protocols, and environmental speeches by world leaders is another encouraging sign. The Paris summit meeting in July 1989 of the heads of the seven industrialized nations produced, for the first time in any summit meeting, a communique that dealt with environmental issues. Although it noted many of the critical problems, it committed no funds and didn't even mention the greatest threats to the environment, nuclear weapons and exponential growth in population and in consumption of resources. Nevertheless, this was a major milestone. Let's hope that communique is a precursor to much-needed action.

What needs to be done is known. We must use energy more efficiently. Develop alternative sources of energy. Plant trees. Recycle materials. Further family planning and develop better contraceptives. Practice more sustainable agriculture. Establish and enforce more restrictive environmental laws. Presume new chemicals guilty until proven innocent. Further safer natural agents for pest control. Develop industrial processes and products that reduce pollution and waste. Stop squandering resources on killing machines and wars. And elect people who recognize all these needs and are willing to put saving the world ahead of reelection.

The resources to do the job are available. What is required is the political will to allocate the resources. The person with the greatest authority and greatest responsibility to face up to the global crisis is President Bush, backed up by the person he has chosen to lead his environmental program, EPA's Administrator William Reilly. It is exciting what EPA has done recently in facing up to critical environmental problems, such as banning most uses of asbestos, supporting strong clean air legislation, stopping construction of the Two Forks Dam, furthering international cooperation on the global warming and ozone layer depletion problems, and pushing for legislation to give EPA authority to ban hazardous pesticides more promptly.

President Bush, in addition to appointing Bill Reilly, has expressed his support for the environment, spoken out for clean air legislation, and joined with other heads of state in putting the environment on the agenda for the summit meeting for the first time in history.

There has clearly been a break with the Reagan era, but this is not the time to relax. It is only the end of the beginning.

Now the president and the Congress must put their money where their mouths are, and the whole cabinet must get in line with the president's environmentalism. As yet, no additional funding has been provided, and the cabinet members' track records indicate that they will have to undergo a major conversion to be helpful to Bill Reilly. Not one of them in the past has demonstrated a commitment to protecting the environment.

The League of Conservation Voters, on a scale of zero to one hundred, scored Secretary of Defense Cheney and HUD Secretary Kemp zero, Interior Secretary Lujan 13, and Vice President Quayle 20 for their environmental performance during the last congress. Secretary of State Baker was chief of staff in the Reagan White House, when they devastated the nation's environmental institutions and budgets. Energy Secretary Watkins's record shows him a strong proponent of nuclear energy. Chief of Staff John Sununu earned no plaudits from environmentalists when he was governor of New Hampshire. These people have all strongly pushed exponential growth in development, resisting any environmental regulations that they thought presented any potential injury to business, real or perceived.

In the critical population era, the Bush administration, led by the president himself, has continued the Reagan administration's policy. It has gone all out to support the right-to-life forces in strongly opposing family planning, the principal means of reducing population growth.

Thus, to deal with the two basic causes of the global environmental predicament—exponential growth in development and in population—this team will have to get a new religion.

It is of concern to me that the new administration, during its campaign to spend tens of billions of dollars on new nuclear weapons, has not, publicly at least, acknowledged that they understand or are concerned about the long-range biological consequences of the deliberate or inadvertent use of nuclear weapons. All other threats to the climate, to ozone layer, air and water quality, plant and animal species, and agriculture pale in comparison.

It seems to me the EPA should be given the charter and the resources to deal with a whole range of causes, symptoms, and cures of national and global and environmental degradation. This should include deep involvement in the energy, population, and economic development areas.

And EPA should be given cabinet-level status. Its concerns cut across all of the areas of national and international responsibility assigned to the other departments, and demonstrate the need for integrating the plans and programs of the whole government. Certainly the protection of Earth's life-support systems is every bit as important to our security as the military and the economy.

EPA's authority within the government also needs to be strengthened so it can force such gross offenders as the Department of Defense and the Department of Energy to abide by the nation's environmental laws and regulations. How can the government claim to be a protector of the environment while excelling in polluting the environment?

Just to carry out its current assignment, EPA needs a doubling of its current $1.7 billion operating budget. The Reagan administration's drastic cuts in its funds and staff were outrageous. In light of the serious environmental crisis facing our nation and the world, it is downright criminal that the agency has less purchasing power today than it had eight years ago, even though the workload has doubled or tripled.

It is difficult to believe that the American people wouldn't consider their security more enhanced by spending another $1.7 billion on your research, monitoring, and enforcement to protect their environment than, for example, $5 billion spent on research on the dream of shielding us from incoming missiles. But no token increase such as $1.7 billion in the environmental programs will suffice. A much more significant investment in saving the biosphere is called for.

An initial infusion worldwide by governments—say, $140 billion per year—on replicating the successful programs I listed earlier would have dramatic impact on altering today's life-threatening trends. How much is $140 billion? Well, that's the amount by which the United States increased its military budget over the past eight years.

The U.S. government might respond over the next few years to the strong current wish of the American people to reduce military spending, taking $50 billion from the Pentagon's budget to invest in protecting the biosphere, thereby truly increasing the world's security. Western Europe, Japan, and the Soviet Union could be encouraged to put up the remaining $90 billion. The heads of states of these nations could then speak with authority about saving the world, and together spark a worldwide moral commitment to mutually assured survival.

Today we have superpowers in the military field, superpowers in the economic field, but nary a superpower in the environmental field.

In his *State of the World, 1988*, Lester Brown, president of World-Watch, developed a proposal for the world to build up its annual "investment in environment security" by $150 billion per year over the next ten years, while reducing its military expenditures from $900 billion per year to $750 billion. He defined specific programs for protecting topsoil and croplands, reforesting the Earth, slowing population growth, raising energy efficiency and developing renewable energy, and retiring Third World debt. His proposal might be expanded by including programs to develop industrial processes that reduce waste and pollution at the source, to further integrated pest management, and to recycle materials. Such planning involving these large expenditures has been criticized as trying to solve the problem by "throwing money at it." On the contrary, it offers the opportunity to invest in a sure thing. Each of the technologies or processes recommended has already been demonstrated on a large scale. Let me illustrate with two examples.

Hundreds of millions of women from both affluent and poor countries, when given the knowledge and wherewithal to practice family planning, have done so, and thereby reduced their countries' population growth. The hundreds of millions of others who want to avoid unwanted pregnancies need to be given the same choice.

By using energy more efficiently and by developing renewable forms of energy, people all over the world have demonstrated how to reduce the use of fossil fuel and nuclear energy, thereby reducing the production of greenhouse gas, acid rain, urban smog, and radioactive waste. Although this so-called soft energy path is the least expensive and most effective way of coping with global warming, acid rain, urban smog, and oil import problems, the Reagan administration almost terminated an effective large-scale government program in this area while continuing to subsidize fossil fuels and nuclear energy. Now is the time for the Bush administration to reverse this direction and put a major effort behind the soft energy path.

As I said before, EPA needs to be involved in these two fields—population and energy—both so fundamental to EPA's assignment to protect the environment. A staff is required to carry out ongoing studies of the impact of population growth and the consumption of resources on the environment, to promote the establishment of a U.S. population policy, and to further increased funding for contraceptive research and for family planning around the world. An additional EPA group is required to function in government somewhat as Amory Lovins's Rocky Mountain Institute does in the private sector, developing and promoting soft energy paths, seeing that our government plays a major role in furthering this most promising route to environmental protection.

EPA is clearly the agency that needs to lead the way and to coordinate our country's overall efforts to save the biosphere in concert with the world community. The people of our country are now strongly behind the agency, giving it great power—the power to stand up to OMB, the cabinet, and the Congress—in fighting for what we all need.

I have focused much of my attention here on areas outside EPA's normal sphere of activity. This should not connote any lack of respect for the agency's important current assignments and its major contribution to protecting the environment. I admire and thank you for your loyalty and persistent dedication to your job during a difficult period. Now is the time for the president and the Congress to give you the resources, reinforcements, and greater authority you require.

The world cannot wait much longer for invigorated action on a comprehensive global environmental agenda. It is time for more people everywhere to become environmental activists—to be part of the solution rather than remain part of the problem. Each of us can make a difference, and the greater one's authority, the greater one's duty to this cause.

## Questions from the Audience

*Q*  You have talked about the importance of market forces and of education in protecting the environment. EPA has been involved to some extent in these. Should it play a larger role?

*A*  I certainly would recommend a larger role for EPA, certainly in educating society, educating the executive branch of the government, educating the Congress, educating the people about the problems involved. There are many examples of problems that we are coping with today that certainly, with hindsight, we could have avoided or minimized with a little attention to their potential implications.

I think that you can also see the incentive to the marketers to get aboard this kind of program. I don't think my suggesting $140 billion a year is reckless. It could be an early type of infusion that will grow, as the whole world gets involved. And that would provide a great market for earnings opportunities and for jobs. I can't understand why anybody who knows anything about business or economics can oppose spending this money. What do you spend $100 billion for? Buying equipment, hiring people to do things, both of which add to the GNP, if that means anything. It certainly provides jobs and income. It's a new market.

When I was at Du Pont, for a while one of my jobs was to look to the future—to decide what products the people were going to want and need, so that we could invent them and make them available. Society's growing demands for environmental protection should lead today's research directors and new product managers to say, "My gosh, what a golden opportunity there will be in the environmental area for our free market economy. Let's get with it!"

Some of them are already doing it. I just saw an article in the *New York Times* about a new business newsletter for people involved in protecting the environment. It's a growth industry. Invest your money there!

You at EPA could be teaching ideas like that—teaching people in the Department of Commerce, the Treasury Department, and the White House who, historically, have been principal propagators of the false message that environmental programs harm the economy. Certainly the need to be environmentally sound may put out of business some plants that are out of date, broken down, and polluting our homes. That's great. Replace them with modern facilities that operate more efficiently and do not foul up the environment. Most progressive companies, by the way, put their own outmoded processes out of business regularly.

Q  Both Gus Speth and you have talked about the need for an elemental change in the way society operates. How do you think that's going to come about?

A  Today, there is a rapidly growing concern by people all over the world (including in the developing countries) about the way their life-support processes are being threatened. People in the business community are concerned about the well-being of their children and grandchildren. I believe that that concern is going to lead to the elemental change to which you refer.

I do a lot of talking around the country on some of these issues, and it is amazing how people respond to it. And that goes for Republicans and Democrats and, regarding the population issue, Catholics and Protestants, Hindus and others. The people are ripe for such a move.

President Bush and President Gorbachev are the most effective teachers in the world, for better or for worse. Imagine—they can go anywhere in the world and talk to hundreds of millions of people, and everybody else writes about it and discusses it. Fantastic.

But when President Reagan was using the pulpit to teach that there wasn't any environmental problem, and was acting to destroy our environmental institutions and regulations, he set our country back. A lot of people were relieved by his optimistic message, but it was wrong. We need a president who is willing to get in tune with the long-term wishes of the people, such as the desire for our provision of a decent environment for future generations, and to use his pulpit to teach how we can work together to make that happen.

Ed Woolard, who recently became chief executive officer of Du Pont, in a speech to the U.S. Chamber of Commerce in London said he now recognizes that industry as a whole has not really faced up to environmental issues. Although he thought Du Pont had done a better job than some others, even they hadn't faced up to the problem adequately. Now that he was the CEO, he had to be the chief environmentalist as well. He said he was going to work to be a steward of the environment. He said that it is important not only to our children and future generations, but to the economic health of the company as well.

Q  Would it be a good idea to give an environmental seal of approval to businesses that do a good job?

*A* Yes, I think it would be a very good thing. Everybody likes to be recognized. And when you acknowledge that a person is doing a good job, that is a way of educating and teaching others.

The Better World Society, in which I am involved, gives five awards annually for work toward building a world that provides a decent quality of life on a sustainable basis. We've given several awards to corporations. We gave one to Merck, for example, which puts up the money for providing the means to eliminate river blindness. Merck is determined to continue until river blindness is eradicated. Their own funding and their own research developed the drug that does the job. They have received a lot of publicity for this.

We also gave an award to Chico Mendez of Brazil, who was fighting corporations. He was a rubber tapper who organized the rubber tappers to block the cutting of trees in the Amazon. He was assassinated this past year by people who want to cut down the trees for grazing land. We have publicized that award in Latin America and in this country on major television programs, pointing out what Chico Mendez did and telling the story of the forests.

[JULY 25, 1989]

---

BIOGRAPHY

Russell W. Peterson, a Ph.D. chemist, was employed for twenty-six years by the Du Pont Company, serving for fourteen of them as a director of research and development.

From 1969 until 1973 he was governor of the State of Delaware. He was chairman of the President's Council on Environmental Quality under President Ford, and then director of the Office of Technology Assessment of the U.S. Congress.

Dr. Peterson has been president and CEO of the National Audubon Society, president of the Better World Society, vice president of the International Union for the Conservation of Nature, and founding chairman of the Global Tomorrow Coalition. He is currently president of the International Council for Bird Preservation, and an active member of the boards of the Population Crisis Committee, the Alliance to Save Energy, and Governor Mario Cuomo's Environmental Advisory Board.

---

# Croesus and
# Cassandra

## Policy Response
## to Global Change*

Apollo, an Olympian, was god of the sun. He was also in charge of matters other than sunlight, one of which was prophecy—that was one of his specialties. Now the Olympian gods could all see into the future a little, but Apollo was the only one who systematically offered this gift to humans. He established oracles, the most famous of which was at Delphi, where he sanctified the priestess. She was called the Pythia. Kings and aristocrats—and occasionally ordinary people—would come to Delphi and beg to know what was to be.

Among the supplicants was Croesus, King of Lydia. We remember him in the phrase "rich as Croesus," which is still nearly current. Part of the reason he was so rich is that he's one of the people who invented money—the first coins were Lydian, and were minted during Croesus's reign. (Lydia was in Anatolia, contemporary Turkey.) His ambition could not be contained within the boundaries of his small nation. And so, according to Herodotus's *History,* he got it into his head that it would be a good idea to invade and subdue Persia, the superpower of the 7th century B.C. Cyrus had united the Persians and the Medes and forged a

*Copyright© 1990 by Carl Sagan. A similar talk was delivered as the Oersted Medal Acceptance Address, American Association of Physics Teachers, Atlanta, January 23, 1990, and is published in *The American Journal of Physics.*

CARL SAGAN, creator of the TV series *Cosmos*, is professor of astronomy and space sciences at Cornell University.

mighty Persian Empire. Naturally, Croesus had some degree of trepidation.

In order to judge the wisdom of invasion, he dispatched emissaries to consult the Delphic Oracle. You can imagine them laden with opulent gifts—which, incidentally, were still on display in Delphi a century later, in Herodotus's time. The question the emissaries put on Croesus's behalf was "What will happen if Croesus makes war on Persia?"

Without hesitation, the Pythia answered, "He will destroy a mighty empire."

"The gods are with us," thought Croesus, or words to that effect. "Time to invade!"

Licking his chops and counting the satrapies shortly to be his, he gathered his mercenary armies. Croesus then invaded Persia—and was humiliatingly defeated. Not only was Lydian power destroyed, but he himself became, for the rest of his life, a pathetic functionary in the Persian court, offering little pieces of advice to often indifferent officials—a hanger-on ex-king. It's a little bit like the Emperor Hirohito living out his days as a consultant on the beltway in Washington, D.C.

Well, the injustice of it really got to him. After all, he had played by the rules. He had asked for advice from the Pythia, he had paid handsomely, and she had done him wrong. So he sent another emissary to the Oracle (with much more modest gifts this time, appropriate to his diminished circumstances) and asked, "How could you do this to me?" Here, from Herodotus's *History*, is the answer:

> The prophecy given by Apollo ran that if Croesus made war upon Persia, he would destroy a mighty empire. Now in the face of that, if he had been well-advised, he should have sent and inquired again, whether it was his own empire or that of Cyrus that was spoken of. But Croesus did not understand what was said, nor did he make question again. And so he has no one to blame but himself.

If the Delphic Oracle were only a scam to fleece credulous kings, then of course it would have needed excuses to explain away the inevitable mistakes. Disguised ambiguities were its stock in trade. Nevertheless, the lesson of the Pythia is germane: Even of oracles we must ask questions, intelligent questions—even when they seem to tell us exactly what we wish to hear. The policy makers must not blindly accept; they must understand. And they must not let their own ambitions stand in the way of understanding. The conversion of prophecy into policy must be done with care.

This advice is fully applicable to the modern oracles, the scientists and think tanks and universities. The policy makers send, sometimes reluctantly, to ask of the oracle, and the answer comes back. These days the oracles often volunteer their prophecies even when no one asks. In either case, the policy makers must then decide what, if anything, to do in response. The first thing to do is to understand. And because of the nature of the modern oracles and their prophecies, policy makers need—more than ever before—to understand science and technology.

But there's another story about Apollo and oracles, at least equally relevant. This is the story of Cassandra, princess of Troy. (It begins just before the Greeks invade Troy to start the Trojan War.) She was the smartest and the most beautiful of the daughters of King Priam. Apollo, constantly on the prowl for attractive humans (as were virtually all the Greek gods and goddesses), fell in love with her. Oddly—this almost never happens in Greek myth—she resisted his advances. So he tried to bribe her. But what could he give her? She was already a princess. She was rich and beautiful. She was happy. Still, Apollo had a thing or two to offer. He promised her the gift of prophecy. The offer was irresistible. She agreed. *Quid pro quo.* Apollo did whatever it is that gods do to create seers, oracles, and prophets out of mere mortals. But then, scandalously, Cassandra reneged. She refused the overtures of a god.

Apollo was not amused. But he couldn't withdraw the gift of prophecy, because, after all, he was a god. (Whatever else you might say about them, gods keep their promises.) Instead, he condemned her to a cruel and ingenious fate: that no one would believe her prophecies. (What I'm recounting here is largely in Aeschylus's play *Agamemnon*.) So Cassandra predicts to her own people the fall of Troy. Nobody pays attention. She predicts the death of the leading Greek invader, Agamemnon. Nobody pays attention. She even predicts her own early death, and still no one pays attention. They didn't want to hear. They made fun of her. They called her—Greeks and Trojans both—"the lady of many sorrows." Today perhaps they would dismiss her as a "prophet of doom and gloom."

There's a nice moment when she can't understand how it is that these prophecies of impending catastrophe—some of which, if believed, could be prevented—were being ignored. She says to the Greeks, "How is it you don't understand me? Your tongue I know only too well." But the problem wasn't her pronunciation of Greek. The answer (I'm paraphrasing) was, "You see, it's like this. Even the Delphic Oracle sometimes makes mistakes. Sometimes its prophecies are ambiguous. We can't be sure. And if we can't be sure, we're going to ignore it." That's the closest she gets to a substantive response.

The story was the same with the Trojans: "I prophesied to my countrymen," she says, "all their disasters." But they ignored her prophecies and were destroyed. Soon, so was she.

The resistance to dire prophecy that Cassandra experienced can be recognized today. If we are faced with an ominous prediction involving powerful forces that may not be readily influenced, we have a natural tendency to reject or ignore the prophecy. Mitigating or circumventing the danger might take time, effort, money, courage. It might require us to alter the priorities of our lives. And not every prediction of disaster, even among those made by scientists, is fulfilled: Most animal life in the oceans did not perish due to insecticides; despite Ethiopia and the Sahel, worldwide famine has not been a hallmark of the 1980s; supersonic transports do not threaten the ozone layer—although all these predictions had been made by serious scientists. So when faced with a new and uncomfortable prediction, we might be tempted to say: "Improbable." "Doom and gloom." "We've never experienced anything remotely like it." "Trying to frighten everyone." "Bad for public morale." What's more, if the factors precipitating the anticipated catastrophe are longstanding, then the prediction itself is an indirect or unspoken rebuke. Why have we permitted this peril to develop? Shouldn't we have informed ourselves about it earlier? Don't we ourselves bear complicity, since we didn't take steps to insure that government leaders eliminated the threat? And since these are uncomfortable ruminations—that our own inattention and inaction may have put us and our loved ones in danger—there is a natural, if sometimes maladaptive, tendency to reject the whole business. It will need much better evidence, we say, before we can take it seriously. There is a temptation to minimize, dismiss, forget. Psychiatrists are fully aware of this temptation. They call it "denial." The rock group Dire Straits has a line in one of their songs: "Denial ain't just a river in Egypt."

The stories of Croesus and Cassandra represent the two extremes of policy response to predictions of deadly danger—Croesus himself representing the pole of credulous, uncritical acceptance, propelled by greed or other character flaws; and the Greek and Trojan response to Cassandra, representing the pole of stolid, immobile rejection of the possibility of danger. The job of the policy maker is to steer a prudent course between these two shoals.

Suppose a group of scientists claims that a major environmental catastrophe is looming. Suppose further that what is required to prevent or mitigate the catastrophe is expensive: expensive in fiscal and intellectual resources, but also in challenging our way of thinking—that is, politically expensive. At what point do the policy makers have to take the scientific prophets seriously? There are ways to assess the validity of the modern prophecies—because in the methods of science, there is an error-correcting procedure, a set of rules that have repeatedly worked well, sometimes called the scientific method. There are a number of tenets: Arguments from authority carry little weight ("Because I said so" isn't good enough); quantitative prediction is an extremely good way to sift useful ideas from nonsense; the methods of analysis must yield other results fully consistent with what we know about the universe; vigorous debate is a healthy sign; the same conclusions have to be drawn independently by competing scientific groups for an idea to be taken seriously; and so on. There are ways for policy makers to decide, to find a safe middle path between precipitate action and impassivity.

We sometimes hear about the "ocean" of air surrounding the Earth. But the thickness of most of the atmosphere—including all of it involved in the greenhouse effect—is only 0.1 percent of the diameter of the Earth. Even if we include the high stratosphere, the atmosphere isn't as much as 1 percent of the Earth's diameter. "Ocean" sounds massive, imperturbable. But the thickness of the air, compared to the size of the Earth, is something like the thickness of a coat of shellac on a globe. Many astronauts have reported seeing that delicate, thin, blue aura at the horizon of the daylit hemisphere and immediately, unbidden, contemplating its fragility and vulnerability. They have reason to worry.

Today we face an absolutely new circumstance, unprecedented in all of human history. When we started out, hundreds of thousands of years ago, say, with an average population density of a hundredth of a person per square kilometer or less, the triumphs of our technology were hand axes and fire; we were unable to make major changes in the global environment. The idea would never have occurred to us. We were too few and our powers too feeble. But as time went on, as technology improved, our numbers increased exponentially, and now here we are with an average of some ten people per square kilometer, our numbers concentrated in cities, and an awesome technological armory at hand— the powers of which we only incompletely understand and control. The inhibitions placed on the irresponsible use of this technology are weak, often half-hearted, and almost always, worldwide, subordinated to short-term national or corporate interest. We are now able, intentionally or inadvertently, to alter the global environment. Just how far along we are in working the various prophesied planetary catastrophes is still a matter of scholarly debate. But that we are able to do so is now beyond question.

There are three key indicators of technology-driven global atmospheric change: nuclear winter, ozonosphere depletion, and greenhouse warming. This talk is mainly about the last, although all three are intimately connected. There may be—indeed I think it is inevitable that there are—other global environmental catastrophes driven by our technology that we are not yet wise enough to recognize. Perhaps the science and policy debates on global warming will be useful for addressing these still undiscovered perils as well.

To start, let's consider a category of molecules known as chlorofluorocarbons (CFCs). The simplest of them has a carbon atom in the middle; poking off in four other directions are chlorine or fluorine atoms. Chlorofluorocarbons were developed for, and are widely used for, a set of benign activities: as the working fluid in refrigerators and air conditioners, the propellant in aerosol spray cans (in many countries still, but not in the United States), fast food packaging, and so on. CFCs are designed for safety. They are chemically inert. They're not corrosive or poisonous; they don't make you sneeze or itch; they don't burn your eyes; they're transparent; they're odorless; they don't bother the cat. They're brilliantly engineered not to bother anything. Except the Du Pont chemists who designed them overlooked one small fact: Precisely because these molecules are so inert, they survive for long periods of time down here in the bottom of the atmosphere—so long that there's time for them to be carried to high altitudes.

Imagine it's the 1960s and you're getting ready for the big date. Here's an aerosol spray can of deodorant. In it there is a CFC propellant that carries the deodorant out of the can. You raise your arm, press the button and go "psssst." Now you smell terrific and you're ready for the big date. What happens to those CFCs in the propellant? They bounce off the mirror, they bounce off you, they hit the ceiling. You've got to open the door to walk out of the bathroom, so some of them sneak out after you. Others trickle out through the window or under the door. As time passes, they diffuse out of the room. Eventually they get outside. What happens there? They bounce off telephone poles and nothing happens. They bounce off other molecules in the air and nothing happens. They are after all, inert. But eventually they get carried to high altitudes.

A few tens of kilometers up there is what is called the ozone layer. Ozone is a gas that absorbs near-ultraviolet radiation from the sun, radiation that is very dangerous to life on Earth. The ozone layer protects us from solar ultraviolet radiation. The amount of ozone there is very little. If it were brought down to the temperature and pressure in this room, it would be something like 3 millimeters thick, the thickness of a pencil point. Not much protection. The CFCs get up into the ozone layer, and their chlorine atoms start presiding over the destruction of ozone molecules. With fewer ozone molecules, more ultraviolet light gets through to the surface of the Earth. What are the consequences?

The most widely advertised consequence is skin cancer. By the way, such skin cancer occurs in light-skinned people much more often than in dark-skinned people. Dark-skinned people are nicely protected with melanin, so they don't get skin cancer from amounts of ultraviolet light that will produce it in whites. And so the number of incremental skin cancer deaths in whites who go outside may be substantial, courtesy of the Du Pont Corporation and others. But that's the least of it.

A more serious danger is that sublethal doses of ultraviolet light can attack the immune system, the body's ability to protect itself against disease. If there's substantial increase in ultraviolet light and if the light-skinned people persist in going outdoors without protection, they can get the equivalent of a case of AIDS. In this case, you don't have to do anything special—beyond continued political complacency—to get it.

The most serious consequence of an increase in ultraviolet light probably has to do with the tiny microorganisms at the base of the food chain. For example, in the oceans there are little one-celled plants called phytoplankton that harvest sunlight. They have to live near the surface of the water to use the sunlight. So they are vulnerable to an increase in ultraviolet light. If those guys are in trouble, the guys who eat them are in trouble. Eating the phytoplankton are zooplankton, little one-celled animals. Eating the zooplankton are tiny shrimplike crustaceans called krill. Eating the krill are little fish. Eating the little fish are big fish, and eating them are dolphins, whales, and people. This is a very simplified version of the food chain. If you remove the base of the food chain, you remove the subsequent steps. You can kill almost everyone in the chain. Some similar, but much more complicated, set of food chain vulnerabilities applies to life on the land.

Significantly increasing the ultraviolet flux at the surface of the Earth is perilous and stupid. But notice how nobody meant to do it. The active agent was developed by people committed from the start to safety. The CFCs are a relatively minor industry compared to some, and the amount of CFCs put into the atmosphere is by most standards tiny. It's understandable that nobody guessed the consequences until rather late. Perhaps—without making a concerted and systematic effort—we are not smart enough to foresee many other consequences of our technology. This story speaks, I think, to the need for higher standards of vigilance.

Now I want to raise a related question: Who discovered that CFCs were dangerous to the ozone layer? Was it, for example, the Environmental Protection Agency protecting us? Nope. Was it the Department of Defense defending us? Nope. Was it the Du Pont Corporation exercising corporate responsibility? Nope. It was two ivy-tower, white-coated, academic scientists minding their own business in some laboratory not even in an Ivy League university—it was at the University of California, Irvine. Sherwood Rowland and Mario Molina are their names. They ought to be household words. We ought to know who they are. What they mainly got for their research—especially at first—was trouble. There was a major campaign to discredit their work led by the Du Pont Corporation, which was selling $600 million a year in CFCs. Du Pont took out big ads in scientific and general readership magazines, essentially saying, "It's only a theory. Not everybody agrees. Probably they made some mistake. When it's definitively shown that CFCs pose a serious threat to the health of everybody on Earth," said the Du Pont Corporation, in effect, "then Du Pont will stop making them." Very nice of them. If many people are sick or dying from CFCs, then there might not be much of a continuing market. It's easy to stop then.

This is a modern example of something like the Cassandra Effect. Not only were the corporations making money from CFCs reluctant to take the evidence seriously, but so were ministries of health and governments worldwide. Are we to interfere with corporate profits in a free enterprise economy on the say-so of two scientists from Irvine? Are we to do without air conditioners or fast foods because of some photochemical theory no politician can understand? What if the chemists made a mistake, and policy makers, believing them, rush off half-cocked, alienating consumers and corporations, voters and campaign contributors? And after all, it was noted, there is debate on the matter in the scientific community. Everyone agreed that some of the input parameters are not measured well enough. Better to be careful. Better to temporize. Better to commission more research and make no policy changes.

There is, of course, much merit—particularly short-term political merit—to this stance. The trouble is that every CFC molecule released to the atmosphere poses a danger to the ozone layer for the next hundred years. It's not enough to say we will make policy changes when the danger is unambiguous. By then it might be too late.

Actually, we were lucky in this case. After a decade and a half of temporizing and debate, the science finally permeated into the policy realm. What did it was the unexpected discovery by a British team of a huge hole in the Antarctic ozonosphere. Nobody had predicted it—not even Rowland and Molina. Then the Du Pont Corporation announced itself ready to start phasing CFCs out, a process to be completed by the year 2000. Adequate substitutes for CFCs are somehow being found. Other corporations, worldwide, followed suit. Governments decided they better do something. There is now the Montreal Protocol and its London amendments, an agreement to phase out production worldwide of CFCs and allied molecules—although in my view, still too slowly. Remarkably, these agreements were achieved before it was clear that acceptable substitutes for CFC would be available.

Let me now address the issue of global warming. What determines the temperature of Earth? The amount of heat trickling up from the center of the Earth is negligible compared to the amount falling down on Earth's surface from the sun. Indeed, if the sun were turned off, the temperature of Earth would fall so far that the air would freeze solid, and the planet would be covered with a 10-meter-thick layer of nitrogen and oxygen snow. Can't we calculate what the average temperature of the Earth's surface ought to be? This is an easy calculation—taught, for example, in elementary astronomy and meteorology courses. The amount of sunlight absorbed by the Earth has to equal on average the amount of energy radiated back into space by Earth.

The flux of energy coming in depends on how bright the sun is and how reflective the Earth is. (Whatever isn't reflected back into space is absorbed.) This sunlight, of course, is mainly in the visible part of the spectrum to which our eyes are sensitive. The radiation from the Earth back into space depends on the temperature of the Earth and is mainly in the infrared part of the spectrum to which our eyes are not sensitive. Set the two sides of the equation equal and out comes the predicted temperature of the Earth. Fantastic! Couldn't be easier! You calculate it, and what's the answer?

Our calculation tells us that the average temperature of Earth should be some 30 degrees C below its actual, measured value. The oceans ought to be blocks of ice and we ought all to be frozen stiff. What's wrong with the calculation? Did we make a mistake? Maybe the fact that we came within 30 degrees of the right answer is good enough, and we should now go on to some other problem. But after all the exact answer affects us. We depend on that 30 degrees. It's life or death for us, so we can be excused for wanting to get the right answer to within a degree or less.

We didn't exactly make a mistake in the calculation. We just left something out. What did we leave out? The greenhouse effect. In effect, we assumed the Earth had no atmosphere. While the air is transparent at ordinary visible wavelengths (except in places like Los Angeles), it is not transparent in the infrared part of the spectrum, where the Earth likes to radiate to space. And that makes all the difference in the world. Some of the gases in the air in front of us—carbon dioxide, water vapor, some oxides of nitrogen, methane, chlorofluorocarbons—happen to absorb strongly in the infrared, even though they are completely transparent in the visible. If you put a layer of this stuff above the surface of the Earth, the sunlight still gets in, but when the surface tries to radiate back to space the way is impeded by this blanket of infrared absorbing gases. As a result the Earth has to warm up some, to achieve that equilibrium between the sunlight coming in and the infrared radiation going out. If you calculate from how much opacity these gases provide, how large the greenhouse effect ought to be, you come out with the right answer. You get that 30 degrees.

Our lives depend on a delicate balance of invisible gases. A little greenhouse effect is a good thing. But if you add more greenhouse gases—as we have been doing since the beginning of the industrial revolution—you absorb more infrared radiation. You make that blanket thicker. You warm the Earth.

Incidentally, the phrase "greenhouse effect" is a misnomer. Greenhouses don't work through the differential transparency of glass between the visible and the infrared. The Johns Hopkins physicist R. W. Wood once built a greenhouse with panes that were nearly transparent in the infrared as well and found no significant decrease in effectiveness. Florists' greenhouses work by preventing convective cooling. The same is true of automobile interiors heated by sunlight on a summer's day. But the phrase is so widespread in atmospheric physics that we are stuck with it.

For the public and policy makers, all this may seem a little abstract—invisible gases, infrared blankets, calculations by physicists. If difficult decisions on what we spend money on are to be made, don't we need a little more evidence that there really is a greenhouse effect, and that too much of it can be dangerous? Nature has kindly provided, in the character of the nearest planet, a cautionary reminder. The planet Venus is a little closer to the sun than is Earth, but its unbroken clouds are so bright that the planet actually absorbs less sunlight than does Earth. Greenhouse effect aside, its surface ought to be cooler than Earth's. It has very closely the same size and mass as Earth, and from this we might naively conclude that it has a pleasant Earthlike environment, ultimately suitable for tourism. However, if you were to send a spacecraft through the clouds—made, by the way, largely of sulfuric acid—as the Soviet Union did in its pioneering *Venera* series of exploratory spacecraft, you would discover an extremely dense atmosphere made largely of carbon dioxide with a pressure at the surface ninety times what it is on Earth. If now you stick out a thermometer, as the *Venera* spacecraft did, you find that the temperature is some 470 degrees C (about 900 degrees F)—hot enough to melt tin or lead. Venus turns out to be no vacation spot. The surface temperatures—hotter than those in the hottest household oven—are due to the greenhouse effect, largely caused by the massive carbon dioxide atmosphere. (There are also small quantities of water vapor and other infrared absorbing gases.) Venus is a practical demonstration that an increase in the abundance of greenhouse gases may have unpleasant consequences.

As there get to be more and more humans on Earth, and as our technological powers grow still greater, we are pumping more and more infrared absorbing gases into the atmosphere. There are natural mechanisms that take these gases out of the atmosphere, but we are producing them at such a rate that we are overwhelming the removal mechanisms. The abundance of these gases is going up with time.

Figure 1 is a representation of the abundances, for Earth, of three different greenhouse gases, as time goes on. In the first graph, the vertical axis shows how much carbon dioxide there is (in parts per million). The horizontal axis is the year (1955 at the left). The curve shows the increase with time of carbon dioxide in Earth's atmosphere. The data come from the Mauna Loa atmospheric observatory in Hawaii. Hawaii is not highly industrialized and is not a major place where forests are burned. The increase in carbon dioxide with time detected over Hawaii comes from activities in other places on Earth. The carbon dioxide is simply carried by the general circulation of the atmosphere—including

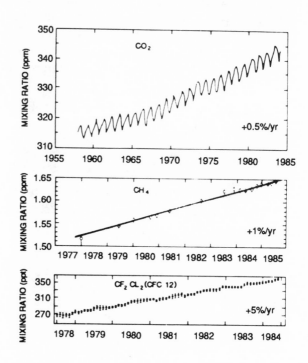

Figure 1
Increase during recent years of three of the principal greenhouse gases $CO_2$, $CH_4$, and $CF_2Cl_2$ (one of the chlorofluorocarbons).

over Hawaii. You can see that every year there's a rise and fall of carbon dioxide. That's due to deciduous trees, which, in summer, when in leaf, take carbon dioxide out of the atmosphere, but in winter, when leafless, do not. But superimposed on that annual oscillation is a long-term increasing trend, which is absolutely unambiguous. The $CO_2$ mixing ratio reached 300 parts per million in this century—higher than it's ever been during the tenure of humans on Earth. Carbon dioxide absorbs in the infrared, we know its abundance is increasing, and this ought to produce an increase in temperature. The question is how much?

Figure 1 also shows the increase of methane with time, and that of one of the chlorofluorocarbons, the one with two fluorines and two chlorines. These increases are steep. As with carbon dioxide, major methane increases began with the industrial revolution. Chlorofluoro-carbon increases are the quickest—by about 5 percent a year—because of the worldwide growth of the CFC industry. Note that CFCs are dangerous in two different ways: They attack the ozone layer, and they are greenhouse gases.

Various scientific groups—modern equivalents of the Delphic Oracle—have calculated with computer models what the temperature increase ought to be. Table 1 compares the results of five different groups working essentially independently with three-dimensional general circulation models, predicting how much the temperature will increase if there is a doubling of the amount of carbon dioxide in the atmosphere, which there will be by the mid-twenty-first century. The oracles are the Geophysical Fluid Dynamics Laboratory of NOAA at

*Predicting the Greenhouse Effect*
*with Global Climate Models*

| Model | Global Change in: | |
|-------|------------------------|----------------------|
| | Temperature (°C) | Precipitation (%) |
| GFDL | 4.0 | − 8.7 |
| GISS | 4.2 | −11.0 |
| NCAR | 3.5 | − 7.1 |
| OSU | 2.8 | − 7.8 |
| UKMO | 5.2 | −15.8 |

Result of doubling atmospheric $CO_2$ using equilibrium climate conditions

Table 1
Projections for the current state-of-the-art three-dimensional general circulation models of global temperature increase and precipitation decrease following a doubling of the atmospheric carbon dioxide mixing ratio.

Princeton; the Goddard Institute of Space Studies of NASA in New York; the National Center for Atmospheric Research in Boulder, Colorado; Oregon State University; and the United Kingdom's Meteorological Office. You can see that there is a difference of opinion by almost a factor of 2, but the average temperature increase is something around 3 or 4 degrees C (in Fahrenheit it's about twice that). Over on the right are predictions of variation in the amount of precipitation. Again there are differences of opinion. Nobody claims that the predictions are perfect.

But note that none of the groups claim that doubling the carbon dioxide content of the atmosphere will cool the Earth. None of them claim that it will heat the Earth by tens or hundreds of degrees. We have an opportunity denied to many Greeks who consulted oracles—we can go to a number of oracles and compare prophecies. When we do so, they all say more or less the same thing. The answers in fact are in good accord with the most ancient oracles on the subject—including the Swedish Nobel Prize winning chemist Svante Arrhenius, who around the turn of the century made a similar prediction using, of course, much less sophisticated knowledge of the infrared absorption of carbon dioxide and the properties of the Earth's atmosphere. The physics used by all these groups correctly predicts the present temperature of the Earth, as well as the greenhouse effects on other planets such as Venus. Of course, there may be some simple error that everyone has missed. I'll say a word about possibly neglected factors shortly, but surely these concordant prophecies deserve to be taken very seriously.

We can take another approach to the problem. We can look at the actual record of global temperature change. In figure 2 are the results from an ensemble of temperature-measuring stations all over the world—in which allowance is made for the fact that the cities are hotter than the countryside because of industrialization and higher population densities, as well as the fact that cities tend to be darker and so absorb more sunlight. The temperatures shown range from the beginning of the century to 1988. You can see substantial wiggles, noise, in the global climatic signal. But there also seems to be a clear upward trend. The 1989 average global temperature is almost as large as the 1988 value. The five hottest years in the entire twentieth century occur in the decade of the 1980s. This is the sort of evidence that has led at least some scientists to conclude that the signature of the increasing greenhouse effect is already here—not just something calculated for the twenty-first century, but here now. This is not to say that the drought of a particular summer was necessarily due to the increasing greenhouse

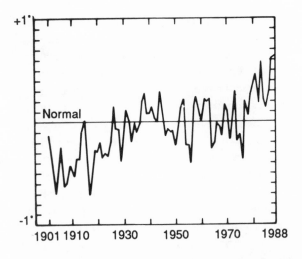

Figure 2
Global mean temperatures during the twentieth century. Data courtesy University of East Anglia and British Meteorological Office.

effect, but rather that the probability of such droughts and the probability of hot years is increasing as time goes on. It would be a very strange coincidence if the hottest years of the twentieth century occur just when the abundance of greenhouse gases is at its maximum, but that the two events are not causally related.

Figure 3 offers a very broad perspective. At the left, it's 150,000 years ago; we have stone axes and are really pleased with ourselves for having domesticated fire. The global temperatures vary with time between deep ice ages and interglacial periods. The total amplitude of the fluctuations, from the coldest to the warmest, is about 5 degrees C (almost 10 degrees F). So, the curve wiggles along, and after the end of the last ice age, we have bows and arrows, domesticated animals, the origin of agriculture, sedentary life, metal weapons, cities, police forces, taxes, exponential population growth, the industrial revolution, and nuclear weapons (all that last part is invented just at the extreme right of the solid curve). Then we come to the present, the end of the solid line. The dashed lines show some projections of what we're in for because of greenhouse warming. This figure makes it quite clear that the temperatures we have now (or are shortly to have if present trends continue) are not just the warmest in the last *century*, but the warmest in the last *150,000 years*. That's another measure of the magnitude of the global changes we humans are generating, and their unprecedented nature.

These temperature increases have secondary consequences that are also very serious. The temperature rise of a few degrees Centigrade by

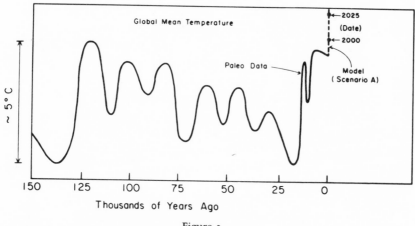

Figure 3

Evolution of the global temperature over the last 120,000 years. Major glaciations (ice ages) are shown. Recent and projected near-future temperatures from the intensifying greenhouse effect (assuming significant efforts to reduce emissions of greenhouse gases to the atmosphere) are the warmest on record in this period. Schematic diagram courtesy James Hansen, NASA Goddard Institute of Space Sciences (GISS).

the middle of the twenty-first century is predicted to cause a thermal expansion of sea water and, to a lesser extent, a melting of polar and glacial ice. The consequence is a rise in sea level. Calculations suggest a worldwide average rise by a few tenths of a meter to a few meters by the second half of the twenty-first century. In the longer run, still more dire consequences may follow, including the collapse of the West Antarctic ice sheet and the inundation of almost all coastal cities on the planet. Heroic worldwide engineering would seem called for to prevent or even ameliorate the flooding.

Before I go on to explore further consequences of greenhouse warming and the nub issue of policy implications, let's consider some other aspects of validating the science. If you go to Antarctica or Greenland and you dig a deep boring core in the ice, the deeper down you dig, the further back in time you are. It doesn't go back very far in geological terms, but it's a very nice recent stratigraphic record. At a given depth, corresponding to a given time in the past, examine the ice. There are various indicators of what the temperatures were when that ice was laid down—from pollen (different plants proliferate at different temperatures), from radioisotopes, and in other ways. In the ice, there are also trapped bubbles of air. You can extract the air and measure the amount of carbon dioxide. There is a striking correlation: When the carbon dioxide abundance was high, the ancient temperatures were high; when the carbon dioxide abundance was low, the ancient temperatures were low. Clearly, this is consistent with the greenhouse story.

I promised I'd say something about feedbacks. This is one of the areas of uncertainty that policy makers should understand. There are both positive and negative feedbacks possible in the global climate system. Here's an example of a positive feedback: The temperature increases a little bit because of the greenhouse effect and some polar ice melts. But polar ice is bright compared to the open sea. So as a result of that melting, the Earth is now darker; because the Earth is darker, it now absorbs more sunlight; so it heats some more, so it melts some more polar ice, and so on. That's a positive feedback. Another positive feedback: A little more carbon dioxide in the air heats Earth's surface, including the oceans, a little bit. The now warmer oceans vaporize a little more water vapor into the atmosphere. Water vapor is also a greenhouse gas, so it holds in more heat and the temperature gets higher—positive feedbacks, the dangerous kind.

Then there are negative feedbacks. They are homeostatic, like a thermostat. An example: Heat up the Earth a little bit by putting more carbon dioxide, say, into the atmosphere. As before, this injects more water vapor into the atmosphere, but this generates more clouds. Clouds are bright, they reflect more sunlight into space, and therefore, less sunlight is available to heat the Earth. The increase in temperature produces a decrease in temperature. Or, put a little more carbon dioxide into the atmosphere. Plants generally like more carbon dioxide, so they grow faster, and in growing faster, they take more carbon dioxide from the air—which in turn reduces the greenhouse effect. Negative feedbacks are like thermostats in the global climate. If, by luck, they were to be very powerful, maybe greenhouse warming would be self-limiting, and we could have the luxury of emulating Cassandra's listeners without sharing their fate.

The question is: Balance all the positive and all the negative feedbacks and where do you wind up? The answer is: Nobody is absolutely sure. A recent estimate by Daniel Lashoff, then of the Environmental Protection Agency, is that the sum of all the positive and negative feedbacks could double or maybe even triple the temperature changes predicted for the next century that I've just summarized. Wallace Broecker of Columbia University points to the very quick warming that happened about 10,000 B.C., just before the invention of agriculture. It's so steep that he believes it implies an instability in the coupled ocean-atmosphere system; and that if you push the Earth's climate too hard in one direction or another, you cross a threshold, there's a kind of "bang" and the whole system runs away by itself to another stable state. He proposes that we may be teetering on just such an instability right now. Again, this consideration only makes things worse.

In any case, it's pretty clear that the faster the climate is changing, the more difficult it is for whatever homeostatic systems there are to catch up and stabilize. Also, I wonder if we're not more likely to miss unpleasant feedbacks than comforting ones. We're not smart enough to predict everything. That's certainly clear. I think it's unlikely that the sum of what we're too ignorant to figure out will save us. Maybe it will. But would we want to bet our lives on it?

Even very cautious projections into the middle of the next century imply major decreases in agricultural productivity because of global warming. Many nations are even today submarginal in their ability to feed their citizens. The decline of indigenous agriculture and the decreasing availability of import food subsidies might be enough to produce global famine. Drought in continental interiors would intensify; fresh water would become increasingly unavailable; desertification would accelerate; and, for variety, coastlines would be flooded. Some regions might get a little better; most regions, according to the projections, will get worse. You could say, "Okay, so the American Midwest will become scrub desert, but then we can plant our wheat in northern Canada. What's the problem?" Well, even if the topsoil in northern Canada were suitable for transplanted agriculture, and even if it really would be significantly cooler in northern Canada, moving all U.S. farming there is going to be enormously expensive. Also the Canadians might have their own ideas on the matter and might not relish being flooded with this new variety of migrant farmer. But as figures 2 and 3 suggest, Canada might not be much better off than the American Midwest. Essentially there seem to be no winners in the era of global warming. It's not that some places are going to get better, others worse, and so on the whole if we are sufficiently detached, it's going to be a wash. The net result is predicted to be a thoroughgoing, equitably distributed disaster.

Consider sea level rises of 1 to 3 meters. That will displace tens of millions of people in Bangladesh alone. There will be a vast new problem of environmental refugees. Where are they supposed to go?

Think about shared river basins, where two or more countries share a river. What happens when the water level gets dangerously low? Will there be water and food wars? Consider Japan, which imports more than half its food today; the Soviet Union, which in an odd relationship between the usually contentious superpowers, depends upon grain from the United States (and Argentina and Australia). What happens to the Soviet Union if it continues to be non-self-sufficient in agriculture and if grain imports dry up?

Think about how the global system works. People in the United States can't be bothered to drive fuel-efficient cars. They need gas guzzlers because cars are symbols—of status, freedom, manhood. So we put a lot more carbon dioxide into the atmosphere than would otherwise be the case, time passes, and then there are millions of refugees in Bangladesh and elsewhere who have nowhere to go. It's an interesting connection. It makes you think.

The biggest carbon dioxide emitter on the planet is the United States. Accordingly, it seems to me, the United States must bear a proportionate degree of responsibility for making sure the problem doesn't get worse. The next biggest carbon dioxide emitter is the Soviet Union. The third biggest, if we combine them, is all the developing countries together. That's a very important fact: This isn't just a problem for the highly technological nations—through slash-and-burn agriculture, burning firewood, and so on, developing countries are also making a major contribution to global warming. Next in order of complicity is Western Europe then China and only then Japan, one of the most fuel-efficient nations on the planet. Just as the cause of global warming is worldwide, any solution must also be worldwide.

The scale of change necessary to address this problem at its core is nearly daunting—especially for those policy makers who are mainly interested in doing things that will benefit them during their terms of office. If the required action to make things better could be subsumed in two-year, four-year, or six-year programs, politicians would be more supportive, because then the political benefits might accrue when it's time for reelection. But twenty-year, forty-year, or sixty-year programs, where the benefits accrue not only when the politicians are out of office, but when they're dead, seem less attractive.

Certainly we must be careful not to rush off half-cocked like Croesus and discover that at huge expense we've done something unnecessary or stupid or dangerous. But it is even more irresponsible to ignore an impending catastrophe and hope it will go away. Can't we find some middle ground of policy response, which is appropriate to the seriousness of the problem, but which does not ruin us in case somehow—by missing a negative feedback *deus ex machina*, for example—we have overestimated the severity of the matter?

Say you're designing a bridge or a skyscraper. It's customary to build in, to demand, a tolerance to catastrophic failure far beyond what the likely stresses will be. Why? Because the consequences of the collapse of the skyscraper or the bridge are so serious, you must be sure. You need very reliable guarantees of protection. The same approach, I think, must be adopted for local, regional, and global environmental problems. And here there is great resistance, in part because large amounts of money are required from government and industry. For this reason, we will increasingly see attempts to discredit global warming. But money is also needed to truss up bridges and to reinforce skyscrapers. This is considered a normal part of the cost of building big. Designers and builders who cut corners and took no such precautions would not be considered prudent because they don't waste money on implausible contingencies. They would be considered criminals. There are laws to make sure bridges and skyscrapers don't fall down. Shouldn't we have similar laws and similar moral proscriptions for the potentially much more serious environmental issues?

I want now to offer some practical suggestions about dealing with climate change. I believe they represent the consensus of a large number of experts, although doubtless not all. They constitute only a beginning, only an attempt to mitigate the problem, but at an appropriate level of seriousness. To undo global warming and bring the Earth's climate back to, say, the 1960s will be much more difficult. The proposals are modest in another respect as well—they all have excellent reasons for being carried out, independent of the global warming issue:

We need a quick phase-out of CFCs (chlorofluorocarbons), which constitute about 25 percent of the greenhouse effect and are its most rapidly growing component. The Montreal Protocol calls for complete phase-out by the turn of the century. While a significant step forward, this is too leisurely a pace. (But the Protocol provides an existence theorem: It is possible for major industrial states to take common action in the face of a serious global environmental threat. Perhaps it is not impossible that we will see a similar international protocol on carbon dioxide and other greenhouse gases before too long.)

We can require much higher energy efficiencies, and it's clear that it can be done with very little discomfort. Some of us remember Jimmy Carter shivering in his cardigan sweater in the White House. If that's what it takes to produce a world that is not significantly worse for our children and grandchildren than the one we were given, we should do it. But that's not even necessary. With tax-relief carrots and tax-penalty sticks, it should be perfectly possible to improve the efficiency of electrical power generation, make large-scale replacement of incandescent by fluorescent lamps, establish fuel efficiency requirements for automobiles, and so on. (Cars are responsible for more than a third of the carbon dioxide generated each year in the United States. Why do we tolerate autos that get only 20 or 30 miles per gallon, when it's entirely feasible to manufacture autos in the 60-to 100-miles-per-gallon range?)

We must put much greater effort into renewable energy resources, especially solar energy. There was another small political drama in the White House on this matter. In the Carter administration, they put in a solar thermal heating system—not a solar-electric system, but one in which sunlight heats water and the hot water is used for various heating purposes, such as presidential showers. Its principal value, I suppose, was symbolic. The moment that Ronald Reagan became president, the solar heating system was ripped off the White House roof. The money allocated to research on renewable energy was cut by enormous factors by the Reagan administration, and we have marked time over the last eight years on this extremely sensible way to deal with the greenhouse issue. Meanwhile, as we saw, all those greenhouse gases have been building up.

And yet solar power systems are nearly competitive with more traditional means of generating electricity, and if we include the environmental costs into the price charged per kilowatt-hour, solar power is probably already competitive. Nevertheless, much more research needs to be done on increasing the efficiency, and on transmission lines to carry power from the arrays of light-harvesting solar cells in sunny environments to more cloudy and more densely populated regions. Superconducting transmission lines need to be explored. Some studies suggest that this may be workable even if we never get room temperature superconductivity; transmission lines cooled even to liquid air temperatures may be economically feasible.

Other systems should of course be developed—especially wind, tidal, and hydrothermal technologies that are renewable and nonpolluting. Systems that chemically burn hydrogen (with the only waste products being water) are possible and need further research and development. For a moment recently there seemed to be some prospect of low-temperature nuclear fusion, which under certain circumstances might have been the ideal solution to the combined greenhouse/energy problem. But that prospect has now rapidly faded, and we are left with hypothetical, enormous, expensive, high-technology fusion systems that even their proponents do not imagine being available on a commercial scale for many decades. In any case it is hard to imagine such systems as the answer for the developing world.

That leaves fission nuclear power, which under some circumstances might be considered as the stopgap between the present reliance on fossil fuels and whatever technology it is that does not generate greenhouse gases that will be adopted in the future. But as Three Mile Island and Chernobyl and the delinquency of many of the facilities supervised and run by the U.S. Department of Energy remind us, there is another price to pay if we adopt fission power. No greenhouse gases are generated, but serious accidents can happen (the total costs of Chernobyl may be hundreds of billions of dollars). A deadly witch's brew of long-lived radioactive elements is generated that will burden our descendants for centuries and millennia to come. Especially after Chernobyl, worldwide public opinion seems dead set against major reliance on new fission power. If such power plants can be made safe and cost-effective, if there is an extremely reliable way to dispose of the radioactive wastes, and if there is no way to divert the fission products into making nuclear weapons, maybe fission power is the stopgap. But the burden of proof surely lies with the manufacturers and supporters of such facilities.

A large-scale worldwide research and development effort is urgently needed for the development of alternative energy sources economically and technologically appropriate for various regions of the world. Note, incidentally, that a mix of technologies will almost certainly be needed for a long time to come. High-intensity industrial power needs—for example, in steel foundries and aluminum smelters—are unlikely to be provided by sunlight or windmills.

Then there is the question of forests. Trees eat carbon dioxide, removing it from the atmosphere. We need massive reforestation. Something like the area of the United States needs to be reforested to stabilize the global carbon dioxide budget at its present value in the face of anticipated carbon dioxide emission in the next century. What's happening today is the exact opposite. On the Earth at this moment, an acre of forest disappears every second. There are only so many acres on the planet. This is something, it seems to me, it is possible to do something about. Nations can plant trees. Individuals can plant trees. In recent years, Japanese companies have been the principal despoilers of tropical forests (especially hardwood), but there is a growing environmental consciousness in Japan. There are also nations such as Brazil that are permitting their forests to be cut down by foreign lumber companies (for a fee, of course), or are permitting their own citizens to cut down tropical forests to generate farmland (especially quixotic, because the tropical topsoil tends quickly to erode away in one or two growing seasons, after which, where there was once a great forest, there is nothing but scrub desert). Perhaps such nations can be convinced in suitable ways—by better environmental education, say, or with reference to their international indebtedness—to reverse their course.

However, on such matters the industrialized countries do not arrive on the scene with clean hands. American admonitions to Brazil about environmental responsibility do not carry much weight unless the United States acknowledges its abysmal environmental record and demonstrates major departures from business as usual. China, with the second largest coal reserves in the world, is not likely to find credible pleas from Western nations that China not industrialize as they did, not unless those industrialized nations can demonstrate a willingness to make environmental sacrifices themselves—and perhaps also to provide the necessary alternative technologies. No nation is beyond reproach on global environmental issues. We must help one another.

Applied Energy Services (AES), an Arlington, Virginia, company, has recently announced its intention to compensate for the carbon dioxide produced over the lifetime of a new industrial facility it intends to build; it has arranged to plant new forests in Guatemala that will remove from the atmosphere the same quantity of carbon dioxide its new facility will inject into the atmosphere. The intention seems fully meritorious, and I hope it will actually come to pass. This is model behavior. Shouldn't lumber companies be required to plant more forests—of the fast-growing leafy variety, used for mitigating the greenhouse effect—than they cut down? What about the coal, oil, natural gas, petroleum and automotive industries? Why not a massive international commitment to replant forests?

There is one other matter that is central to global warming, especially in the long run, and that is world population growth. People make carbon dioxide. People have to stay warm. People have to cook food. People have to get to work. And these activities often involve putting greenhouse gases into the atmosphere. The more people, the more serious these problems are, and the more difficult it is to solve them. Curbing population growth is essential. The way to do it is not just making contraceptives available and explaining family planning. Poor people are not too dumb to limit their family size, although that's a widespread misunderstanding in the West. People in developing countries have large families not only because of deep-seated human feelings, but also as a kind of insurance, as a result of a cost-benefit analysis, because the government does not provide social security. Children cost very little to raise, and will be useful in farming or whatever the meager family occupation is. You have a lot of children because it is unlikely that most of them will survive to adulthood, and you need someone to help with the work and look after you in your old age. All over the world there is an extremely interesting phenomenon called the demographic transition. It works in communist and capitalist countries, in Buddhist and Christian countries, East and West. It's a transideological, transcultural reality: When the per capita income gets above a certain level and people have enough to eat, suddenly the population growth rate drops dramatically. The most effective way for the industrialized north to address rampant population growth is to help bring the billion poorest people on the planet to a degree of self-sufficiency. That's part of the solution to global warming as well.

Every one of the foregoing approaches to ameliorating global warming is desirable on quite separate grounds: Quick phase-out of CFC production is essential to safeguard the ozone layer. Higher energy efficiencies and the search for alternative—especially renewable—energy sources is desirable for economic reasons, to minimize dependence on foreign oil and other energy sources, and as protection against the eventual depletion—whenever it comes (a controversial issue)—of fossil fuels. We are willing to allow environmentally risky off-shore oil-drilling because it is important to preserve "energy independence." Doesn't this argument apply much more forcibly to supporting research and development on alternatives to fossil fuels? Planting and preserving forests is important to preserve species diversity and for powerful emotional reasons: our ancestors used to live in trees and we have a deep affinity for them. Curbing global population growth is one of the imperatives of our time for reasons that are well-known. Greenhouse warming is a policy issue that cuts across many other contemporary environmental and political issues.

Global warming—as well as ozonosphere depletion, nuclear winter, acid rain, and other of the new global environmental problems—has a new character. The key aspect is the irrelevance of national boundaries to the problem. Consider some country where they're burning fossil fuels. The carbon dioxide goes up into the atmosphere. Does it stay over that country? No. A carbon dioxide molecule doesn't know about political boundaries. It's never heard of passports. It has no brain, so it doesn't understand the profound idea of national sovereignty. It's just blown by the winds, moved by the general circulation of the planet. If it's produced in one place, it can wind up in any other place. The planet is a unit. No one nation can solve the greenhouse problem alone. Whatever the ideological and cultural differences, the nations of the world must work together; otherwise there will be no solution to greenhouse warming and the other global environmental problems. We are all in this greenhouse together.

Notice also that there are no short-term solutions to this category of problems. You put something up into the air and it stays for a long period of time. We have no way to flush it out. It may well be that what we do today affects our children, our grandchildren, our great-grandchildren a hundred or more years into the future. If we mess up now, our children and their descendants pay the consequences. These environmental issues force upon us not just a transnational, but also a transgenerational ethic. If we want to save ourselves, we are going to have to adopt—as Einstein said in 1945 in an only slightly different context—a new way of thinking. I don't think it will be impossibly hard to do. Many major world religions have been teaching such doctrines for a long time.

I'm haunted by a phrase in the Book of Proverbs: "They set an ambush for their own lives." We cannot continue mindless growth in technology, with widespread negligence about the consequences of that technology. It is well within our power to curb technology, to direct it to the benefit of everyone on Earth. Perhaps there is a kind of silver lining to these global environmental problems, because they are forcing us, willy-nilly, no matter how reluctant we may be, into a new kind of thinking. We are a resourceful species when push comes to shove. We know what to do. Out of the environmental crises of our time should come, unless we are much more foolish than I think we are, a binding up of the nations and the generations, and the end of our long childhood.

# Questions from the Audience

Q   People have a natural tendency to concentrate time and attention on selected problems—the current "war on drugs," for example. What would have to happen to focus an equal amount of public attention on major environmental problems such as global warming and depletion of the ozone layer?

A   What will it take to get us going against global environmental problems? There is a pessimistic view that until agriculture starts failing in a major way, *nothing* will get us going, that short-term, local vested interests and the wishes of politicians to be reelected will take precedence over wisdom.

But there is also an optimistic view, which says that if the people understand the nature of the problem, they will demand a solution. I myself would give odds slightly in favor of the latter view. But it's by no means guaranteed.

Q   How do you rate EPA's performance in its twenty years of existence?

A   I certainly have the view that from 1981 to 1989 EPA was not courageously in the forefront of global environmental issues, or even local ones. I believe EPA's enforcement powers could have been used much more strenuously and much more responsibly.

I'm surprised that there weren't a lot of people in EPA resigning publicly during that period of time, because of the clear dissonance between the ostensible objectives of EPA and the actual accomplishments of EPA. There *are* other jobs available. (Which, of course, is easy enough for me to say; I recognize the penalties attached to such resignations—but still I'm surprised.)

In many areas of government, I believe the successful administrator is the one who's on the thin edge of being fired. If a sizable number of your executive staff ever felt that the agency was not doing its job, and there was a chance of mass resignations or firings, no president would readily risk the public outcry that would result. The dissidents could have real leverage.

Q   Do you think EPA should take a more active role in educating people about the environmental problems we face?

A   I am surprised that EPA does such a poor job in public education on environmental issues. Public education, I would have thought, is the key to making possible everything else that EPA stands for. By public education I don't mean just broadcasting emergency announcements that say, "Oh my goodness, there's a chemical that maybe makes apples dangerous." I mean informative, professionally done messages that simply and clearly explain.

You could find other ways to tell the public about the long-term consequences of radiation. [Here Dr. Sagan sings a jingle, with enthusiasm but somewhat off-key:] "Here is what a rem [a measure of radiation] is. It's not so hard to understand. A hundredth of a rem, fine. One rem, not so good. A hundred rem, really bad." Maybe you could do a little TV cartoon about rems, radon, medical X-rays, fission power plants, nuclear war.

Another subject for a public education message might be the matter of controlled experiments, explaining the applicability of data from animal experiments to people. How do toxic or carcinogenic or mutagenic doses of some chemical in an 8-ounce mouse translate into doses for an 80-kilogram human?

I think it might even be useful for EPA to state explicitly in its educational messages that there may sometimes be a conflict between the objectives of a corporation—which is trying to maximize profits and provide golden parachutes and executive perks—and the interests of the general population. Sometimes there are conflicts in interest between the two, pulling in opposite directions. Why be afraid to say so?

Q Dr. Allan Bromley, who was recently confirmed as the president's science adviser, testified at his Senate confirmation hearing that he had not seen sufficient scientific evidence to convince him we ought to reduce carbon emissions significantly. This is from the man who has breakfast with George Bush to advise him on science policy. What would you say to Dr. Bromley, to try to convince him?

A I would ask him to look at the correlation between past temperature and carbon dioxide abundance in samples of Antarctic boring cores. I'd ask him to think about why the five hottest years of the twentieth century happened in the 1980s. I'd ask him to look at the concordance between the five different general atmospheric circulation models. I'd stress the other benefits of dealing with greenhouse warming—the economic benefits of energy efficiency, the argument for energy independence, the ozonosphere protection benefits of a CFC ban, etc. And I guess I would ask him what it would take to convince him, short of being too deep into the global catastrophe to do anything about it.

Certainly there is a danger of the Croesus fallacy here. But the Cassandra danger, it seems to me, is much more serious. If this were a risk-free situation, then we'd be doing the right thing already. But there are risks both ways. There is a middle course that we must take.

Q  Do you have an opinion about using animals for research?

A  Nothing that's not completely obvious. For ethical reasons we certainly are not going to perform large-scale controlled experiments on people. Yet we are fouling the environment with tens of thousands of chemicals, the consequences of which we understand poorly.

The alternatives are: a) Stop producing the chemicals, all of them. b) Start experimenting on people. c) Let everybody look out for themselves, and if there are chemicals and pollutants that bother them, that's their problem. I think all three of these courses are unacceptable. That leaves d) Experiment on animals.

You have to do it responsibly. You have to care about animals. They are fellow inhabitants of this planet and our relatives. They can feel pain. They have feelings. The problem is most agonizing for the primates, as I tried to suggest in my book *The Dragons of Eden*. But I think (d) is the least undesirable option.

I'm sure that animal rights people are correct in some instances, where great and unnecessary cruelty has occurred. If we can be cruel to each other in systematic ways, it's very clear we can be cruel to other animals who don't even have the protection, the very meager protection, of being called human beings. But we can be much more scrupulous in animal experimentation than we've been.

Q  Would you comment on the moral dilemma of our trying to tell developing nations that they should slow down industrial development, or perhaps consider alternatives—given that industrialized nations have consumed so much of the world's reserves and caused so much environmental degradation?

A  China has the world's second largest coal reserves. China clearly has ambitions, which we fully understand because we had exactly the same ambitions, to industrialize exponentially. What will be the energy source for China's industrialization? Clearly, its coal reserves.

So now imagine the American secretary of state and the Soviet foreign minister knocking on the door of the Chinese foreign minister. "Excuse us. Sorry to bother you. We recognize that we've done some really bad things in the past about burning fossil fuels and committing many other environmental sins. But please, don't you burn your coal, because it's going to produce this terrible greenhouse effect, and we're not going to be able to produce any food and we're going to be hungry." Maybe China would find that a compelling argument, but I'm a little skeptical.

China has coastal cities. If the sea level rises substantially—in another century or so—it inundates the coastal cities of China. That's an argument which would make some sense to China. But "Don't do as we did" doesn't work in this case any more than it does when you tell your child, "Do as I say, not as I do." That is widely acknowledged to be ineffective advice.

Effective action by the United States and the Soviet Union would begin by cleaning up our own act, to have increased moral leverage when we talk to other countries. And then we could try to provide alternative energy sources at costs competitive with those of coal, even if it requires subsidies by the United States and the Soviet Union. Here again, there's a cost-benefit analysis. It's very clear that those alternative energy sources ought to be made inexpensive, efficient, and widely available. Also, it is especially important to use homegrown technology in less-developed countries.

This is a very serious technological challenge. I don't think it's an impossible one. But we're not working on it at all.

Q Can we digress a bit? We know you are deeply interested in space exploration. But why do you feel so strongly that there is life in other parts of the universe?

A I don't feel strongly that there are other forms of life out there. I don't believe there's life out there. I don't *dis*believe there's life out there. I say the existence or absence of life out there is one of the most important scientific problems ever posed. And here for the first time in history we have the technology perhaps to find out. So let's try.

Your question reminds me of a point I wanted to make to this group about the connection between space exploration and the concerns of EPA. I mentioned something about Venus before, but I believe this is a much more general issue.

Some of the other planets are worlds that have followed different evolutionary tracks. Put another way, they represent alternative fates of Earthlike worlds. Venus is an example of a runaway greenhouse effect. Mars has a surface so antiseptic that you can't find an organic molecule on it, much less a microorganism. And it has a hole in its ozone layer of planetary dimensions. There's hardly any ozone there at all. Ultraviolet light strikes the surface unimpeded. And it was the study of Martian dust storms that set us on the course that eventually led, about a decade later, to the discovery of nuclear winter.

By studying other planets, you learn about your own planet. Many of the leading practitioners of the earth sciences cut their teeth on studies of other planets. Jim Hansen, whom I mentioned earlier as a leading student of greenhouse warming, first began studying greenhouse effects in his doctoral thesis at Iowa State University. That thesis was an attempt to disprove the greenhouse model of the high surface temperatures on Venus. So he started studying greenhouse effects in a planetary context. This is true for an astonishing number of students of the subject.

I participated in a conference on greenhouse warming in Sundance, Utah, this summer, which was attended by high-level U.S. and Soviet officials. There were two keynote speakers and a panel of three scientific experts. Four out of those five people were planetary scientists.

So there is important justification for examining other planets. EPA, if not funneling a little money to NASA, ought to at least encourage NASA.

Q Some scientists suggest that as a result of global warming from the greenhouse effect, additional cloud cover will be generated around the world, serving to counteract the warming trend. What are your thoughts on this?

A I've discussed positive and negative feedbacks in the body of my talk. Recent work by V. Ramanathan of the University of Chicago suggests that the water vapor feedback loop is overall of the positive—i.e., the dangerous—variety, making the greenhouse effect worse.

I've mentioned a recent estimate by Daniel Lashof, recently of EPA and now at NRDC [Natural Resources Defense Council], that the sum of the positive and negative feedbacks would double or maybe even triple the temperature changes I was talking about earlier. In other words, the bad, positive kind of feedback greatly exceeds the good, negative kind.

But maybe that's wrong. Maybe we will be very lucky, and the feedbacks will exactly balance. I think, however, that it's very unlikely that the sum of all the things we're too dumb to figure out will save us. Maybe events will work out that way, but I sure wouldn't want to bet my life on it. Clearly, there are things we don't understand about the climate system.

I'd like to make one last remark here:

Nuclear winter was discovered, absolutely to our astonishment, in 1983. The widespread presence of radon in homes, I learned at lunch today, was discovered in 1984. The hole in the Antarctic ozone layer was discovered in, I think, 1986.

Isn't there something really worrisome about the fact we are making these discoveries as recently as we are? Doesn't it make you wonder what other major catastrophes we haven't discovered yet? Things that will sweep from your desks all the environmental problems you are worrying about today, and make you say, "Oh, my God, look at this one! We have to address this right away."

Where in the United States is there an institution of very high quality scientists devoted to finding the new catastrophes? The answer is, nowhere. There is no systematic effort.

The discovery by Rowland and Molina that CFCs endanger the ozonosphere was an accidental discovery. Finding nuclear winter was accidental. Finding the hole in the ozone layer was accidental. And the discovery that radon in homes is serious and widespread was accidental. All these discoveries could perhaps have been made years sooner, by systematic study by first-rate people. That didn't happen.

There is something extremely stupid about this setup. For a relatively small amount of money, it would be possible to establish first-rate research institutes. There are all sorts of scientists who would love nothing better than to work to help save the planet. Scientists have at least as much interest in preserving the environment as anybody else.

Why doesn't EPA commission summer study programs for first-rate scientists to work on these problems? Or hand out a few blank checks with instructions to "Go find us a new, important problem that we have been too dense to see up to now?" That's small change. Why not do it?

Wouldn't it be a good idea to find out about these problems before they blow up in our faces?

[SEPTEMBER 21, 1989]

Carl Sagan is the David Duncan Professor of Astronomy and Space Sciences, and director of the laboratory for planetary studies at Cornell University. He has played a leading role in the Mariner, Viking, and Voyager expeditions to the planets, for which he was awarded the NASA Medals for Exceptional Scientific Achievement and (twice) for Distinguished Public Service. His scientific research has enhanced our understanding of the greenhouse effect on Venus, dust storms on Mars, the origins of life on Earth, and the prospects of finding life elsewhere.

Dr. Sagan was chairman of the planetary sciences division of the American Astronomical Society and of the astronomy section of the American Association for the Advancement of Science. He has published more than six hundred scientific papers and popular articles, and has authored or edited more than twenty books, including *Broca's Brain* and *The Dragons of Eden*, for which he received the Pulitzer Prize. His TV series *Cosmos* won Emmy and Peabody awards, and was the most widely watched series in the history of public television. The accompanying book of the same title is the best-selling science book ever written in the English language.

In part because of his warnings concerning a nuclear winter following nuclear war, he received the Annual Awards for Public Service of Physicians for Social Responsibility and of the Federation of American Scientists. He is also a recent recipient of the United Nations Environment Programme Medal, the Leo Szilard Award for Physics in the Public Interest of the American Physical Society, the Honda Prize in Ecotechnology, and eighteen honorary degrees.